THE CASE OF
THE HELMETED AIRMAN

A STUDY OF W. H. AUDEN'S POETRY

The Case of
The Helmeted Airman

A STUDY OF
W. H. AUDEN'S POETRY

By

François Duchene

1972
CHATTO & WINDUS
LONDON

Published by
Chatto & Windus Ltd
40 William IV Street
London W.C.2
*
Clarke, Irwin & Co. Ltd
Toronto

ISBN.O 7011 1785 0

© François Duchene 1972

Printed in Great Britain by
Butler & Tanner Ltd
Frome and London

Consider this and in our time
As the hawk or the helmeted airman sees it

ACKNOWLEDGMENTS

Grateful acknowledgment is made to Faber & Faber Ltd, London, and Random House, Inc., New York, for permission to quote from the copyrighted works of W. H. Auden, and from *Memories and Commentaries* by Stravinsky and R. Craft; also to Faber & Faber Ltd, London, and Harcourt Brace Jovanovich, Inc., New York, for the extract from *Ash Wednesday* by T. S. Eliot from his *Collected Poems* 1909–1962.

CONTENTS

NOTE

The titles of volumes by Auden are printed in italics; those of poems, however long, are in roman type. Thus *The Age of Anxiety*, where the volume and the poem are identical, is italic. But 'For the Time Being' and 'New Year Letter' which appear in the volumes of the same names along with other works, in the first case 'The Sea and the Mirror' and in the second the sonnet sequence 'The Quest', are in roman.

Some of Auden's volumes have appeared under different titles in Britain and America. *Look, Stranger* in Britain was called *On This Island* in the United States. *New Year Letter* in Britain was *The Double Man* in the United States. The titles used here are the British ones.

Prologue

THE APATHETIC FALLACY

In his essay on Robert Frost in *The Dyer's Hand*, Auden distinguishes between two ideals of poetry, Ariel's and Prospero's. For Ariel, as for the potter of the Grecian Urn in Keats's Ode, 'Beauty is truth, truth beauty'. For Prospero, art is epitomised by Dr Johnson's dictum that 'the only end of writing is to enable the readers better to enjoy life or better to endure it'.[1] As Auden remarks, every poem shows some signs of rivalry between Ariel and Prospero (and so, one might add, does every poet), but in him more than most Prospero holds the upper hand. Auden certainly can write excellent Ariel poems, like the first section of the 'Ode to St Cecilia', or 'Look, stranger'. Yet, in general, he is, more than almost any poet who comes to mind, a Prospero. His art, despite his emphasis on its nature as a game, derives from the struggle with living and with thinking on living. This is more than a matter of the subjects he treats, though these, from politics to religion, hardly smell of 'pure' art. It is built into his process of writing itself.

> Looking up at the stars, I know quite well
> That, for all they care, I can go to hell.
> But on earth indifference is the least
> We have to dread from man or beast.
>
> How should we like it were stars to burn
> With a passion for us we could not return?
> If equal affection cannot be,
> Let the more loving one be me.[2]

'The More Loving One', the late poem which contains these lines, is unlike the approach to the night sky of any poet one can remember. It is not at all a joke and its playfulness in fact emphasises how serious it is. Yet it conveys neither plaint, nor protest, nor overt ritual, only the thinker's conclusions drawn from the human predicament which inspires them: even its

I

provocative humour quite lacks the 'anti-poetic' violence of the surrealists. The statements in the piece are not, as in nearly all the usual approaches, an emotional release with objective trappings. They are objective comments which draw the frontier round an emotional situation. Their poetic force depends on the urgencies of feeling which gave rise to them, but those urgencies make no appearance in their own right. The ideas are flatly stated, emotions are deliberately subordinated to the situation in which they operate. This is still very much poetry, because the inferences are obvious and compelling. Nevertheless, the disciplines of objectivity, or balance, are stressed more than the urge which calls them forth. Where most poets' attempts to communicate are subjective, one man's experience speaking through loaded language to another man's intuition, Auden's is indirect: he moves by the statement not of feelings, but of conclusions and psychological events whose interrelations imply, but do not insist upon, the feelings and impulses which evoked them.

This method of composition could be called simply classic, which is exactly what the poet called it in his youth:

> And through the quads dogmatic words rang clear,
> 'Good poetry is classic and austere'.[3]

That, no doubt, is all he meant to mean by his famous doctrine of Necessary Impersonality. Perhaps, if more of his verses were like 'The More Loving One', fewer people would have read other judgements into them. This is a classical piece in the classic mould, where detachment is a form of distillation. Its concentration and poise enhance the sense of the poet's personal involvement: a great deal of thought and experience are necessary to attain such potent clarities. The trouble is that often Auden's detachment is not of this quality. It frequently suggests quite an astonishing *lack* of involvement. The unusual contrast between his universal terms of reference and his unattached manner, his 'odd impersonality',[4] is the central puzzle of a very individual, even eccentric, talent. It explains the unstable solution of admiration and unease in which so much of the comment upon him is suspended. On the one hand, the breadth of horizons and variety of scenery of Auden's poetry carry the marks of a major talent. There is in his work a great deal of light poetry, nearly all of it highly metropolitan, from nightclub songs and formal occasional pieces to chatty autobiography; much love poetry; political poetry; satire, frequently bordering on farce; poetry of conversation with friends, turning latterly to cultural talk; poetry for the platform; musical poetry, that is, either about music or with a strong musical content; poetry of self-interrogation; religious poetry; even nature poetry: every kind of poetry, in fact, which can easily relate to a man's personal problem and his place in the world. Although there is not the poetry of emotional extremes —or perhaps because of it—Auden's verse comes nearer to a universal range of interests and themes than any other in the English (or American) language this century. On the other hand, Auden has a disconcerting air of knowingness—of coming to know experience rather than of undergoing it. In his youth, he tacked images onto his lines like a common stock of impressions card-indexed for scientific research. In his later work, he somehow has contrived to make every feeling or image a symbol of something else. In either case, he exudes a rather sterilising air of consciousness as if he himself were only involved at second-hand in all the patterns of words and ideas he handles with such consummate ease.

When Eliot, who is in many ways Auden's poetic antitype, describes Magnus Martyr's 'inexplicable splendour of Ionic white and gold',[5] he is attached and detached at the same time, at once the observer and devotee, the critic and votary, of his image. He is 'aware that a phenomenon, being wholly itself, is laden with universal meaning. A hand lighting a cigarette is the explanation of everything; a foot stepping from a train is the rock of all existence'.[6] Auden frequently lacks this reciprocal relationship with his metaphors: he rarely seems to have met them looming through a yellow fog or even on equal terms. He appears abstract in two senses—in the obvious one that, like Eliot, he often generalises in abstract ways; and also in the underlying one that he frequently gives the impression of not being fully engaged by the objects of his attentions. Particularly in his youth, taking off with the typical illusion fostered by an overdose of education relative to experience, he embraced it,

3

'as the hawk sees it or the helmeted airman', from a great height of speculation and moral (disguised as clinical) judgement.[7] There is a violent contrast between Eliot's artistic concern with things, as if for themselves, and the aggressive, repressive way in which Auden reduces the inmates of the Sport Hotel, the

> insufficient units
> Dangerous, easy, in furs, in uniform
> And constellated at reserved tables [7]

to a culture for the social biologist of the political weeklies. His all-embracing eye is able to single out the salient points and guiding principles of

> infinite
> Populations
> Of possible cases,[8]

but there is always a distance between him and them. He enters all too rarely into the skin of experiences momentarily all-important and totally preoccupying in themselves.

One might easily deduce that Auden's image-making faculty is weak. This is not so. On the contrary, he has, or has had, an astonishingly ebullient faculty for vivid visual instances. He can go on for page after page flashing cinematic shots at breakneck speed before his invisible audience. It is hard to believe that such inventiveness, extravagant to the point of genius, can be anything but a transposed emotional force, some kind of upheaval of the personality. Indeed, Auden's visual invention was incomparably richer in his eruptive youth than it now is in later life. Yet the images *are* only flashes projected on a screen. There is no hint of immediate life, no relationship between the visual idea invoked and the relatively low level of participation required from the audience. The majority of Auden's images are strangely two-dimensional.

> Trains keep stopping regular as dogs by certain posts. The red dormitory wing of the Academy extrudes a succession of white and black particles which, obedient to laws of attraction and repulsion, quickly assume group patterns, and caught by a northerly current, stream slowly toward the green square. Nurse-maids pause on the esplanade for mutual investigations. The band is leaving the Winter Gardens by an emergency

exit. A lady has fainted. Time for lunch. There isn't going to be
very much lunch unless you all wake up.[9]

One must make allowances for fashion at the time this was
written—the influence of cubism and the German expressionist
cinema. All the same, black comedy and surrealist menace
apart, here is the world of Wodehouse in which policemen
exist to have their helmets stuck on lamp-posts on Boat-race
night; take it how one will, this is algebraic farce. There is
what seems an internal contradiction, by ordinary standards,
between Auden's power to conjure up images in crowds and his
frequent failure to give them independent life.

Even when he leaves satire for the lyric, this habit of mind is
apt to control the outcome.

> May with its light behaving
> Stirs vessel, eye, and limb;
> The singular and sad
> Are willing to recover,
> And to the swan-delighting river
> The careless picnics come,
> The living white and red.[10]

This is, or should be, full-blooded with carnal images of Spring,
and 'vessel', Biblical for 'prick', is the proper word for the time
of year.[11] Yet, in seven lines, May has been extracted right out
of the vegetation of the spring and landed in the rarefied world
of its abstract qualities. Categorising 'the's abound and isolating absences of any article at all. These vessels, eyes and
limbs are disembodied images for a Picasso canvas, an eclectic
montage giving the impression they satisfy the artist primarily
because they confirm him in what he already proposes to know.
It is in character that both in this and in its sister-piece, 'Fish
in the unruffled lakes', the only lines suggesting a direct experience and starting-point are the last ones, which, in the
shape of 'The endearment and the look', or still more as 'Your
voluntary love',[12] are the dying falls and weakest verses in
either poem. Auden has written, in his later self-corrective days,
that 'one must be passive to conceive the truth'.[13] If there is an
important poet of recent years seemingly innocent of negative
capability, Auden is the one.

The same incompleteness of response tends to limit the music of his verse. He is very conscious of the musical properties of poetry. 'I know', he told an Oxford audience in 1956, 'that through listening to music, I have learned much about how to organise a poem, how to obtain variety and contrast through change of tone, tempo and rhythm, though I could not say just how'.[14] He has pointed out that the Elizabethan song-writers discovered metrics through setting words to music which they would not have found by purely verbal experiment.[15] He himself is the most assiduous and successful writer of songs and lyrical pieces of this century. And yet one can take a wide range of poems throughout Auden's career—highflown ones, light-hearted ones, ballads, lyrics, farcical sermons, meditations—each as different from the others as one could well imagine, and find that their tonal patterns vary surprisingly little. They are apt to be vigorous and active and bear down decisively on what they have to say; they verge, at times, on vulgarity. They lack the rhythmic variousness, the linguistic delicacy, the touch of the vulnerable, which is the supreme quality of more Protean, and even of more fastidious, artists. Auden's work is masculine in a limiting way, which suggests a certain rigidity in his nature or at least in his conception of himself. It is striking that once he has set the tone of a poem it hardly varies. A lyric may have a music of melancholy, but it will not have the internal variations, the modulations and changes of pace which are so crucial to Eliot's art. The result is that though Auden despises a slavish adherence to metrics, his own conception of writing, as seen in action, not in theory, is apt to be rather mechanical: subtly mechanical, for Auden is far too self-aware to be oblivious to such a temptation, but mechanical all the same. Auden's style, in short, is neither so malleable nor so varied as it aims to be in the infinite variety of its technical means. It can be put to a host of uses, but the quality of mind behind it will tend to remain stubbornly, even sometimes rather monotonously, the same. One normally reacts to Auden as to the insistent personality of an actor-manager recognisable as his own familiar self whatever part he plays.

In an age of relativity and free verse, washed by the eddying

streams of the unconscious, the evidence of a man's commitment tends more than ever to rest on the rhythms of his
phrases. His intensity replaces the lost certainties about the
world on which earlier artists could count. Eliot is the modern
master of such phrasing and an anguished intensity of music is
the hallmark of his verse.

> Because I do not hope to know again
> The infirm glory of the positive hour
> Because I do not think
> Because I know I shall not know
> The one veritable transitory power
> Because I cannot drink
> There, where trees flower, and springs flow,
> for there is nothing again . . .[16]

Here, virtually shorn of images, and indeed of punctuation, is a
poetry so powerful in rhythm it almost punctuates itself. Part
of the impact of Eliot's lines comes from the fact that most of
them—even when he gives himself objective airs—are really
muted cries of pain: Eliot's poetry is first of all a record of
suffering. Auden, by comparison, is loose and unselective. This
is not because the rhythms of his famous conversational style are
nearer those of prose than either Eliot's or Yeats's—though
they often are; nor because the finest of his poems, like 'Musée
des Beaux Arts' or 'Atlantis', could be spoken in a drawing-
room and do not even have Eliot's agonised drawing-room
politeness. It is because their music and phrasing seem less
apposite, less perfectly tailored, to the immediate moment of
what the poet has to say, and to that extent less charged.
Auden writes brilliantly from within the conventions of the
language, but he lacks that formal tension which gives Eliot or
Yeats the faculty to lead up to and deliver a phrase so that it
seems an ideal version of itself, just that Platonic bit more perfect than life. Auden has neither the rigorous concentration of
the modern selective artist, nor, though he is 'a marvellous
talker, with all the gifts of an orator at his finger-tips', that
elastic syntax of the emotions which is the glory of the greater
Jacobeans.[17]

Finally, and related to all this, there is Auden's tendency to formlessness, especially in his appreciable number of longer works. This is not true of his earliest, mainly short, poems which on the contrary, are striking for their formal strictness. Nevertheless, from the nineteen-thirties onwards, Auden's poetry tends to looseness. It uses forms which often, at first sight, look regular enough, and even ape metrical stanza patterns on the page. It is part of Auden's mastery that he can handle any metric with great fluency and loves to test himself with the most elaborate ones, like canzones and villanelles or to experiment with alliterative and quantitative verse forms as well as those within the post-renaissance iambic norm. Yet all this wardrobe of the poet's calling seems oddly removable. Auden's eloquence works from within the formal framework rather than through it; as with Dylan Thomas, his stanzas often give the impression of fancy dress for what is really a kind of semi-surrealist prose-poetry. It may be significant that many of the best passages in the longer works actually are written in an excellent though almost over-elaborated prose. It is characteristic of Auden that his real contribution to prosody is a whole family of loosely flowing stanzas in which the tone is more important than the stanza pattern. Auden writes 'as a peculiarly free agent, easily, restlessly and voluntarily turning from style to style and from subject to subject, exploring the potentialities of a situation or an idea, an image or a tone of voice, a verse-form or a rhythmic cadence'.[18] Whether or not one agrees with the implication here that the poet is singularly free from inner compulsions, a Master in the most dissociated sense of the word, this does convey the surface impact of much of his poetry. Stephen Spender who, in a rather fleeting and impressionistic way, has written some of the most balanced criticism of Auden's work, goes further: 'his skill conceals a defect which he has never entirely overcome—a lack of the sense of the inner form of a poem. By this I mean that with Auden form hardly ever seems to grow out of the experience which is the centre of the poem, out of what Henry James would call its "felt life". The form is imposed from the outside by the force of a didactic idea or by those stanza patterns in which the later poet shows such virtuosity.'[19]

In the circumstances, it is not surprising that the main response to Auden, after the period of his early triumphs, has been hesitant, with, one sometimes suspects, an element, especially in British academic critics, of the fear of being taken in. It is hazardous to dismiss Auden as a mere word-spinner: the fertility of his invention, the richness and independence of his intellect and his capacity, when he wishes, to speak directly to the reader's feelings, all argue the contrary. At the same time, he seems not merely frequently impersonal but at times (Spender's phrase again) almost 'depersonalised' and facile.[20] It is hard to find firm ground in this treacherously brilliant landscape: is it fertile? is it marsh? and if in patches one or the other, where? The contrast between Auden's universal terms of reference and his unattached manner has contributed more than anything else—certainly more than the reaction against the excesses of the poetry of opinions of the Thirties—to the wariness about him, sometimes bordering on aversion. The phenomenon is British more than American, but it exists to some extent on both sides of the Atlantic. It is summed up in a non-committal query which appeared in 1968 in *Encounter* asking whether he were 'a major artist, a simply important one, or a mere index in the history of taste'.[21] The one point on which there is general assent is that Auden is a brilliant technician, a virtuoso. This in itself is far from reassuring. Literary Limbo is littered with virtuosi, and recognition of the master craftsman, as with Eliot's *miglior fabbro*, Ezra Pound, turns easily into suspicion and even rejection of his products. Only Ezra Pound comes anywhere near Auden in the mixed feelings he arouses. Such feelings have done a great deal to devalue Auden's reputation since its palmy days in the far from palmy Thirties.

*   *   *

Characteristically, Auden himself has provided clues to the paradox of an art in which certain states and emotions are expressed more nakedly perhaps than in the work of any other reputable modern poet and yet the general effect of which is one of detachment and impersonality. Speaking at Oxford, in 1956, of the poet's 'Primary Imagination', his primitive awe in the presence of 'Sacred Objects', he explained how his adolescent

passion for geology had been steeped in the magic of naming
the ores and mines encountered on his moorland walks:

> Looking back, however, I now realize that I had read the
> technological prose of my favourite books in a peculiar way.
> A word like *pyrites*, for example, was for me, not simply an
> indicative sign; it was the Proper Name of a Sacred Being, so
> that, when I heard an aunt pronounce it *pirrits*, I was shocked.[22]

The late, critical Auden, like Napoleon on St Helena, is not
above polishing up the more controversial aspects of his legend
for posterity, so one must always be wary of his latter-day
revelations. When stressing piety he cannot be entirely unaware
of the world's assumption that he is, if not impious, at least 'rude
to the infinite', as Geoffrey Grigson once (and approvingly)
wrote of him.[23] Nevertheless, Auden offers what seems a
genuine insight into his own attitude to images. His aunt's
'impiety' in pronouncing 'pyrites' as 'pirrits' was 'ignorance'
and the ignorance an inability to give the right pronunciation
for a name. Poetry, he adds, underlining the hint, 'pays
homage by naming'.

> I suspect that the predisposition of a mind towards the poetic
> medium may have its origin in an error. A nurse, let us suppose,
> says to a child, 'Look at the moon!' The child looks and for
> him this is a sacred encounter. In his mind the word 'moon' is not
> the name of a sacred object but one of its most important
> properties and, therefore, numinous.[24]

Auden goes on to explain that poetry cannot occur before one
has grown to appreciate that names are *not* identical with
things. Yet there is something in his own verse which suggests
the opposite, and that the prepubertal fetishism has remained
more alive in him than in many of his peers. Do most poets
really pay homage by naming? They certainly expend a great
deal of effort isolating what is for them mysteriously exciting in
an experience or thought, the energy of which they strive to
convey. They are extremely busy re-creating the emotional
rhythm and visual or dramatic setting of the moment and
evoking its awe. But it seems a very truncated view of this
effort to think, as Auden apparently does, that one need only
name a Sacred Object in order to invoke it.

Why Auden should take such a view is an intriguing question. Here again, he himself offers random but frequent clues. The most direct example is perhaps the passage in *The Dyer's Hand* where he expatiates on the psychology of obesity. 'If my own weight and experience give me any authority, I would say that fatness in the male is the physical expression of a psychological wish to withdraw from sexual competition and, by combining mother and child in his own person, to become emotionally self-sufficient. The Greeks thought of Narcissus as a slender youth but I think they were wrong. I see him as a middle-aged man with a corporation, for, however ashamed he may be of displaying it in public, in private a man with a belly loves it dearly; it may be an unprepossessing child to look at, but he has borne it all by himself.'[25] Auden, then, thinks of himself as a Narcissist, a notion which would occur to any reader of his verse, particularly in the Thirties, where this is frequently implied. Such an attitude matters, because Auden is steeped in Freud and, in Freudian terms, Narcissism is closely related to homosexuality, and both with an incapacity for emotional development.

Auden's work is littered with discreet associations of love with 'a crime', with 'uncles', with 'one an aunt refers to as a friend', with bicycles and bicycle-pumps, threatening soldiers and all the rest of the modern panoply of homosexual symbols.[26] As the poet grows older the references grow more direct so that, by the Sixties, Auden speaks of himself as one of the world's 'unwilling celibates' and remarks that

> about
> blended flesh, those midnight colloquia of Darbies and Joans
>   I know nothing, therefore about certain occult
> antipathies perhaps too much.[27]

All this helps to connect many elements in Auden's work which might otherwise seem hard to relate to each other or to its overt purposes. It makes plausible the rather camp whimsies of the public-school spirit in decline, the sixth-form cliquishness, the undergraduate confessions, the Boy Scout and gang spirit, which pop up so oddly through the 'clinical' rationalism of the early verse. It also casts light on the psychological interests which are one of the few constants of Auden's many changes in *Weltanschauung* and some of the compulsions behind the sometimes apparently gratuitous ritualism of his later verse. These in turn are only sub-categories of a crucial aspect of Auden's approach to his art: this is his elaborate strategy of indirection.

Auden wears his evasions almost outrageously on his sleeve. His secretiveness about his private life is ostentatious, one might almost say exhibitionist. He goes out of his way to advertise his determination to establish his personal reserve and, characteristically, generalises this into a general standard of behaviour. When writing Louis MacNeice's obituary, Auden praised him for his 'stoic reserve' in hiding much depression from his friends and seemed to regard it as the height of friendship that he should do so.[28] When, on the few occasions that Auden himself, as a poet, has been emotionally rather explicit, he has subsequently tried to cover up his tracks with an almost comical, because necessarily ineffective, ferocity. The number of poems he has excised from the latest edition of his supposedly collected works would almost fill an anti-anthology of the public's favourite pieces. He has, for instance, left out the rather breathless but striking 'O love, the interest itself in thoughtless Heaven'; and one of the most famous of all his paragraphs, the one ending: 'We must love one another or die'.[29] To the post-Freudian mind, there is something suspect about this tense parade of privacy. Suspicion grows when one realises that, like Montaigne, Auden repeatedly takes himself as an illustration for his *obiter dicta* on life and manners and that a cunning selection of his statements would go far further to establishing his autobiography than one would expect of a champion of detachment. One cannot help feeling the poet, far from being impersonal, is in fact trying to suppress the effects of an unwilled but highly conscious isolation in self. The impassiveness of his verse has something of the corrective effect of the night sky in 'A Walk after Dark':

> A cloudless night like this
> Can set the spirit soaring;
> After a tiring day

> The clockwork spectacle is
> Impressive in a slightly boring
> Eighteenth century way.
>
> It soothed adolescence a lot
> To meet so shameless a stare;
> The things I did could not
> Be as shocking as they said
> If that would still be there
> After the shocked were dead.[30]

Might not the clockwork spectacle of Auden's detachment offer his equivalent of the shamelessly soothing stare of eternity?

Auden expresses the emotional logic of this in an early poem where he tells his lover that

> . . . since our desire cannot take that route which is straightest,
> Let us choose the crooked, so implicating these acres,
> These millions in whom already the wish to be one
> Like a burglar is stealthily moving.[31]

Here, reduced to essentials, is the psychological mechanism of so much of Auden's art: the poet calls in the entire universe to redress the balance of his feelings. For all its multifarious political and social activities, his poetry about external themes is in many ways only a vast and varied extension of his poetry about internal ones. Take for instance his psychoanalytical approach to politics in the Thirties. At one pole he set the refusal to adapt to life,

> The high thin rare continuous worship
> Of the self-absorbed,[32]

in which Narcissism, political reaction and the death-wish are all equated; and at the other the duty to 'rebuild our cities not dream of islands',[33] islands being, in Auden's canon, almost always symbols of Narcissism. It would be hard to interpret collective phenomena in ways more narrowly based on an argument from the plight of the individual.

For a man like Auden, struggling to be the whole acceptant man, the reproach of Narcissism and self-regard must have been most difficult to bear, since it implies—or implied to the young poet—eternal exclusion from the Freudian paradise of

emotional maturity. His compulsion to stand aside as an observer, to generalise, would arise naturally from an attempt to
find the counterpoise to such a sense of incompleteness in himself. Auden's poetic method transcribes a determination to
grow from an unbalanced to a balanced mode of feeling. His
passion for clinical detachment when young, for Christianity
when not so young, and throughout for psychoanalysis; his insistence that poetry is not self-expression but a solemn game
and that Sacred Objects can be conjured up by being named;
all have one conviction in common—the desire to raise objective standards and abjure subjective attitudes: the fear of
self. He is perpetually standing away from his own experience,
in order to take cognisance of everything about him, the
universe, the community of other men, himself, as if it were
only by embracing the whole world that he dare embrace anything at all. Little has value in itself, its force derives almost
entirely from its contribution to the general scheme of things,
the necessary universal harmony. Auden cannot give his heart
to anything until he has first satisfied himself that his reactions
stand up to his own categorical imperatives. He is creating an
intellectual frame of relationships to replace the emotional one
he fears he cannot carry in himself.

Yet, however plausible such a psychological determinism is
in explaining Auden's art, there are clear limits to its power to
convey that art's principle of life. For one thing, Narcissism may
imply detachment in relation to others, it certainly does not
suggest this in relation to one's own pain: it cannot be equated
with immunity from feeling. In fact, his poetry expresses certain
kinds of emotion, particularly a kind of melancholia, more
simply and abundantly than that of any other prominent
modern writer of verse. That is obvious from his lyrics in the
Thirties if from nothing else. Some of his poetry stubbornly
refuses to enter into the depersonalised patterns to which it
would be irremediably predestined if it were wholly governed by some iron law of detachment. Both the music and the
imagery of a poem like 'Look Stranger' are of the most traditional empathic type. Moreover, his early poetry proves that
he is quite capable of producing the received kind of imagery
(for the lack of which he is frequently reproached), where pre-

cise conscious metaphors open a window on the powerfully imprecise stirrings of the unconscious:

> I, crouching behind a sheep-pen, heard
> Travel across a sudden bird,
> Cry out against the storm.[34]

> . . . lonely on fell as chat,
> By pot-holed becks,
> A bird stone-haunting, an unquiet bird.[35]

Such images as symbols of menacing restlessness or awakening life, where Auden identifies the outward event and inward state in a perfectly orthodox way, show that his detachment should not be taken too literally. His impersonality is not a congenital mental or emotional structure, a built-in limitation. It may be indirectly related to one, but in itself it is in some sense a choice deliberately made.

The choice, I think, has been conditioned at least as much by Auden's cultural background as by his personal psychology. This can be illustrated by John Bayley's interesting, and to some extent convincing, thesis that Auden, like Tennyson, is a poet of childhood fixations. If these were really the dominant source of their art, one would expect to see a striking similarity between the two. Yet it would be hard to think of a difference greater than between the styles of Auden and Tennyson. Tennyson's 'dreadful hollow behind the little wood' to which Bayley refers, is full of the ghosts who terrorised a small child wandering round the vicarage garden at Somersby.[36] Poems like 'Tears, idle tears' have the same quality of naked and defenceless feeling. That is the last thing one would say of most of Auden's poetry. Talk as he may of Sacred Awe, there is nothing superficially awestruck about anything he does.[37] One might find a psychological explanation of this too. Auden's poetry might be seen as tied to the fixations not of the infant in the vicarage garden but of the later, though still prepubertal, conspiracies of Tom Sawyer or William Brown heaving stones through the neighbours' greenhouses. Yet the arbitrary glibness of such distinctions is singularly unconvincing beside the simple fact that Tennyson and Auden seem, each of them, to epitomise an age. Auden has written that 'great changes in artistic style always reflect some alteration in the frontier between the sacred and profane in the imagination of a society'.[38] It is hard to conceive of Tennyson's looming emotions outside the nineteenth century or Auden's reductive self-consciousness away from the ironies of the twentieth.

Although 'implicating these acres, these millions'[31] no doubt has private roots in Auden's personality, this should not lead one to ignore the obvious point that Auden's morally encyclopaedic attitude is far more natural in our modern culture than critics repelled by the generalising spirit implicitly assume. True, Auden's intensity and clarity of purpose in seeking to identify with the world may arise from a need to transcend what he feels to be personal limitations, but in itself the identification is one of the understandable, indeed required, responses from a citizen of the twentieth century. Though the intellectual manifestations of the ambition to be universal include gross over-confidence, their emotional cause is rather the reverse. When poets were confident enough of their relations to the gods—or, more accurately, when they still thought of nature in the emotional categories of their personal experience — the lyrical stance went without saying. The Elizabethans were gloriously subjective even in what they thought to be their objective thinking. The chain of being, in which one could discuss the music of the spheres, or grade angels, animals or stones in endless arbitrary and beautiful analogies, was essentially a cosmological view in which a man could, without even knowing it, imprint his own patterns of feeling on the world. The writer affirmed his conviction of the universe and, like the astrologer, conjured up his own destiny, almost magically, by his verbal spell. It was almost literally — if unconsciously and sometimes in a terrifyingly inverted way, as when men felt they were puppets of the movements of the stars—an act of arbitrary creation. It was always a kind of ritual, in which thought and emotion, not yet truly conscious of their context, spontaneously blend. The situation today is utterly different. One who is aware of the individual impulse as a tiny element in an infinitely complex universe, and of the limits and temptations of the individual's vision, cannot accept feelings as accurate barometers of reality. The modern jansenist or puritan cannot, like Pascal, swell emotionally with the sense of the infinite and shrink with the infinitesimal in Man, for he is conditioned by the detached scientific spirit to abjure such identification of the universe with himself. Nor, however, can he identify himself with the universe and assume, like the Victorian prophet of science, that matter is at his disposal, for he knows far too acutely his own limitations and his inner chaos. To such a man, the command to know the 'data of an unyielding universe' can be all-compelling.[39] To know exactly what he can and cannot encompass is the nearest he can come to re-establishing the safe old family relationship with the Universe. Auden himself has written that 'to see the individual life related not only to the local social life of its time, but to the whole of human history, life on earth, the stars, gives one both humility and self-confidence'.[40] In this sense, he is far closer to the mainstream of the modern consciousness than Eliot or Yeats, who were almost eccentrically preoccupied with the evidence of their own inner selves. He has, laudably, made a far greater effort to come to equal terms with his surroundings. Auden's attempt to know his world has been governed by a very typical need to release his own feelings from crippling uncertainties and doubt. His art is a common predicament made manifest by a temperament peculiarly vulnerable to it.

Auden was brought up on the first vulgarising wave of an intellectual revolution. His was the generation after the first world war, when liberal capitalist society was on the verge of nervous breakdown. Freud, Marx, the anthropologists, who had been unearthing every kind of illiberal irrationality with the tools of scientific enquiry and rational analysis, were becoming the mentors of the marching wing of society. Their discoveries fitted in with the disillusion of people who had seen the creed of progress founder in the most industrially murderous of wars. Only the spirit of objective consciousness seemed to contain within a civilised crust of order the underworld of half-tamed forces which politics and the theorists alike revealed. Consciousness had a confessional, almost a medical, role and scientific analysis held the throne of an almost Papal infallibility.

Every eye must weep alone
Till I Will be overthrown . . .
But I Will can be removed
Not having sense enough
To guard against I Know.[41]

Communists would 'objectify' the class struggle of greedy, irrational men into the free society of brothers by their scientific
understanding of the laws of history. Men moved by the new
rules of rationalised Unreason 'converting number from vague
to certain'.[42] The 'change of heart' required to transform a
rotting society was hardly distinguishable from the 'new styles
of architecture'[43] or, even as late as 1937, from

the research on fatigue
And the movements of packers; the gradual exploring of all
the
Octaves of radiation;
To-morrow the enlarging of consciousness by diet and breath-
ing.[44]

In the circumstances, the attempt to reach wisdom by objective thought, in so far as this is possible, thought at any rate
passionate in its precision, was one of the most obvious courses
for a poet seeking to transcend the stifling conventions of
George V's England.

Accordingly, Auden's poetry is a curious mixture: questing
in its fundamental urge to achieve a personal balance, but
didactic in its way of presenting each intermediate conclusion
as a moral imperative, a panacea, for all men. The didacticism
is apt to present itself as the real motive force, but it comes in
the last resort less from the desire to teach than from the
author's own need to be in tune with universal imperatives as
he sees them at the moment of utterance. Like all born teachers,
he is more concerned to share an experience he is undergoing
and to impart his tentative conclusions (even if the very excitement of his discovery makes them look anything but tentative),
than to present *ex cathedra* statements of 'the truth'. His career
has been a bewildering succession of apparently absolute
'truths' which he has been the first to discard when they had
served their turn and a new hypothesis had led to a new con-

viction. Each system has, in short, been an experiment as Auden picks his way forward to his own peace of mind. Relative as each proved to be, while it lasted as the most closely approximate image of the hidden imperative Auden was looking for, each had something of the absoluteness of the hope of harmony that lay behind it. While ostensibly dedicated to the truth about the human condition, Auden has in fact been, in his own phrase, fumbling 'about in the Truth for the straight successful Way'.[45] His obsession has been his personal peace of mind, the Good Place to which 'the Truth' might lead him.[46]

Since ideas, conclusions and psychological events exist in their own right and not that of the artist, Auden's poetic voice is rarely pitched high. Truth is not a city to be taken by storm nor a girl to be swept off her feet. It can be discovered but it cannot be seduced. It can be raised, but not possessed. Nor is it an ego to be expressed, mirrored or launched: truth is, or is not.

> Truth, like love and sleep, resents
> Approaches that are too intense.[47]

In fact, one can only bear witness to the truth. Even a highly musical poem like 'Look, stranger, at this island now', conveys experience through the eyes, the dispassionate observer's 'look' and 'watch' which recur again and again in Auden's early verse. He is somewhat like Wordsworth in that his writing most often rises to its peak through the value of its insight, rather than by an overpowering appeal from the poet's emotions to the reader's sensibility. When that comes through his poems have a quality of quietness, which is spiritual and distinct from their surface noises. It is the very English quality of a shaft of light on a cold-coloured landscape, as in 'Perhaps I always knew what they were saying'. When the insight fails, the verse tends to fall flat, or entertain for secondary reasons, such as a witty aside or formal and verbal virtuosities which have lost their point. Like Wordsworth, Auden, when not at his best, easily seems to be at his worst.

Wordsworth, partly because of the period when he wrote, saw and felt and judged very much as an individual, and a quirky one at that. When he went wrong, it was in a parody of the unimproved plain man, but his individualism also served to put him in a personal relationship with his themes. His great verse has a kind of petrified passion, its music bearing traces of the waves of emotion from which it sprang. Auden, over a hundred years later, is much more wary of his impulses: his whole life has been an attempt to educate them. He is very much the eclectic intellectual, the freelance teacher. In verse, this intellectuality tends to invention and mobility. When he is excited, Auden usually throws up a firework display of ideas, images and musical patterns. He is in constant danger of dispersal and artistic irrelevance, because his raw material is the whole field of modern culture, from geology to politics and from painting to religion. When he goes wrong, it is in a parody of the unstaunchable professor on whose opinions the sun never sets.

These are normal hazards of a poetry of contexts such as Auden's. Poetry of this kind is bound to be 'impure', that is, full of elements which belong not to the representation of the poet's nature but to the world about which it is necessary for him to reach a judgement. Such poetry is also likely to have an unscrupulousness which is more than a matter of Auden's superficial weaknesses, like condescension towards failures: this is, that anxiously seeking the Good Place, he is in danger of selling an argument, not least to himself, instead of expressing conviction as a state of being. A subtle tone of bullying and preaching, symptomatic not of the poet's ostensible beliefs but of his deeper uncertainties, tends to creep in. Worse still, the poet, who has to identify with the whole universe in order to believe in himself, must, as a *means*, ape the supposed detachment of the scientific attitude to attain the *end* of attachment to his immediate world. The result is a certain loss of tactual contact not only with things and with people, but with the very experience he has himself undergone.* This apathetic fallacy which stands the old pathetic fallacy on its head, mimicking the

* Take for instance Auden's description of a nightmare from which he seems frequently to have suffered:

Across [plains], spotted by spiders from afar,
   I have tried to run, knowing there was no hiding and no help;
On them, in brilliant moonlight, I have lost my way
   And stood without a shadow at the dead centre
Of an abominable desolation,
   Like Tarquin ravished by his post-coital sadness.[48]

indifference of Nature even in the apprehension of one's own most powerful emotions, is one of the traps for the sensibility of a scientific age. In a certain type of artist, caught, like Auden, in the intellectual assumptions and mechanisms of his time, it is perhaps *the* temptation. It turns him into a poet whose images, all too rarely dredged as numinous forms out of his troubled feelings, normally figure as the victims of his ulterior motives. It is this which makes his verse, for all its ebullience, variety and visual precision, nevertheless seem to have 'little colour, smell or touch'.[49] Auden likens his 'singing robe' to a 'cotton frock', but this is too gaudy: in some ways, it makes one think more of the grey flannel of the traditional English prep-school uniform.[50]

The apathetic fallacy so evident in Auden's work can, then, be seen as a product of the poet's general environment as well as his personal psychology. It may well be that Auden's solipsism has made him specially sensitive to the modern sense of isolation, but his keen awareness of the need to identify with the cosmos, derived from the culture, is also powerful in shaping his art. A seventeenth-century solipsist might have been still more allegorical, still more emblematic and fantastical than Auden, but he would never have been to the same extent the observer trapped in his observation post. He could always take refuge in mythical relations with the Godhead, the Virgin or some Impossible She. He would at least have given the impression of a relationship with his anthropomorphic mental universe, and almost certainly even fooled himself. He would have been neither so isolated, nor so obsessed by the awareness of isolation, nor so much in need of coming to terms with it as a way of life, as a twentieth-century solipsist of Auden's stamp. For the heir of the scientific culture who has to stand aside and

---

Loneliness and anxiety could hardly go further. Yet it is hard to say of these verses, as of the surrealist paintings which they recall, that the mere representation of the inner desert really stirs one to an apprehension of its horror. Though there is a great deal of fussing with psychological symbols and dream states in Auden's verse, I do not know of a single case where he conveys the heightened emotions of a dream as elsewhere he conveys the adult frustrations of love, the excitement of political hope and despair, or even the anxiety of a half-grasped intuition.

be detached, the clash between objectivity and isolation is inherent. Because he instinctively accepts this, Stephen Spender in his reminiscences, in *World Within World*, of his friend up at Oxford, has perhaps come closer than anyone to stating the nature of Auden's restlessness:

> Auden . . . sometimes gave the impression of playing an intellectual game with himself and with others, and this meant that in the long run he was rather isolated. His early poetry also gives the impression of an intellectual game . . . of impartial objectivity about catastrophes, wars, revolutions, violence, hatreds, loves, and all the forces which move through human lives. . . . Auden himself was too human, moreover, for it to be an attitude which he could for long maintain in the face of experiences that wrung his heart. . . . In the next phase an answer is rather promiscuously provided: and this answer is Love. However, the love which is supposed to save both the individual who is aware of his own subconscious depths, and the society which has repented of its evil exploitation . . is too analytic, too adaptable and adjustable to every occasion, too sterilized, too much the love in a psychoanalyst's room. So with the other answers: from psychology to Communism to Christianity; they remain a little arbitrary: and perhaps the root of this arbitrariness is the poet's own isolation.[51]

This seems to me to go deep because of its stress on the relation between the two key ideas of 'objectivity' and 'isolation'. The objectivity is the standard one sets oneself, the isolation, whether as cause or effect, is the mental state built into the effort itself. The energy behind most of Auden's poetry is generated by this sense of an impasse in which intellect and emotion cannot help but war.

As a result, the last response one should have to the impersonality of Auden's work is to take it at face value. One has only to enter into the moods of the poetry to realise that indeed the most superficial thing about it is its air of indifference. This is not the cause but the symptom of the mental purgatory from which the poet instinctively struggles for release. The striking difference between Auden and other poets who were, or claimed to be, men of their world, like Byron, Browning or Kipling, is that their works are finally a ragbag of comments on the world about them, with unifying characteristics but no clearly unifying passion, whereas his have an extraordinary singleness of purpose. His development has not been, like that of many artists, a growth as of a plant or tree, but a pilgrimage, a deliberate painful journey from a Limbo of inner doubt to an Eden, or more modestly, Arcadia of ordered and more or less accepted values. His verse has always been a parable of the individual struggling up his spiritual mountain. Almost from the first, this has been virtually the one and only theme behind the bewildering variety of his interests; and, in the last resort, it is a profoundly introspective one.

Auden differs fundamentally from the sociologist, the extra-vert observer, in that his strength is in introspection, which he then extends, often over-confidently, to generalisations about the world around him. It is hardly too much to say that despite his immense culture and astonishing mental activity, Auden's first and only reliable source of information has been himself. This has too frequently made him brash and slick in his esti-mates of others, but it has also given him a far above average insight and emotional awareness and a rich sense of the con-trary powers contained in any ethic worthy of the name. Thus while at his worst he produces advice which is self-revealing in its plausible coarseness—

> Writer, be glib: please them with scenes of theatrical bliss and horror,
> Whose own slight gestures tell their doom with a subtlety quite foreign to the stage[52]

—at his best one also finds the quite exceptional clear-sighted-ness about his own feelings that he displayed even as an under-graduate. Already in *Poems*, his first volume published in 1930, he hit on lines that were penetratingly, even painfully, true:

> Love by ambition
> Of definition
> Suffers partition
> And cannot go
> From yes to no
> For no is not love, no is no
> The shutting of a door
> The tightening jaw
> A conscious sorrow.[53]

'Conscious sorrow' is pretty good: at an age, and in an age, when aspiring, lustful young men were still given to pretending that their sorrow was not self-conscious, Auden was already rooting out what his sharp eyes saw was make-belief: 'no is not love, no is no'. Whenever Auden is writing about himself on a subject close to his fundamental preoccupation with finding himself, the tone changes: it ceases to be a performance and becomes charged with feeling, responsible, full and strong.

From the very beginning of Auden's career, such passages express the conflict between an attitude of intellectual mastery and a personal though unprofessed pain. Originally, Auden tended to blame this anxiety on a society which was undeniably out of joint but, reading even the early poems with a little hindsight, one can see that his problem was far more personal, intimate and difficult to eradicate than that:

> Love by ambition
> Of definition
> Suffers partition.

The bald matter-of-factness of this statement conceals what has since proved to be a deep and lasting conflict between the emotional obsession of the artist and the scrutatory attitudes of the modern intellectual induced by a culture which he has embraced more heartily than most.

Eliot has written of the 'dissociation of sensibility', Yeats of 'division', Auden himself of 'duality', Matthew Arnold, in 'The Scholar Gipsy', of 'divided aims'. Outside poetry altogether, R. H. Tawney has spoken of the Puritan ethic as

> a dualism which regards the secular and the religious aspects of life, not as successive stages within a larger unity, but as parallel and independent provinces, governed by different laws, judged by different standards, and amenable to different authorities.[54]

This sense of division amounts, in short, to an intuition of the disintegrative effect on the modern spirit of the intellectual revolution of the past three centuries. One may choose to regard this from the cultural angle as the secularisation of a dualism implicit in Christianity; from the Christian point of view as a failure of humility; from the liberal one as Man's reluctant awakening to the real nature of his relationship with the universe around him; or from the Marxist one as the expression of the inhuman relationships engendered by Capitalism. In each instance, the sense of conflict, of a divided mind, is fundamental. If this is so, one would positively expect poets to betray the tension in their works. Evidence of duality, such as the apathetic fallacy, would not be a mark of shallowness but of honesty. This, it seems to me, is precisely the case with Auden.

From start to finish, his poetry is driven by the metaphysical distress of the intellectual harrowed by the emotional vacuum of his broad but abstract knowledge of the world. He is a space-man uncoupled from the earth of his too easy observation but unable to survive in the solution of emptiness in which he and his planet appear to be suspended. In retrospect, it is plain that this motivated the generalised and undefined menace of Auden's youthful work far more than fear of any external event, however frightening, such as impending war or revolution. The un-ease was, at heart, an unfocused awareness of the isolation inherent in the confidence that the poet could deal with his life, and the world around him, as with so many scientific data. The very effort to be objective and in league with the universal re-quires a suppression of self that is emotionally impossible, at least for an artist who lives, vocationally, for the exploration of feeling. It implies a confidence in the material reality and spiritually fulfilling character of man's accumulated body of knowledge which the individual patently cannot have as soon as he becomes self-aware. What use is such knowledge, essen-tially a technique in the services of the species, and sometimes only a convention, in helping the single man to define his private emotional purposes?

Even the various reasons we construct — or, as Auden has in effect said throughout his career, above all the reasons we con-struct—disseminate their own emotions. The twentieth-century belief in progress through science has been no exception. Its categories and laws, its analytic ways of wisdom, make a dramatic language, but emotionally a comfortless one. Applied to human feelings, analysis always seems to end up by stressing the conflicts and reducing the triumphs over them to the least evocative word. Freud has shown, to our vulgar prejudice at least, that love is not Love, but the drive of the libidinous Ego at grips with its environment. Marx has shown that freedom is not Freedom but the satisfaction of one class at the expense of another. The anthropologists have shown the gods are no God but the varieties of human hope and terror striving to tame the Unknown. The physicists have shown that the universe is not made in the image of Man, or even of his works as one could imagine Newton meant, but is to be apprehended only through a network of equations which traditionally educated men cannot understand. All these views, garbled or not, stress the conflicting or impersonal elements of our world and disintegrate the human person as a separate, distinctive unit whole and active in himself. To anyone who has absorbed their influence, the world is a struggle of forces of which he is an incidental, very temporary, expression. The human being becomes, on analytical assumptions—we need no Freud to point it out—an aggressive, lonely animal seeking out his own purposes. His loves are an accidental coming together, his constant departures a proof of his self-absorption. It is striking how many modern poets consumed, like Valéry, by self-devouring consciousness, harp again and again on the Narcissus theme. Auden's own conclusion was 'we love ourselves alone'.[55] At this stage even the vocabulary conveys despair. 'Alone' is a word which echoes desperately through Romantic verse. This is not just self-dramatisation. It is the despair of the mind which has assaulted Nature till it has turned the old soil of feeling into a desert of its own abstractions.

Auden's art is not, then, a 1200-page self-indulgence in the virtuosity of his own literary talent and the ideologies of the day. Whatever its superficial temptations, it has been fired by an underlying conflict to which an artistic ethic of detachment is a form of adaptation. That detachment is no doubt also the product of a psychological propensity to self-absorption. But this in itself is part of the pain that begets the pearl and has opened the poet to the larger and similar pain of a culture equally conscious of its being immured in self. Auden's art is exemplary of an age in which metaphor is no longer man's link with the universe, but only an extension of himself; where the conceit is not a facet of external reality but a fancy of his own;

a world not of Gods who offer a protective shell but of consciously supreme fictions which are too fictitious to offer supremacy. Auden's history is one long attempt to outgrow the tyranny of the analytical spirit over his own feelings and to evolve an outlook that will reconcile them with each other. By nature, this implies a highly intellectual art, and Auden has many of the limitations of the brilliant intellectual, including a mobility of mind which outranges his emotional grasp. Yet the very force of his personal involvement in the culture's inner contradiction has enabled him to embrace its tensions more explicitly perhaps than any other poet and to find a form of clarity in the depths of his own entanglement. Struggling with the unresolved dilemmas which more or less affect us all, he has won through to a poetry which not only is always interesting but also spans a growth of thought and feeling as strongly founded and as broad as any in recent English literature. Auden has often been compared with Yeats and Eliot in terms which suggest that the titans before the flood of modern poetry have been succeeded, as is the way with later generations, by a giant with feet of clay. Such comparisons are rather misleading. Auden is not an 'expressive' artist, as Yeats or Eliot are; he does not so much affirm feelings as seek the setting for his inner world. This leads to another kind of poetry, which has to be assessed in other terms. Auden's art may well become more, and not less, appreciated when its implications cease to be as entangled as they are today in controversies which, because they have not fully surfaced, naggingly confuse judgement and debate.

THE NOVELTY OF *POEMS*

AUDEN now preaches from Anglo-Catholic pulpits, but his first volume, *Poems* (1930), had a quality which could better be described as nonconformist rigour. Its verse evoked

> The slow fastidious line
> That disciplines the fell.

This is not just a matter of landscape, though Auden's fondness for windswept rocky scarps is almost the *griffe* of his early style. The whole tenor of *Poems* expresses a desire to discover the bedrock of values that remained after the Edwardian clouds of Platonic absolutes, from Beauty onwards, were dispersed by the grapeshot of 1914.

> Heroes are buried who
> Did not believe in death
> And bravery is now
> Not in the dying breath
> But resisting the temptations
> To skyline operations.[1]

Thoughts of heroism and tragedy are for relatively secure, self-confident and imperial generations, not tested by withering fire. Such people can afford to dramatise their achievements and themselves. Their descendants, however, who have experienced tragedy in the flesh, are purged of grand opera. Armchair warriors cultivate their heroisms, not, usually, front-line warriors, still less inmates of concentration camps. Most of these look instead for values which will help them prevent a repetition of the horrors they have witnessed and undergone. Values can only be acquired by comparison, balance, judgement and care. In their service, inflation turns to deflation, vague aspirations to precise comparisons, collective dreams to a hard look at the consequences for individual citizens, Platonic ideals to scientific analysis. The post-tragic attitude is matter-of-fact, concrete, and, above all, moderate: in a violent age, moderation speaks for the hold of the mind on reverence. The 'technocratic' voice, present from the beginning in Auden's verse, is first and foremost a post-tragic one. Its guiding light is the desire for constructive clarities in place of death-dealing dreams.

This ambition determined the characteristic qualities of the *Poems*: extreme concentration, in the hopes of punishing all vagueness of thought or sentiment; detachment, the better to conduct a strict self-criticism; ruthless honesty with oneself:

> Voices explain
> Love's pleasure and love's pain . . .
> Hushed for aggression
> Of full confession
> Likeness to likeness
> Of each old weakness;
> Love is not there
> Love has moved to another chair.[2]

'Aggression of full confession', 'Likeness to likeness of each old weakness', 'Love is not there'—by systematically stripping the polite veils from banal or unsightly realities, Auden strikes his characteristic note, harsh in the first instance, but with a humanising aftertone of pain. Though labials and vowels are cunningly aligned and rhymes, irregularly spaced, echo one another in little spirals of sound, sensuality is officially played down in this verse. Its power to move one is to a large extent rooted in the unspoken assumptions, the contrast between its austere demeanour and the emotional burden hinted at by the very temptations it resists. The postponed afflatus of understatement leaves the reader to infer for himself the gravity of the pose. It is ultimately just as deliberately noble a style as those it implicitly rejects, but what others achieved by heightened expression this attains by reticence. Anything more overt would, in such a puritan mental climate, be a form of reliance on artificial aids and a shirking of the duty to grapple with oneself. By its very nature, the form of speech insists on the moral courage required to be so brutally impartial with one's own feelings.

The complexity of attitudes and modes of thought in this

poetry is already great. The source of its unusual beauty is in fact a peculiar sensibility to the relations of feelings one with another, the interweaving of emotional cause and effect. It is a mesh of conclusions, each implying the trials and errors that have been lived through and overcome for present understanding to be reached. We react to the interplay of many sentiments, whose very conjunction multiplies their meaning. *Poems* (1930) offers in a highly concentrated form much of the experience of groping self-discovery that most people go through, not at university, but over a period of many years. Where the basic intuitions are so sophisticated, literary elaboration would be out of place. Instead of the common kind of ornament—the birds and bees which Cecil Day-Lewis, though superficially Audenesque, floated quite expertly through the pylons of his early verse—*Poems* display what their author has praised in Milton: a remarkable mastery over syntax, 'the structural element in style'.[3]

This is partly the simple consequence of compression: where you strip away the flesh, the skeleton necessarily stands out. There is more to it than that, though, as one can sense from the extraordinarily positive uses to which Auden forces almost every part of speech. The starkness of the numerous verbs is frequently reinforced by putting them in the imperative, and even adjectives play a quasi-verbal role. Indeed, as often as not, they are present participles used with a curiously transitive effect:

> Doom is dark and deeper than any sea-dingle.
> Upon what man it fall
> In spring, day-wishing flowers appearing,
> Avalanche sliding, white snow from rock-face,
> That he should leave his house,
> No cloud-soft hand can hold him, restraint by women;
> But ever that man goes
> Through place-keepers, through forest trees,
> A stranger to strangers over undried sea . . .[4]

'Day-wishing flowers', 'avalanche sliding'—presented in such an active form, these seem to be not nouns, that is states of being, but events under way, and thereby almost verbal clauses. Even 'place-keepers' has oddly mobile connotations. The

accumulation of purposive words gives the passage a dynamism
that would not emerge from its otherwise quite elementary
development of narrative and ideas. This is further heightened
by the ingenious syntax of the paragraph:

> Upon what man it fall . . .
> That he should leave his house,
> No cloud-soft hand can hold him

is a particularly deft modulation from the passive feeling of the
pressure of doom on the individual to the man's own active
Odyssey driven forward by it. The change of mood hinges upon
a couple of subjunctives and a mere 'that'. This is an illustration
of what is perhaps the most original and insistent feature of
Auden's early style, the use he made of prepositions, con-
junctions and imperatives, all of them impersonal in their final
effect:

> Enter with him
> These legends, Love;
> For him assume
> Each diverse form
> To legend native,
> As legend queer;
> That he may do
> What these require,
> Be, Love, like him
> To legend true.[5]

'To legend native', 'As legend queer', 'That he may do',
'What these require'—instead of being modestly invisible as
in most writing, here the joints of language point the corners of
the route until it is largely on their well-articulated twists of
direction, their 'flick of wrist' that the poem glides and turns.[6]
The short lines still further stress their frequency, counterpoint
and force. It is a highly dexterous exploitation of the mech-
anics of speech to create a kind of personality out of thought, to
present it not in two dimensions as is the danger with verse so
full of abstractions, but in three.

There is a curious physical depth, attained largely by sound
effects, in some of the *Poems*:

> Again in conversations
> Speaking of fear

And throwing off reserve
The voice is nearer
But no clearer
Than first love
Than boys' imaginations.[7]

At first flush, 'again' and 'but' and the twice-repeated 'than' look dialectical enough, though this, obviously, cannot be their main function. 'Again', as the first word in the poem, cannot be truly argumentative. In part, it simply suggests informality. But, placed where it is, it also creates a kind of emotional and rhetorical echo, as if to stress the number of times confession has occurred and how much of a *ronde* the repetition all is. Like the other prepositions, 'again' seems to isolate the key words that follow so that every impression comes through on its own. The rhyme also helps.

The voice is nearer
But no clearer

slowed up by the booming penultimate syllables ('near-', 'clear-') and dragging feminine endings ('-er'), sounds with the hollowness of a dream. The aftertones of 'nearer' and 'clearer', the rounded space of 'than first love/than boys' imaginations' (where 'imaginings' would have been more obvious but less ample) close the stanza on a long enveloping line and give the 'voice' a room and a distance out of which to reverberate. To write of such things, even briefly, exaggerates their impact. Nevertheless, the cumulative effect, as the ear takes the fleeting hints, is of a restrained incantation, a resonance that fractionally outlasts the poem. The delicate music of abstract thought, chamber music, which results, is the great aural attraction of many of the best *Poems*.

*   *   *

The virtues of *Poems*, highly distinctive as they are, look familiar enough, even traditional, today when it is difficult to speak of Auden without some reference to Skelton, Hardy or Graves. Their triumph has been so complete that it is difficult to think oneself back into the literary conventions their vigour assailed, breached and supplanted. Just how new they were can only be gauged by disinterring neglected works, like Robert Bridges' *Testament of Beauty*, the fruit of his old age, which came out in 1929 and impressed and influenced Auden himself. The *Testament of Beauty* is in some ways a powerful meditative poem with lines condensing the conclusions of a lifetime:

> Our stability is but balance, and conduct lies
> in masterful administration of the unforeseen.

Bridges, then over eighty, was visibly concerned—probably with the example of Yeats's self-transformation before him—to strip his style of the clichés of romance. Despite this, Bridges' language and rhythm are not inventive enough and the sentiment comes perilously close to the hackneyed at crucial moments. One is not surprised to learn that

> Man's happiness, his flaunting honey'd flower of soul,
> is his loving response to the wealth of Nature.[8]

Auden's detached pose was one way of deflating the high-toned insufficiency of this late Victorian tradition, even at its most honourably ambitious in *The Testament of Beauty*, and of replacing it with a little raw Nature.

> The silly fool, the silly fool
> Was sillier in school
> But beat the bully as a rule[9]

was an abrupt return to simple statements and first principles, reminding one of the brute facts behind the public-school values of the Georgians and their pseudo-Athenian trappings.

More to the point for the impact Auden made on the young, he was new even in relation to Eliot and Pound. They, not he, were the literary revolutionaries. In literary terms, he merely built where they had first cleared the ground. Still, their radicalism was peculiarly backward-looking, very much of the right and, in many ways, only a transplant of literary attitudes long familiar on the continent. Perhaps because they were American expatriates, they were obsessed by the vision of a lost classic poise. Their nostalgia for the Golden Age of their imagination is often put down to 'postwar disillusion', but this is one of history's optical illusions. Eliot's *Waste Land* and Pound's *Hugh Selwyn Mauberley* are soaked in the cyclical view of civilisation stated in its most pessimistic form by Spengler and later Toynbee. Though all four achieved fame after 1918, all four were twenty and crystallised their essential vision well before the Great War. Culturally, they belong not to the post-war period but to the *fin de siècle* reaction against crude mid-Victorian positivism which dominated European culture from the 1880s onwards. Eliot learned, after all, from Laforgue. Eliot, Pound and Yeats, in their denunciations of postwar society, were unconsciously having the best of both worlds, com-bining the anti-bourgeois cultural superiority of Baudelaire with mourning over a heyday full of the values of the Victorian *bourgeoisie*. Auden, though starting with the same bitterness against the present as Eliot, Pound or Yeats, looked in the opposite direction, towards the future. He reflected a partial renewal of the old faith in science. Human reason, triumphing over reactionary vested interests could, tomorrow, through 'Socialism' and the fulfilment of reason in society, bring nearer the Golden Age. The 'few score of broken statues', far from deserving to be worshipped as fetishes, must, now they were broken, be swept away. Auden was necessarily an activist, a radical egalitarian, for, to hope at all, he had to be the enemy of all the privilege—that is, of the selfishness and irrationality in high places—which turned possible happiness into omni-present misery. The political contract between Eliot, Pound and Yeats, whose youth lay on the far side of the war, and Auden, who was at prep school during the war, was not a superficial affair, divorced from their wider inspiration. It derived from their whole attitude to the culture around them, coloured by differences of philosophic outlook and of the generations.

Eliot, Pound and Yeats, like the prewar characters they were, all accepted Bloomsbury's variant of the older humanism with its stronghold in the older universities (though none of them was English, and, from an academic point of view, Pound's quali-fications and personality were highly suspect). Auden broke away from their implicitly upper-class belief in a cultural élite, by being less a literary reformer than a new animal in writing. He introduced into poetry the technical terms of the new, or newly accepted, sociologists, Malinowski, Rivers, Marx, Freud,

Groddek and the rest, whose collective tone was foreign to the British oligarchic tradition in which Oxbridge was steeped. Himself the son of a scientist, 'from my sixth until my sixteenth year I thought myself a mining engineer'.[10] But his family was upper middle class and Anglo-Catholic with a long line of parsons in the background. Auden was thus a living bridge between the two cultures. In this sense, he really was the spy, the intruder, of his own early mythology.

Auden's use of language as a branch of engineering, his parody of the schoolmaster's manner, his determined toughness of statement, expressed an attitude now found with only slight transpositions throughout the establishments of the industrial world. It is a technical, presumptuous, egalitarian spirit which measures, codifies and plans. It stands heir to the older liberal humanism which still lived on, in 1930, in the weak-kneed hellenism of the universities, but its priorities are utterly different. The older humanism, rooted in the classical revival of the Renaissance and the aristocratic urbanity of the eighteenth century, tended to assume that a man should cultivate himself in the Augustan, latinate mould and be a model of civilisation to others. The ghost of Lord Chesterfield hovered like an aesthetic imperative at the back of its ideas of comportment. The new, rooted in the egalitarian and scientific cast of mind of the industrial revolution, does not expect any man to be a model of comportment for anyone, but demands that he should supremely fulfil his social function. The older humanism was individualistic, moralising and highly literate, asking of a man the kind of character and polish which could only be gained from belonging or being co-opted to the dominant minority. Its temptations were blatant snobbery; and a complacent stoicism for the privileged, based on the feeling that nature was too subtle to be controlled, let alone changed; that human misery, being inevitable, need not be rooted out; that it was faintly ill-bred, because naïve, to try; and that culture was somehow more important than the messiness of mere life. The new believes that man himself can become so subtle that, for all practical purposes, he can outwit and enslave nature. It stresses knowledge and social utility, is classless and believes that misery is a form of incompetence. Its temptation, as the later Auden might put it, is to think of human beings in masses and averages or, to put it in a more old-fashioned way, to ignore the tragic element in life.

Auden, himself a vulgariser of the New Thought, was half a product, half a producer, of this transformation in outlook. Indeed, to the extent that 'coming out of me living is always thinking', he was almost a popular poet in the world of spreading education, though his popularity extended only to the rank and file of undergraduates. Auden's thoughts were, or seemed to be, only a step or two ahead of what any bright chap with a university training and literary interests might have picked up as he sauntered between pub and digs. His aspirations answered to common needs. His curtness appealed to people surfeited with Georgian white-flannel verse. His radical political morality pleased those disgusted with 'the old gang' of title-selling, Versailles Treaty politicians.[11] His world of undergraduate confessors, cinematic cowboys and strolls on moors corresponded to the increasingly collegiate ways of life, tastes and recreations of a new generation. Even the obscurities of his poems, ordered round mental associations not cartesian logic, and yet retaining a flavour of systematic rationalism, were a badge of progress on the one road where Eliot had shown the way. Better still, the comparison with Eliot made Auden's verse seem deceptively easy and companionable. Anne Ridler has testified that 'for myself . . . it was Eliot who first made me despair of becoming a poet; Auden (with, of course, dead poets, notably Sir Thomas Wyatt) who first made me think I saw how to become one'.[12] Eliot wrote mandarin English, unattainably remote and erudite. The very quality of his phrasing made it hopeless to copy him; he could only be parodied, and that poorly. As for his views, High Church and monarchy made no appeal to most of the young, even though he cast a halo of intellectual dignity around both which made them more difficult to disparage. In Auden, there was, at least at the time, nothing of all this. Here was the bright boy incarnate, self-confident to a degree, writing, though perhaps a little obscurely, about recognisable but new things in a recognisable but radical way. What could be more modishly modern than 'telegraphese'— chaplinesque, expressionist and technical sounding all in one?

What could be more aseptically and rigorously of the intellect than the refusal to give names to *Poems*, the insistence that they be known by their numbers in Roman numerals? What could be more socialist than a style whose clipped precision alone proclaimed its allegiance to science and its hatred of the confusions which camouflaged the bastions of privilege? What could symbolise the generation gap more dramatically than the guerrilla warfare of 'Control of the passes was, he saw, the key'?[13] Everything about the *Poems* was the radical manifesto of a youth crying out against the postwar *Weltschmerz* and sheer mismanagement of England and calling for something new. As Walter Allen has testified 'those of us who had been children during the first world war' suddenly found their spokesman. 'It is doubtful whether any first volume of poems since Byron's *Hours of Idleness* has made such an immediate and, so to speak, stunning impact on the young who are interested in poetry.'[14]

*　　*　　*

One consequence of this has been that the *Poems* have been judged by the pretty misleading stereotypes which usually go with a movement. Even where these correspond to realities, it is normally to characteristics more typical of Auden's later verse, in the Thirties. The tendency is to read into the *Poems* systems of psychiatric and Marxist thought which, with them, are secondary. And when this view is corrected, it is replaced by a dualism with, on one side, the 'pure-in-heart' who are 'never ill' and, on the other, 'the old gang' doomed to disappear.[15] Similarly, the same words continuously recur in describing the verse, 'tight-lipped', 'clinical', and so on.[16] This is natural enough, for Auden himself gave them currency, but it traps one into mistaking stylistic tricks for imaginative qualities and slogans for themes. In fact, the ideas and attitudes the *Poems* contain are at once firmer, more varied and less systematic than those often read into them in the light of later events.

This is true even of Auden's politics, the area where he was often at his crudest. It would be quite wrong to identify him with the flag-wagging into the hinterland of the future of which Day-Lewis and Spender were guilty. His example probably led them on but, as often happens, the leader sensed the limits of his myths better than his followers. There was in him an element of prudence which they lacked. He talked abundantly of secret agents and of the old gang, several of his poems are miniature manuals for maintaining the morale of revolutionaries, and above all he became more and more concerned with the role of the Leader: 'Leaders must migrate: "Leave for Cape Wrath to-night" ' he said—too often perhaps.[17] Yet most of the things he had to say were firm enough as far as they went. He was quite aware that the historic role he and his friends felt they must assume might be a histrionic over-estimate of themselves:

> Always the following wind of history
> Of others' wisdom makes a buoyant air
> Till we come suddenly on pockets where
> Is nothing loud but us.

He did not think the process of change could be quick or simple, a revolutionary's rapid thrust:

> The future shall fulfil a surer vow
> Not smiling at queen over the glass rim
> Nor making gunpowder in the top room,
> Not swooping at the surface still like gulls
> But with prolonged drowning shall develop gills.[18]

He was, in fact, a moral evolutionist:

> as foreign settlers to strange county come,
> By mispronunciation of native words
> And by intermarriage create a new race
> And a new language, so may the soul
> Be weaned at last to independent delight.[19]

It was only gradually that frustration goaded Auden into more simple-minded views; and that justifiable impatience with a leadership whose code was demonstrated by events to be totally at variance with the needs of the time degenerated into banner slogans. In essence, his early poetry did not offer a political programme but an imaginative vision of change.

What is true of their politics in particular is true of the *Poems* as a whole: despite their pretensions, their world is an imaginative not an analytic one. With their air of critical in-

telligence, their abstract and generalising ways, they seem to
have an underlying logical structure, but this is largely make-
believe, the ritual of a faith in rationality. Almost any poem
under the microscope yields quite a different reading. Take, for
instance, 'The summer quickens all'. Despite their economy of
phrase (a programme in itself for the time at which they were
written), the first two lines,

> The summer quickens all,
> Scatters its promises[20]

lands one squarely in the heady world of wishes and of the
young sap rising. Burgeoning desires are essential to the dramatic effect of many an early Auden poem. They are the starting
point of all action and lead to a whole constellation of related
themes: love—of course—migration, hope and, in its distorted
forms, the will to live in fairy-tales and even the promise of the
second coming. The element of yearning is compulsively present
in these poems: it is essential to their inner drama. The hint of
it is flashed in front of the reader so that he can never forget its
existence; but before he can rise to the bait—at that time the
familiar 'poetic' response—the world of wishes is subjected to
the tests of the world of responsibilities, of acts. The correction
of the impulse follows hard on the heels of the impulse itself.
While the summer scatters its promises 'to you and me no less',
nevertheless we must be reminded of our limits: 'neither can
compel'. Neither of 'us' has real control over the process of
growth which is working through us and of which we are the
accidental and temporary vessels, no more, no less. Though the
second stanza,

> The wish to last the year,
> The longest look to live,
> The urgent word survive
> The movement of the air

continues to state a world of wishes—to win over fears of death,
the passing of love and the failure to achieve fame—it does so
in a way whose very affirmations imply scepticism and irony.
These are etched into the curt abstract phrases symbolic of a
precise and analytical spirit; and become explicit in the third
stanza which asserts that the lovers will have to make 'evil'

39

choices they presumably wish to avoid, since these will be 'divided days', when they have apparently parted.

At first sight, this moralising rationalism might seem too staid, too purely critical to rank as an imaginative quality. Yet it is vital to the imaginative strength of Auden's early poetry. In some ways, indeed, it is only the rationalising, or at least technical, air of Auden's thinking which allows him to renew old imagery. The fact that he identifies landscapes with psychological states, mountains with mothers and so on, makes it possible for him to put new blood into the worn-out imagery of nature. His doctrine of the death wish allows him to give a precise sociological appearance to the ripe old sense of decay. In a very real sense he is able to rejuvenate traditional responses by placing them in a new intellectual framework. Further, Auden's rationalism is not a critical spirit of detached inquiry, but an intellectual passion to control one's environment and destiny; it is linked to the other more moral passion for integrity. There is some of this in the determination with which it is accepted that

> we shall choose from ways,
> All of them evil, one

and still more so in the climax to which the middle passage of the poem rises, the injunction to

> Look on with stricter brows.

It is at this point, when the worldly critique of subjective feeling reaches its peak in the Credo of necessary mastery, that the whole vision is transformed by

> The sacked and burning town,
> The ice-sheet moving down,
> The fall of an old house

in a word, by the sense of fate. What raises Auden's early poetry to a mythical plane is the sense of impassive Nature using her agents of evolution, wearing them out like carpenters' tools, throwing them away and passing on. The demonic power takes many forms—sometimes it is just the Life Force, at others, the illusory refuge of the person who fears the necessary dangerous journey to change oneself and the world, at others still the inheritance the new man must bear: the distortions of a sick society, the mother who, in 'Paid on Both Sides', eggs on the cowboy-bravoes to their endless vendetta, the 'ancestral face'.[21] Though this vision may owe much to Hardy, it powerfully turns the scientific cosmology to a poet's purposes. In a less formidable imagination, the scientific view would merely have led the poet to a rationalist wariness of subjective impulses and helped produce a minor, social art. Instead, Auden has seized on the mythical possibilities of an evolving universe working through astronomical spans of space and time, indifferent to individuals and to species, loyal only to its own processes. He has turned the theory of evolution into an iron law of destiny, a kind of Brahma and Shiva, destructive of individuals in its very power to create, crushing mere hopes and wishes with its awesome self-sufficiency of process. It is this deity, presiding over Auden's early work, who makes it numinous and in its own bleak way magniloquent. Auden has not merely opposed the old vision by a critique; he has set up a countervision by its side.

The triangular system of tensions between Feeling (the aspiration which launches 'the summer quickens all'), Will (asserted through scientific rationalism) and Fate (the 'archaic imagery' which casts doubt and grandeur on every effort) is not logical but psychological. The analytical intellect usually works in antitheses not in triads. A world of three, or more, centres of attraction makes for patterns which are richer than any such dualism could be. The attitudes and insights of the *Poems* are ambivalent, shifting and sometimes even in conflict with each other. Their basic theme, the need to transform the dying world of the past into the brave new world of the future, seems simple enough. But in practice it is only a focus for the most complex and turbid feelings, the uncertainties of which break up into a bewildering variety of postures. There is not only the contrast between will and fate. Auden is also constantly veering between hope and fear. At the heart of the fluctuations lies his typical double optic on free will, most clearly expressed when he has the Life Force tell the young man setting out in life that 'I shifted ranges'

To reach that shape for your face to assume.[22]

Has the Life Force reached 'that shape' or has the young man's face 'assumed' it? The uneasy tension between predestination and free will is never resolved and the Manichean battle rages through the *Poems*—and indeed throughout Auden's poetry. At times he is full of active and busy hope for the future. At others, he is dominated by fear of failure. This opens the door to at least four attitudes in the *Poems* and all do indeed appear there.

One is a kind of evolutionary pessimism, a Hardyesque sense of fate with tragic overtones.

> Though he believe it, no man is strong.
> He thinks to be called the fortunate,
> To bring home a wife, to live long.
>
> But he is defeated. . . .
>
> . . . though later there be
> Big fruit, eagles above the stream.[23]

This mood of ostentatiously stoic non-complaint in a setting of barren uplands avoids self-pity, though only just, for self-pity, finding no echo in the Life Force, seems parochial and irrelevant. This, in turn, gives one incentive to self-improvement: it implies that only science, putting nature to the question, can offer a route, though neither a safe nor rapid one, to the mastery over the context necessary to avoid final defeat. Hence the second attitude of a qualified trust in progress prompting self-interrogation and the prayers for courage of the modern knight of the round table.

> To throw away the key and walk away
> Not abrupt exile, the neighbours asking why,
> But following a line with left and right
> An altered gradient at another rate
> Learns more than maps upon the whitewashed wall
> The hand put up to ask; and makes us well
> Without confession of the ill.[24]

Yet even this is rather patient and passive for a young man in a time which summons him to urgent action. So the wheel turns through a revolutionary quarter, in the passages where the

Leader's duty to show the boys how to gain 'control of the passes' is bracingly expounded:

> Shut up talking, charming in the best suits to be had in town,
> Lecturing on navigation while the ship is going down. . . .

> If we really want to live, we'd better start at once to try;
> If we don't, it doesn't matter, but we'd better start to die.[25]

The last line shows how unstable this mood too can be. If revolution is necessary to rescue society from its distortions and diseases, it is nevertheless almost certain to be unpleasant. It might destroy its very agents. Engulfed, they may, in the light of history, be simply devoured by the Life Force seeking out its purposes as a river breaks its banks to find the sea.

> We know it, we know that love
> Needs more than the admiring excitement of union . . .
> Needs death, death of the grain, our death,
> Death of the old gang.[26]

Such premonitions of destruction bring the poet back full cycle, to the Hardyesque view of fate as looming and terrible. This circular motion, from mood to mood, complex enough in itself, is made the more so by Auden's contrasted public and private impulses. His sense of his obligations as a citizen conflicts with his feeling for the intimate pleasures of friendship, love or simply peace. When all these elements are combined, the permutations are almost endless, dictated by shifts of feeling, which easily embrace opposites, not by formal logic.

A single poem will veer ambiguously from one attitude to another. Sometimes it will be a secular prayer for the moral love which frees a man from his burden of negations. At others, it will praise the new life beyond the inner transformation scene and, at others again, despair of ever encompassing it. Sometimes the young man of Will seems to be climbing over the uplands symbolic of Fate, at others the mountains seem about to crash down on him. Sometimes the poet describes the moment of peace that a love affair brings at the heart of troubled times, sometimes the sense of the insufficiency of any private emotion on the eve of the gathering storm. Sometimes he speaks as the Life Force working through the species or individual, sometimes he will debate with himself, thinking out his inner confusions as one enjoying free will. Sometimes he will sketch portraits of those so weighed down by the past that they have no hope of fathering the future, at others he will burst out in angry denunciation of them. Sometimes he will issue the call to revolution in ringing tones and a few lines later cringe before probable death and less probable rebirth for himself and his friends. In short, the miracle of change, now seen as conscious choice and now as coming revolution, at one moment in the confidence of action and at others in the depression of injured suffering, is almost as Protean as poetry itself. This necessarily precludes intellectual consistency. Only the centre of preoccupation remains consistent. Only the imaginative coherence remains. The *Poems*, which appear to be random, are nevertheless ordered, as it were magnetically, round a few imaginative poles which are the still points of the constantly turning world. The best analogy is perhaps the schema of relativity, with the parts, in their constant motions, being related to each other in spite of everything by their mutual tensions. It leads to a poetry which is inherently—and as it were structurally—rich even when superficially most bare.

Plainly, a poetry of such ambiguities and shifting shades cannot be adequately interpreted in political or moral terms. Auden does often elaborate his themes in social or moral ways, but these remain peripheral to the extent that the over-riding mood is introverted. The *Poems* refer ultimately to the condition of the poet himself, not to society or his own desirable behaviour. If they have a collective significance it is far below the surface at the level of the imaginative style of the modern mind. They are remarkable for the total ambitions of embracing the world to which his expensive education introduces a youngster straight away, the commanding heights of the past, present and even future, the outer and inner space, the beckoning achievements of the Caesars and Homers to which he is immediately summoned by his inheritance of man's collective mastery. He has to absorb a universe; and at the same time can find no significance except in this total control, for the universe is one of energy and processes of change, all of them relative, with no fixed points on which to rest. The expanding universe of his desires explores all the positions of the *Kama Sutra* of self-fulfilment, imagining each event in all its potentialities and not along a single defined logic of settled laws. Hence the bewildering shifts in the poet's attitudes to his own themes. It is not the logical confusion some have taken it for. It is instinctively (and before the idea was clearly stated) the 'thinking in variables' which is supposed to be the hallmark of the most recent intellectual advances. The *Poems* are a field theory of the sense of impending revolution. Moreover, in their occasional despair they also point to another element in the current mental context: the individual's suppressed but never absent awareness that this eclecticism, this *Musée Imaginaire* of his own powers, *is* only imaginary—that he himself is in truth a very small figure in his immensely self-important universe. The cosmogony of the *Poems* is, in the last resort, the dramatisation of a personal predicament.

If one looks at the earliest piece Auden has kept in his collected editions, the quite unpolitical poem written in 1927 and since entitled 'Letter', one finds set out there in private terms the patterns of feeling universalised elsewhere in the volume:

> From the very first coming down
> Into a new valley with a frown
> Because of the sun and a lost way . . .[27]

Here, in the '*very first* coming down into a *new* valley' is the adolescent sense of awakening evident, more grandly, in such lines as 'The Spring unsettles sleeping partnerships', along with the Wordsworthian hint of the lost gleam of childhood in the background. The sense of discovery would be of special importance to an intellectual like Auden for whom so much of life is the exhilaration of *becoming aware*. There is the personal tropism for light, for the blinding consciousness of truth and peace, and the sense of the difficulty of giving oneself up to it, in the 'frown because of the sun'. There is also, equally strong—pessimism is merely the negative reflection of hope—the anguish of 'a lost way'. In 'Letter', this is all purely personal, casual and without cosmic pretensions. Yet, in embryo, it contains all the activist, doom-laden heroics of the poet on the threshold of life which pervade the *Poems*. They dramatise

45

Auden's first contact with the world, his lust to live, to do his duty and, above all to make his mark, and equally his panic fear of failing in any or all of these things. They create a myth of the budding poet's ambition.

This is indeed a young man's poetry. But just as Auden's intelligence and literary mastery save him from the traps of the adolescent dilettante, so his seriousness of purpose takes him beyond mere posturing. Just as it is not enough to describe the *Poems* as moral and social, so it is not possible to contain their personal preoccupations within the frame of adolescent dramatics. In several passages, the poet tries to fine down the idea of salvation through correctly judged action to a razor's edge of definition:

> Calling of each other by name
> Smiling, taking a willing arm
> Has the companionship of a game.
>
> But should the walk do more than this
> Out of bravado or drunkenness
> Forward or back are menaces.
>
> On neither side let foot slip over
> Invading Always, exploring Never,
> For this is hate and this is fear.
>
> On narrowness stand, for sunlight is
> Brightest only on surfaces;
> No anger, no traitor, but peace.[28]

This is an attempt to pinpoint the nature of these 'perfect moments', as Sartre calls them, when consciousness is in complete unison with the reality of a relationship.[29] Behind the apparent, but purely abstract, precision lies a dream of harmony, of perfect love, reached by a discipline of truth, an unmonastic rule,

> Travelling by daylight on from house to house
> The longest way to the intrinsic peace,
> With love's fidelity and with love's weakness.[30]

This is essentially a search for The Way. Not, certainly, a Christian, or formally religious, Way: perhaps a Freudian Way along which one comes to terms with oneself and with others. Secular though it is, this is a manifesto of the spiritual quest which has dominated Auden's artistic life from end to end.

*   *   *

The marked originality, superficial obscurity and recurrent attitudes of the *Poems* give them an apparent evenness of style and quality which tends to evaporate on closer acquaintance. Though all, without exception, are about nearly related subjects, there are considerable differences between them, both of quality and of approach. The biggest differences are chronological. This is concealed by Auden's practice of never printing his poems in chronological order if he can possibly help it. He has always been anxious that readers should be surprised into honest responses to any poem by coming upon it out of context; and there is no better way of achieving this than by creating a confusion from which no context can be confidently inferred. He also seems to be one of those artists obsessed by the fear that Lilliputian critics will tie Gulliver down with their ropy formulas. No doubt, too, he enjoys goading critics into unnecessary detective work and seeing them hunt around for clues in the chaos he offers to the prying eye. One is bound to sympathise with this yearning for camouflage, although there are objections to it even from the artist's point of view. The raw material of poetry is mental associations as well as words. The growth of the poet's mind is the ultimate one behind them all. To deny this merely breaks up the underlying patterns and destroys some of the richness of the poetry itself. Auden apparently felt otherwise, even at the time he published *Poems*. The result is that the volume's corporate personality has something of the misleading regularity of a superimposition of different features in an identikit portrait: it offers an average face which slurs over some of the most expressive traits.

Poems, as we know it, is a second edition combining three separate elements. One is the pieces surviving from an earlier volume, hand-printed by Stephen Spender in the summer of 1928 at the end of Auden's three years up at Oxford. This charming and characteristically amateurish pocket-book of poems was printed in at most 45 copies and is full of misprints corrected in Spender's own hand. As early as 1937 Isherwood asserted that 'the mis-prints alone are worth about ten shillings each' and today the British Museum itself possesses only a facsimile.[31] Nine pieces from this undergraduate volume remain in the later edition of *Poems* now current, five of them embedded in 'Paid on Both Sides', the 27-page playlet Auden began, apparently, at Oxford and finished around Christmas 1928 in Berlin.[32] Most of the rest of the *Poems* consists of work Auden wrote either during his year in Berlin or later in England when he returned to look for a job. All of these pieces must have been ready early enough (perhaps in the spring of 1930) to meet Faber & Faber's deadline for publication in September of the same year. Finally, seven poems of the original edition were replaced in the second edition, dated November 1933, by an equal number, 'all written', Auden says, 'before 1931'.[33] Chronologically, then, the differences between the earliest and latest of the *Poems* are slight: the earliest, Poem V—'Letter', as it has since been called—was written in 1927, the latest less than four years after. However, this early period in Auden's career was one of rapid change; and once one is aware of the stratifications in the volume, at least one significant distinction forces itself on one's attention. This is between the poems written at Oxford, along with 'Paid on Both Sides' which, though finished in Berlin, brings their world to an imaginative climax; and the poems begun in Berlin, or later on Auden's return to England. Auden himself has written that when he left Oxford and went to Berlin, he 'ceased to see the world in terms of verse'.[34] The Oxford poems, and 'Paid on Both Sides', 'see the world in terms of verse'. They are steeped in personal and literary emotions. They present Auden's imagination in a way which is both naked and cosmic, rather like one of those Rodin statues in which a head or hands rise out of a block of unhewn stone. In Berlin and the later poems, the vision, though still present under the surface, becomes clothed in social and political preoccupations.

The Oxford poems are permeated by the adolescent turmoil of the boy wandering on the northern hills. These poems—the earliest, that is, which are still part of his current published

work—are typically formed of taciturn landscapes wracked by
seismic movements underground. There is an almost exagger-
ated contrast between the non-committal surfaces and the tur-
bulence beneath. The formal restraint lies in

> The stone smile of this country god
> That never was more reticent,
> Always afraid to say more than it meant,[35]

the very music of which is reserved. And yet, of course, what is
'meant' is nearly always the divine tumescence of new and
demanding life. The force of the *Poems*, especially the earlier
ones, comes from the way in which they move concurrently on
these two contrasted levels. Consciously and intellectually, they
are the rationalist's grappling with life, the determination to
understand and control of Auden's scientific family background
and early ambition to be a mining engineer. Emotionally, and
under the surface, they declare that life is a passionate dialogue
with the Great Mother in the midnight of Everyman's self-
communing. They have the enormous vagueness of childhood
impressions magnified through the lens of puberty and focused
to consciousness by the adolescent awakening. The budding
professor in the foreground of the *Poems* trails the enormous
shadow of a demi-urge behind him. The result is a style more
powerfully suggestive than at any other stage of Auden's
career. It can be compressed into packed drama:

> one died
> During a storm, the fells impassable,
> Not at his village, but in wooden shape
> Through long abandoned levels nosed his way
> And in his final valley went to ground

or into beautifully precise images with a mysterious undertow:

> Beams from your car may cross a bedroom wall,
> They wake no sleeper; you may hear the wind
> Arriving driven from the ignorant sea
> To hurt itself on pane, on bark of elm
> Where sap unbaffled rises, being spring;
> But seldom this. Near you, taller than grass,
> Ears poise before decision, scenting danger.[36]

These flashes of mute epic move the reader from one vaguely awesome sentiment to another. The powerful linkage of disparate ideas suggests a stream of consciousness controlled by deep subterranean forces. Auden's imaginative power was probably at its peak in this, his earliest, period of creative mastery.

There are not many of these Oxford poems, but they do reach a kind of climax in the one long and systematic piece in *Poems*, the playlet, or 'charade' as Auden calls it, 'Paid on Both Sides'. At the mechanical level, of prose and plot, 'Paid on Both Sides' is ridiculous. At the political level, it is a protest against violence, the gang warfare which was already tearing the Weimar Republic to pieces, delivered through characters of whom, as Isherwood has suggested, it is impossible to say whether they are 'epic heroes or members of the school OTC'.[37] Yet, as soon as, in the poetry, the gang warfare changes into a metaphor of the struggle to live right, 'Paid on Both Sides' shifts into a different key. The reflective choruses, soliloquies and monologues give an air of lofty myth to the sordid succession of shootings. They present the tiny but critical moment, 'poised before decision', where the whole of evolution bears up, and also bears down upon, the New Man who can no longer avoid choices which will determine his whole life. All the warring tensions of the piece intersect at the moment of choice which, though circumscribed and even vitiated by the past, somehow still remains marginally open and free. Because it is so ambiguous and because so many pressures converge on the new soul struggling to find a way, 'Paid on Both Sides' has intense dramatic life of an inner kind. Though no play, it contains some of Auden's most highly charged poetry. By the same token, it represents something more than the saga world to which it eagerly invites comparison. It is more than Schoolboy, more than Icelandic, limited to the warrior's defiance of destiny. It has a touch of Aeschylean moral grandeur in its concern with the umbilical link between a man and his fate, and with what he owes to the gods. There is real power in the primal, though falsely primitive, vision excited by the first encounter between the poet and his world—a vision held in solution, though sometimes imperfectly, in the early *Poems*. They occupy the high ground of Auden's imagination and have a mythical quality his late poetry has partly lost.

The poems Auden began in Berlin seem already to be operating on lower ground. This is not a euphemistic way of hinting that they are less good. Both in literary mastery and as evidence that the poet is moving to a more mature view of the world, they suggest a substantial advance. They are nevertheless more workaday and matter-of-fact. The Oxford mythology still provides the canvas, but it tends to disappear behind the political and psychological pigmentation painted over it. Auden and Spender both agree that Auden's views underwent a change after he left Oxford. Spender says, with the touch of asperity of the half-willing disciple who has been left high and dry by his leader:

> Auden held certain views very strongly at Oxford. These have impressed themselves on me the more because he reversed most of them shortly after he left. Here are a few of his characteristic pronouncements:
>
> A poet must have no opinions, no decided views which he seeks to put across in his poetry.
>
> Above all, poetry must in no way be concerned with politics. Politicians are just lackeys and public servants whom we should ignore.
>
> The subject of a poem is only a peg on which to hang the poetry.
>
> A poet must be clinical, dispassionate about life. The poet feels much less strongly about things than do other people.
>
> Poems should not have titles.
>
> Never use exclamation marks, and avoid abstractions.[38]

Reversing these precepts, on Spender's hint, one would gather that Auden, once in Berlin, turned almost at once into the type of radical, political poet one would expect from his *persona* of the Thirties. Auden, though, puts the change more in moral and psychological than political terms.

> I met a chap called Layard and he fed
> New doctrines into my receptive head.

> Part came from Lane, and part from D. H. Lawrence;
> Gide, though I didn't know it then, gave part.

51

They taught me to express my deep abhorrence
If I caught anyone preferring Art
To Life and Love and being Pure-in-Heart.
I lived with crooks but seldom was molested;
The Pure-in-Heart can never be arrested.[39]

In the later *Poems*, one sees the young man preoccupied with a moral revolution but still not writing what could properly be called political poetry. It is the politics of Purity-in-Heart, a kind of Lawrentian halfway-house between the visions of Oxford and the politics of the Thirties. Auden is still much exercised with finding the Way. Indeed, the poems which define it most closely seem to have been written at this time. However, he is less anxious to elaborate a myth of the fateful choice and more to translate it into action. The poetry becomes a mixture of social judgement and personal self-questioning, the two running parallel, since Love and the Revolution tend to be associated at one end of the scale, while the deathwish and social conservatism are completely equated at the other. 'Easter 1929', the longest and most systematic piece in *Poems* after 'Paid on Both Sides', is strikingly different from the charade, even though written at most a few months later. Where 'Paid on Both Sides' is steep, vatic and timeless, 'Easter 1929' is mostly self-analysis linked to a political situation. It has a definite contemporary setting, Berlin, which is no longer travestied as the Far West; a precise time, as the title—added later—indicates; and above all, it is the only poem of open autobiography in the whole volume. Whereas generalisations in 'Paid on Both Sides' tend to stand on tiptoe like emotional exclamation-marks:

O how shall man live
Whose thought is born, child of one farcical night,
To find him old? — [40]

in the realistic world of 'Easter 1929' they take on the airs of a manifesto:

It is time for the destruction of error.[41]

Where the imagery of the earlier *Poems* stirred the unconscious, that of the later ones is remarkable for a catholic appetite for the social, and above all English, scene. It is much more than the usual caricature of it as pylons, aeroplanes and abandoned sidings. There are certainly a lot of these, but its impressive quality is a broad, observant and relaxed variety. There are railway lines moving up country, drivers leaning out of cars to ask the way (the *narrow* way, of course), young men lying on headlands over bays, others smoking leaning against chained-up gates at the edge of woods, gaitered gamekeepers by rotting stacks (these three in a single poem),[42] gulls sheering off cliffs, moorland market towns, farmers and their dogs listening to the radio, sitting in kitchens 'in the stormy fens', blue smoke rising from garden bonfires, fallen bicycles in a public park— all the paraphernalia of living as the urbanised middle class might see it. It is the first AA member's view of England in poetry, with a poacher's resentment of the Big House lurking in the background. That part of it almost certainly owes as much to Hardy, Edward Thomas and Lawrence as to politics, the social conscience, or any real knowledge of country life.

Yet, with all this liveliness, social observation is far less obtrusive in the *Poems* than it was to become in the Thirties. It is firmly integrated into verses of which the dominating quality is often a subtle self-questioning. These poems are at their best when Auden stresses the issues

> glossed over by the careless but known long
> To finer perception of the mad and ill.[43]

Most of them are written in a Skeltonic style which is the outstanding feature of the later *Poems*. It is as if the fluid Skeltonic mode of unadorned short and not-so-short lines is ideally suited to the fluid processes of self-analysis. This is the verse of organically shifting definitions as part of a process of growth. In certain of the Skeltonic poems, Auden tries very hard to chart the most indefinable states, fixing on the point of difficulty or unresolved understanding in his struggle with himself and lifting it up as far as possible to the light of conscious day. For instance, 'To ask the hard question is simple' is a truly remarkable record of the mental fog in which a half-truth is half-apprehended. Is it about sex? self-knowledge? the narrow way? evolution? all of them and more? As a fragment for a progress of the mind, it is extraordinarily faithful to the kind of feeling a thinker, especially an immature, still half-adolescent thinker, can go through when trying to penetrate beyond the present range of his emotional understanding to a dimly felt insight and new control. This is the kind of frustration, of confused hints of memory and of future apprehensions implied by the trial and error of any evolution, personal or political. It was not the subject of poetry before; poets normally write of their feelings as the result of frustration rather than about the cause of frustration itself. These early poems of Auden's with their self-denying fidelity to the precise states of mind which go with certain moods or thoughts seem to me unique in English poetry.

They also have a strangely evocative charm which it is not easy to pin down. The ideas in them are precise, at least in logical and scholastic terms—Michael Roberts praised their 'Aristotelianism'—though they are not truly thought through in experimental ones. Yet the references to these ideas are so compressed and pass on so rapidly from cause to effect and from notes to overtones, that they become clues rather than statements. This has the curious effect of turning categories of thought into mysterious symbols. At first, this seems a weakness. Before one has mastered the clues, many a passage seems *veiled* in wilful obscurities which one suspects are merely a mask for an incapacity to gauge the properties of each particle of the poem. Once the clues are mastered, one discovers this is not so, and that the images invariably become strong and full without losing the magical glitter, the air of incantation, which comes from the ritualistic way in which they are handled. There is a runic charm in the musical wisps of thought of Auden's Skeltonic verses. In these poems, Auden has found an original language for the adolescent and rationalist *examen de conscience*.

The mechanism of honest and careful heart-searching on which they are based also leads him to isolate themes the full importance of which he could not have known at the time but which have proved crucial since. The outstanding case is 'This lunar beauty', the burden of which is that there is no 'oneness' between man and nature, because man's notion of 'beauty' is rooted in a consciousness alien from the rest of nature. Communion with the moon is impossible; the Wordsworthian view of nature is fallacious and progress lies elsewhere. The poet affirms, with typical evolutionary confidence, that 'time is inches' and men's duty the acceptance of the laws of gradual adaptation and change. In this poem, Auden flatly contradicts the natural religion of the Wordsworthians, without fuss, almost as a matter of course. Plenty of poets in the wake of Eliot and Pound had attacked the vagueness of Victorian standards of spirituality, but they had done so fastidiously, as a matter of good taste. When they went further, as Eliot did, it was to draw the ancestral conclusion, in however new a way, and turn to established Christianity. Auden's originality was that, rejecting the assumption of communion with nature on grounds of substance, not taste, he was content at this stage to draw no systematic conclusion. It would have been so easy to trumpet an anti-romantic manifesto, as others did. Auden resisted the temptation. He stated his position firmly and left well alone. This restraint in suspending generalised judgement, this refusal to swing between the poles of pantheism and traditional religion, was a real innovation. It applied the modern spirit of accuracy where a less exacting intelligence would have jumped to a premature conclusion.

It is astonishing that so many poets in the nineteen-fifties thickly settled this particular tract of land without seeming to realise that it was long ago cleared for them by an elder despised for taking the easy way out. In fact, while they were content to state their reticence, Auden as early as *Poems* saw in the dichotomy of conscious Man and unconscious Nature larger implications which he straightway proceeded to explore. 'Easter 1929', which launches virtually all the main themes of Auden's career, attempts just this. It stresses that *homo sapiens* cannot preserve himself from the isolation of his own distinctive awareness. Together, 'Easter 1929' and 'This lunar beauty' mark the starting-point of the largest theme in Auden's poetry, the new effort demanded of us by the isolating effects of consciousness. It is equivalent to asking all over again the question the Romantics, from Wordsworth to Yeats, begged by the comforting assumption of possible 'oneness' with Nature or the

Universe: how to accept one's life in a world weaned from God? This question running at the back of the *Poems*, is even reflected in their style. Auden's manner of writing, compounded of surface aloofness and concealed involvement, is a way of stressing that man is bound to be an observer, even of himself. He can only treat subjects as an outsider, even when they are of desperate importance to him, because he knows he is not one with any of them, nor even altogether one with himself. He must marry his own life in his own terms and not by assuming communion with objects or with landscapes.

It was a rare achievement at this period, to isolate this elusive but essential theme of the modern mind so firmly and so soon. The *Poems* are extraordinarily close to reality precisely because they are fragments in which the detailed observations matter more than the grand design that it would be tempting to elaborate by forcibly coordinating them. Whether or not this is the scientific puritanism it purports to be, it is, on balance, a very sophisticated, mature restraint.

*　　*　　*

Poems occupies a special place in Auden's work. It is one of those rare first volumes which manage both to make literary history and to justify it in retrospect. They are far fewer than one might suppose. For every collection like *The Lyrical Ballads* which stands the test of time there are many *Hours of Idleness* which seem wooden or impossibly banal in the light of the author's later achievements. *Poems* is one of the handful of exceptions. This is not altogether a compliment: it would stand out a little less if Auden had borne out all its formal promise in his subsequent career. The loosening of his standards in the Thirties endows it by comparison with some adventitious strength and dignity. Yet it remains a remarkable performance: one of the most influential first volumes in twentieth-century poetry, and along with Eliot's *Prufrock* in 1917, one of the most accomplished.

In relation to Auden's own art, *Poems* stands apart in several ways. Most of Auden's work is very much of the world, embedded in the politics or psychology of the human condition.

Only *Poems* exploits his remarkable myth-making powers in anything like their pristine form. One becomes aware of his precocious strength when, very occasionally, one comes upon an image, or a few lines which, with the same general intent as the rest, nevertheless seem relatively derivative:

> Eyes, ears, tongue, nostrils bring
> News of revolt, inadequate counsel to
> An infirm king.[44]

The sudden sixth-form Elizabethanism makes one realise how much weaker Auden's poetry would have been if his intuitions had been dressed up in less original ideas: if, for instance, his sense of the archaic had been vested in Titans rather than cowboys in a titanesque landscape; or if he had rifled the old renaissance vocabulary yet again (as indeed he did in 'the last transgression of the sea')[45] rather than his father's library of old Norse literature and textbooks on geology. Auden gained greatly from the fact that he 'had been brought up on the Icelandic sagas, for they were the background of his family's history'.[46] Moreover, he seems to have renewed his childish vision, as poets often do, in the crucible of adolescence:

> Long, long ago, when I was only four,
>   Going towards my grandmother, the line
> Passed through a coal-field. . . .
> Tramlines and slagheaps, pieces of machinery,
> That was, and still is, my ideal scenery.[47]

It was astonishingly convenient for a socially-conscious poet in the Thirties to be imaginatively as well as doctrinally excited by industrial debris, to think it not only socially necessary to be depressingly urban but also to be able to confess to his lover that:

> When I was a child, I
> Loved a pumping-engine,
> Thought it every bit as
> Beautiful as you.[48]

An apter gift for fashion would be hard to conceive, except that Auden created the fashion himself. It requires great powers to turn a natural predisposition into a complete new set of symbols developed so vividly that a large school of writers afterwards exploits them. Perhaps it needs even greater powers, while breaking free of old associations, nevertheless to exploit these too with confidence and success. For a youthful rationalist who had broken free of traditional religion in favour of the Viking heroics of the sagas, Auden showed a daring *penchant* for cowboys of the Apocalypse and guru-like figures treading the air of rumour:

> Some say that handsome raider still at large,
> A terror to the Marshes, is truth in love;
> And we must listen for such messengers
> To tell us daily 'Today a saint came blessing
> The huts.' 'Seen lately in the provinces
> Reading behind a tree and people passing.'[49]

In imagery like this Auden has not simply learned a new language. He has learned it so thoroughly that he can afford to consort with the old forms of thought and still not lose his new-found personality. The outline and detail of the world of *Poems*, the scenes of industrial decay set in bleak northern uplands, the cowboys speaking tersely of fate, the film shots, all tell the same tale of myth-making power. Though Auden has kept this all his life, he has never exerted it since in such a concentrated or visionary way.

There is a still simpler and more general reason for the marked individuality of the *Poems* within the Auden corpus. Much of Auden's later writing is exuberantly formless; they constitute the formal exception. Almost all the *Poems* are striking for their formal strictness and tension, not least in the use of irregular stanzas. This no doubt is what makes Barbara Everett, who seems disconcerted by Auden's usual manner, say that he rarely makes himself felt as an artist compulsively driven to write 'except in some of his earliest poems'.[50] Whatever the relevance of such assumptions to Auden's later work, it is a fact that in the *Poems* one is constantly aware of a young man of great talent working out his co-ordinates, as a person and as a writer. The air of scientific detachment, the passion for precision in establishing laws of behaviour, bear witness to the author's determination to elaborate his own standards of right reason: there is clearly a search for moral identity in the *Poems*.

The search for identity is also quasi-religious. The notion of the Leader plunging into dark continents is partly political, but it is equally a dramatic metaphor for the metaphysical restlessness, the anxious quest for control of one's world, which has mattered so much to Auden's art.

Then again there is a search for stylistic identity in the *Poems*. The obscurities of manner, the compressions and distortions, are part of an effort to heighten the aesthetic tension and mould tighter patterns—in a phrase, to construct a personal language. Just as a writer needs a private fiction, a legend of the world, out of which to write, so, in purely stylistic terms, he needs to focus his speaking voice to produce his own verbal building blocks. Eliot's important distinction between 'beliefs held' and 'beliefs felt' applies to a poet's language as much as to his ideas. The carefulness of the *Poems* in seeking to achieve that, stands out from every tense yet supple line. Auden condensed them with the deliberation of a prodigy modelling his own artistic personality.

To say that the *Poems* are classically successful may be going too far. The violent compressions postpone the necessary suspension of disbelief and seem at first a trifle muscle-bound. The peripheral antics of 'Paid on Both Sides' destroy its unity too much for the most ambitious piece in the volume to stand as a symbol for the whole. Yet the fact remains that the better one knows them, the stronger the *Poems* appear. With familiarity they lose their first air of awkwardness without becoming merely easy and gain clarity without breaking their enigmatic charm. Above all, they have the difficult virtue of what a French historian has called '*la modération dans les conceptions fortes*'.[51] *Poems* constitutes one of the poles of Auden's art, opposite 'The Sea and the Mirror' written during the second world war. These two works echo one another across the years of Auden's artistic growth. The *Poems* open the movement, stating the fragmentary themes and, in a sense, asking the questions implicit in Auden's view of life; 'The Sea and the Mirror' provides the central development with the poet's matured answers. They speak to one another across the disappointed hopes and harsh disillusion of the 'low dishonest decade' overshadowed by Hitler and the slump.[52]

A BYRONIC RADICAL

EVEN today, the mention of Auden almost automatically conjures up visions of the Thirties. To a lesser extent, the converse is also true: in any discussion of the Thirties the name of Auden is likely to be one of the first to crop up. As far as poetry goes, the two are nearly synonymous. The justice of this may seem debatable to future generations. Why should Auden, and the school of superficially political poets he fathered, appropriate a decade during which Yeats, long ago winner of a Nobel Prize, was consummating his final and finest phase; Eliot, the revolutionary influence in postwar poetry, was still a flaming sword with which to rout the Georgians; David Jones, though out of the limelight, was turning the epic experience of a generation into myth; and even among the young, the rhapsodical Dylan Thomas was hammering out a style far more daring than Auden's own? Auden was only one of the luminaries of a decade luminous with poets and, in retrospect, not even the most secure in the estimation of his peers. It is arguable, too, that the Thirties are in some respects an exception in Auden's own career. The spirit of most of his early or late work is ultimately dialectical. It is idiosyncratic enough to acquire, by this fact alone, a certain privacy. In the Thirties, on the other hand, it is *engagé* and, frequently public in the most topical and assimilable way, easy, flowing and fashionable. Auden is often condemned for not being the poet of the Thirties still, or for having been too much the poet of the Thirties once, while in fact, in his own career, the decade, or the most celebrated part of it, has in some ways been a parenthesis. And yet, when all due obeisance has been paid to pedantic truth, Auden rightly remains the symbol of the Thirties. The *enfant terrible* making verse out of all the odds and ends of a period well christened The Depression reflected the natural reactions of intelligent humanity with a less particular light than Eliot or Yeats; and he was a poet of far more various diet and ambition than Dylan Thomas. He is the one poet in whom the phenomena of the age are mirrored in anything like their daily habit and diversity.

One need only look at an anthology of poetry of the Thirties, like the excellent selection by Robin Skelton, to see why his personality cast such a shadow over contemporaries. For one thing, he gave the younger generation a high proportion of its leading ideas, or more properly, literary *tics*. When Robin Skelton writes that there is 'something curiously adolescent in the use of phrases like "The Enemy", "The Struggle" and "The Country" and in the deployment of such words as "Leader", "Conspiracy", "Frontier", "Maps", "Guns" and "Armies" in much of the writing of the period', he is sticking to the Audenary vocabulary of the time.[1] Most of the poets willingly accepted these terms and images, not as plagiaries but as the world out of which they wrote. Julian Symons quotes Charles Madge, 'the ideal intellectual revolutionary simpleton of the period':

> But there waited for me in the summer morning
> Auden, fiercely. I read, shuddered and knew.[2]

'It was probably just as well', writes Cecil Day-Lewis in his autobiography, *The Buried Day*, 'that I was three years older' than Auden, 'for otherwise his influence might have been too potent for me: as it was, . . . though I had certain half-conscious reservations about him, I willingly became his disciple where poetry was concerned. . . . I found his poems difficult to understand, and sometimes at first unsympathetic; but the vigour of their language, the exciting novelty (to me) of the images and ideas embodied in these early poems, and the delighted sense they gave me of a poetry which, so to say, knew its own mind— all this proved so infectious that my own verse became for a time pastiche-Auden.'[3] Auden was the maker of myths and manners for the majority of poets in the Thirties, good and bad. This perhaps is one reason why 'it is rare for a decade to be so self-conscious'.[4] Auden, simply by striking his attitudes, thinking his own thoughts in his own extravagantly conscious, self-dramatising way, greatly helped to make it so. He projected himself so masterfully that he imposed a style on a whole school of writers.

This capacity to influence others rested, in the last resort, on powers of penetration which always made him seem more *relevant* than others of his age-group. David Gascoyne put this rather well when, referring specifically to Auden, he remarked that 'strength of character and depth of experience are inseparable, ultimately, from important poetry. Without them, poetry may be ravishingly beautiful, but *merely* decorative, *merely* lyrical.'[5] Often, reading verse from the Thirties, one comes acros poetry which is sensually richer and more 'finely' written than Auden's verse: to the point, if one merely looks at a single poem, where one may wonder how Auden could be so much the leader and a man as independent as MacNeice, say, a follower. One understands what Louis MacNeice was hinting at when, in an open letter to Auden, he wrote, 'Your poems are strongly physical, but not fastidiously physical. This is what I should expect from someone who does not like flowers in his room.'[6] There is something bare and bleak about much of Auden's writing, not so much physical as mechanical. Yet compared with the lesser lights, he nearly always writes with the vivid vigour of a synthesising mind. There is usually a clear point to a poem by Auden, even when the details are not so clear. Unlike many modern poets, he is not afraid to be simple and direct. He is brilliant in selecting the material essential to his purpose. His images are effortlessly complete even when mere silhouettes:

> You dowagers with Roman noses
> Sailing along between banks of roses
>   well dressed,
> You Lords who sit at committee tables
> And crack with grooms in riding stables
>   your father's jest. . . .[7]

It is astonishing how rare this talent for lightning caricature is in lesser poets. Some quite valid ones frequently flounder around in search of their images, looking in vain for their outlines; Auden nearly always finds them. The outcome may seem facile, but it is the facility of great powers. So, again and again, in Skelton's anthology, Auden's poems seem less impressive individually than the potentials of other men's 'fine writing' but end, cumulatively, by making far more of an impact. This talent for dynamic relevance must have been even more impressive for Auden's envious competitors, struggling to keep up with him, than it is now in retrospect for the connoisseur. His early work seemed to express everything they would have liked to say before they had become quite aware of it. Naturally, it assumed extraordinary importance in the minds of the rising *literati* of the left. 'Auden's *Poems* (1930) and *The Orators* (1932) belong to that small class of works which have an absolute importance and value at the time of their publication because they express cohesively a set of attitudes which have been waiting for an expositor. There have been one or two such books, not necessarily masterpieces or even works of high talent, in every decade of the twentieth century. Kingsley Amis's *Lucky Jim* was such a book.' Julian Symons, who writes this in his memoir on the Thirties, gives revealing chapter and verse for the impact Auden made on intellectuals at the time. 'I was amused to read the other day in Richard Hoggart's brilliant book about Auden that "In *The Orators* the important figure of the Airman symbolises the forces of release and liberation": amused because I remembered how anxiously this point was debated immediately after the book's publication. Was not the Airman, we asked ourselves, a Fascist?'[8] All this may seem quaint today, but the capacity to move one's audience to such involvement is the acknowledged legislation of which young poets dream.

If one adds to that the sheer quantity of Auden's work and the facility of his talents, it is plain he had all the qualifications for a *chef d'école*. The variety of his inspiration was awe-inspiring. 'It is his astonishing capacity for assimilation and his ability to distill poetry out of the most forbidding retorts of science, which make me think that Auden more than any other young writer has the essential qualifications of a major poet,' wrote Day-Lewis in 1934.[9] Three years later Geoffrey Grigson praised Auden's 'broad power of raising ordinary speech into strong and strange incantation'.[10] Drawing material from such varied sources and transmuting it so easily into verse, Auden published volume after volume in rapid succession: *The Orators* and the revised edition of *Poems* appeared in 1932; the masque, *The*

63

Dance of Death, in November 1933; *The Dog Beneath the Skin*, the first play written with Isherwood in May 1935; and the second, *The Ascent of F6*, in September 1936; while the second volume of short poems, all written in the early Thirties, *Look, Stranger!* came out in October 1936. Somehow, Auden also found time for the schoolmastering which earned him a living between 1930 and 1935. How unlike the costive example of Eliot it all seemed! Not surprisingly, it has become difficult today to be clear whether Auden is typical of the Thirties or the Thirties are typical of Auden.

The only obvious parallel for such a phenomenon is Byron a century before. There is not much in common between Byron and Auden strictly as poets. One has only to glance at Auden's 'Letter to Lord Byron', written in 1936, and its Byronic models, to see the difference. Byron at his best is one of those numerous Romantic geniuses of improvident improvisation, like Shelley in verse, Schubert in music or Géricault in painting, who composed so fast it seems appropriate they died young. *Don Juan* reads like one bright idea sparking off another in the heat of unpremeditated communication. Auden, even imitating the outrageous polysyllabic rhymes of *Don Juan*, seems prudently controlled, consciously professional. A century separates Byron playing the revolutionary individualist, speaking—from however wicked and incestuous a heart—to an ideal order, and Auden, the social engineer of brave new worlds. The intervening years have extracted from the rebel tradition its old confidence in the individual's instinct for rightness. The desire, awakened by Hegel and Marx, to identify oneself with the process of history has taken over. Byron gloried in his ego, Auden likes to give himself objective airs. And yet the similarity of situation remains: both created a style, a myth, for their generation—and that, few poets, including ones finer than either, have achieved in the long roll-call of English poetry. Byron and Auden are at least alike in their situations and, to some extent—though Auden's influence was only English, Byron's European—in their impact on contemporaries.

Poetry is apt to become vital and popular in periods of upheaval. Both the most fertile periods for English poetry in recent times—the thirty year periods in the shadow of the

French and Russian revolutions—have been times of anguish and turmoil. During these two periods, beliefs were breaking down and reforming at an accelerated pace and, in both cases, causing mental suffering and renewal. In poets, anguish is the mother of invention; in potential readers, it opens up a vein of sympathy, a response to the literature of values and feeling, which creates a market for poetry less narrow than in cooler periods when idealism remains relatively private. Years of upheaval, in short, help to produce both major poets and their market. The striking likeness between Byron and Auden is in their relationship to their audience. Both were launched full-fledged, almost from first youth onwards, as poets and as myths. Both dramatised the radical aspirations of a youth impatient with the increasingly self-defeating conformism of the elder generation. Both were morally speaking,—as myths rather than individuals (despite Missolonghi or Auden's abortive visit to Spain)—the leaders at the imaginary barricades, the men who gave embattled youth a style, an awareness of why, how and where it differed from what it saw as a selfish elder generation sitting on immoral thrones of privilege and power. As Julian Symons says of the literary liberalism of the Thirties, it was 'a poetic movement more than anything else, and this was partly because Auden imprinted his personality so firmly upon these ten years and partly because the uplift of spirit in the early Thirties found expression most easily in poetry'.[11] The moment was looking for the man and, in Auden, found him.

It is, however, all too easy to mistake the domain of Auden's influence. Reading today of the doings of the Thirties' poets one might gain the impression that the whole world was hanging on their lips. It is easy, in the memoirs of Spain or the heady politics of golden youth, to forget the pathetic showing of the left at the polls; to forget that the electorally substantial left, in the shape of the Labour party, was itself a parcel of old fogeys in the eyes of the literary radicals. The poets, in their urgent desire to save civilisation from the fatal disease of capitalism and its Nazi metastasis, identified themselves with 'the masses' and claimed to speak in their name. Yet, in fact, the last group they sprung from, or even talked to, were the masses, if by that one means, as they did, the proletariat. 'The poets were, much to their embarrassment, and almost to a man, members of the *bourgeoisie*, and mostly products of public schools, and this may be one reason why almost all their images of communal experience can be so easily translated into terms of the undergraduate reading or climbing party. . . . They talked in an almost empty theatre as if it were a packed Wembley Stadium. They argued, proved, disproved, and judged, as if the whole nation were listening. They had, in fact, discovered a drama and invented an audience. This, of all the thirties phenomena, is perhaps the most fascinating. These poems of social criticism were almost all aimed at people who did not exist, at least in the roles assumed by the poems. Their assurance and poise is a pretence. Their prophecies are made to a handful of the converted '.[12]

Yet, if they were far more of a political minority than they cared to suppose, the pink poets were nevertheless culturally dominant. They not only felt themselves to represent the future, they did in fact influence it. Not in the disastrous Thirties themselves, to be sure. Just as it required the war to turn the massive parliamentary majorities of Baldwin and Chamberlain into the Labour landslide of 1945, so it needed the war to inject many of the attitudes of the anti-fascist minority of Thirties' intellectuals into the orthodoxy of postwar Britain. The victory came too late and in many ways was won in the wrong context, as so often is the case. But that the radicals so influenced the future is a much better measure of their intellectual and artistic primacy, and of its connection with politics, than the undoubted evidence that they were, even in their heyday, only a fashionable minority.

Of no one is this cultural domination truer than of Auden. There is an almost mathematical parallel between the growth of his fame and the rise of the Popular Front. One would never guess from the retrospective nostalgia of men of the Thirties how tiny were the first printings of Auden's works. It took three years to exhaust the thousand copies of the first poorly produced edition of *Poems*; and nearly a year to run through the similar printing of *The Orators*. Auden became really widely known only through two anthologies edited by Michael Roberts, *New Signatures* (1932) and *New Country* (1933). These launched the Thirties Movement on the public. Auden still had to wait, though, till 1936 and the full tide of the Popular Front for a true public success, *Look, Stranger!*, which consecrated his public image as Rebel Laureate. Even then, the 2,350 copies of the volume sold between October 1936 and the reprint (of 2,000 copies) of December, were only a feat by the miserable standards of sales of poetry, then and now. Still, a few months later, Faber & Faber were ready to risk a printing of 10,240 copies of his next work, *Letters from Iceland*, written with Louis MacNeice, which appeared in July 1937. Admittedly, this contained a great deal of prose and was proportionately less forbidding; and, even so, went out of print only in May 1949.[13] Yet such printings were a fabulous performance for a poet and marked the peak of Auden's popular acclaim. In November 1937, when he was just 30, the leading radical poet of England received the King's Gold Medal for Poetry from his monarch, an act so unconventional that the percipient might have guessed Edward VIII would shortly go too far and have to abdicate. In the same month *New Verse*, founded in 1933 by Geoffrey Grigson to propagate the Auden gospel, devoted a double number to him in which nearly all the more important younger writers, of Auden's stable and out of it, paid homage as to an acknowledged master.

This is all history now, or would be, were it not that it so much affected Auden's poetry. An astonishing, and above all astonishingly rapid, change came over his writing after the publication of *Poems 1930*. In an extraordinarily short space of time the discreetly sculptured style of the *Poems* was transformed into the extensive, 'conversational' style Auden has cultivated ever since. The poems of 1928 are steep, pronouncing doom from Sinai; those of 1931 and later are broad, covering the whole plain of society with their poetic pamphleteering. The poems of 1929 are self-questioning; those of a year or two later are as often as not brashly assertive. Above all, the *Poems*, regular or irregular, were remarkable for their formal strictness; from *The Orators* onwards, there is a kind of effervescent formlessness about Auden's work.

The pieces of the Thirties are usually public performances. They are often very brilliant, but whereas the mood of the *Poems* is normally reflected in their music, in the Thirties the music reflects above all the rhetorical excitement or the crowd-swaying mastery of the author. It does not carry a strict connotation of the inner process which might be presumed to have generated the poem. The excitement of the writing tends to break the bonds of discipline and pour out in apparently arbitrary play or a pandemonium of inventiveness. There is an immense expansion of manners and material, counterbalanced by a certain disintegration of the poet's imaginative world. The result is great variety. The *Poems* all had a certain quality which could pass as a common style, a single recognisable rhythm of personality. The work of the Thirties is a dazzling fairground of distinct, though necessarily related, styles. At the very least there are four—a racy Regency conversational style; the poetry of talk based on the classical iambic line, though usually rhymeless; a lyrical style, in which many of Auden's finest effects are achieved; and a popular |style, Auden's celebrated light verse, which is particularly abundant and a good deal of it still uncollected. The mental atmosphere of *Poems* was one of search, almost of research, its emotional one the enormous hinterland of childhood and adolescent myth. Auden's poetry in the Thirties moves rapidly out of these steep shadows into a broader but shallower world of multifarious daylight. His work often inclines to the hectoring tone of the political poems which has stuck in the public memory; and where it is successful, it is frequently in light verse where great powers can skate rapidly over unresistant ideas, or in radical and erotic lyrics which raise the early adult equivalent of childhood myths, but in a noticeably more conventional way. The result is that one finds, on the one hand Dylan Thomas congratulating Auden in 1937 for being 'a wide and deep poet' who has almost worn away 'his first narrow angles of pedantry and careful obscurity'[14] and, on the other, Henry Reed, writing a few years later, shaking his head over large parts of *Look, Stranger!* for being 'disturbingly glib'.[15] No view of Auden in the early Thirties can be complete unless it accepts these contradictions.

*   *   *

The transitional work between the *Poems* and the Thirties is *The Orators*. In theme it is in many ways the culmination of the *Poems*. In treatment, it is already part of the Thirties. It is a long work—in the original edition 108 pages long—and as both its title and its length suggest, an expansively rhetorical one. The first part, called 'The Initiates', consists of four prose poetic essays in what Monroe K. Spears claims is formal rhetoric: 'oration or public speech, argument, statement or scientific exposition, letter or informal style'.[16] If this is correct—and Spears seems to have had excellent access to Auden—it conveys something of the histrionic quality of the work. The two easiest pieces to describe are the initial burlesque of a headmaster's 'Address for a Prize-Day' and the 'Letter to a Wound'. The Address is apparently a perfectly serious exposé of the failures of 'Love', and their consequences, sandwiched between a farcical opening and an ending which sheers off into a fantasy witch-hunt. The Letter is equally ambiguous. It is the first clear statement of Auden's doctrine of neurosis as the source of creativeness, but turns out also to be the narcissistic love-letter to his own wound of a recently operated young man. (Auden himself had recently been operated on and presumably regarded this, after Layard, as a failure of Purity-in-Heart.) In each case, one is asked to take the unconscious message as being virtually the inverse of the conscious one. The whole approach is psychological and ironic, and whatever one is required to understand has to be read between the lines of the speakers' claims and invocations.

This double focus is even more marked in the second and longest section of *The Orators*, the 'Journal of an Airman'. This is a series of notes, snatches of verse, surrealist prose vignettes, even diagrams (suggesting lunatic letter-writers to newspapers?), in which the Airman (a goggled version of the Leader) girds himself busily, but with hints of ineffectuality, for battle against The Enemy (who remains as enigmatic, off-stage and unattainable as Captain Ahab's white whale). The climax is reached with a series of farcical but sinister fifth-column attacks on the defenders of the Airman's unidentified city, so turned that the breakdown seems to occur within the Airman as well as around him. The close is the pilot's log book entry of his take-off, followed by a grim blank in the spirit of Scott's last diary in the Antarctic. The third and last part, of 'Six Odes', rehearses the same themes in verse, with references to 'Christopher',

'Stephen' and 'Warner', from which one gathers that The Orators and Initiates include Auden's literary set duly togged up for the Revolution.

The Orators has an almost Sordello-like reputation for obscurity. This fearsome fame seems due mainly to the impossibility of coaxing any logical progressions out of its kaleidoscopic detail. This is no new problem, as the *Poems* had already shown. Once one looks for coherence, as in the *Poems*, not to the equivocal or frankly contradictory stated attitudes but only to the preoccupations round which they cluster, most of the obscurities dissolve. *The Orators* simply systematises the vision, present in the later *Poems*, of the Leader advancing into the eye of the coming revolution in order to deliver his fellows into the freedom of necessity. In Auden's self-dramatising world, a Leader knows he may be the sacrificial victim of the revolution which it is his historic duty to fulfil. *The Orators* is, then, a kind of inverted epic of funk over the coming catastrophe—

> Proofed against shock
> Our hands can shake—[17]

of which the message is nevertheless a rousing call to action. Though it comes nearest of all Auden's works, both in style and content, to justifying Orwell's jibe about a 'gutless Kipling', it is oddly impressive in its urgent ambivalence.[18] The revolutionary theme brings out all the ambiguities of Auden's psychological view of man—action and defeatism, heroism and cowardice, loyalty and betrayal, reason and irrationality, creation and neurosis, health and illness, suicide and killing, appearing only as opposite colorations of one another. Nothing, subjectively, is quite what it seems from the outside to the observer who believes himself to be objective. What to him seem facts are, subjectively, merely accidental surfacings of a constant mental commotion between the positive and negative poles of experience: only the central and external feature, the imminence of violent change, is constant. *The Orators* carries the approach of the *Poems* to its logical conclusion of a psychological fantasia on the transformation theme.

Although in subject the logical conclusion of *Poems*, in treatment *The Orators* breaks sharply away from them. The syntax, one of the strong points of *Poems*, tends at times to little more than that of ordinary speech and sometimes to rather less. *The Orators* is full of catalogues:

> One charms by thickness of wrist; one by variety of positions; one has a beautiful skin, one a fascinating smell. One has prominent eyes[19]

and so on, with slight interruptions, for several paragraphs, as the encyclopaedist of beautiful boys overcomes the poet. Even when Auden keeps his catalogical mania on a tighter rein, he still indulges in collectors' tricks. He is apt to end subordinate clauses with full-stops and launch the next clause on an 'And', with a capital A, as if it were a new idea and not just another item on a lengthening list. Gaps open up in the previously close-knit texture of the verse. The literary cubism of *Poems*, compounded of neat formulae and neater sounds counter-pointed in tightly modelled patterns, breaks up. Though each individual surface was flat, their close and expert juxtaposition produced high reliefs of depth and shade. In *The Orators*, the separate elements are violently dissociated, the self-contained little phrases shoot off at unpredictable angles like splinters from an explosion. There is an agitation of 'images of cinematic speed and clarity' hustling one another off the retina.[20]

> The hammer settles on the white-hot ingot. The telescope focuses accurately upon a recent star. On skyline of detritus, a truck, nose up. Loiterer at carved gates, immune stranger, follow. It is nothing your loss. The priest's mouth opens in the green graveyard, but the wind is against it.[21]

There is a sense of disintegrating civilisation, even of Malrauxesque violence, in *The Orators*, as in none of Auden's other works. Though the theme is 'England, this country of ours where nobody is well', its bitter, modernistic Expressionism may have been the delayed effect of Auden's year in Germany in 1928–9.[22] Berlin and Hamburg, with their restless theatre and futuristic cinema, their omnisexual and political nightclubs, their warring parties and constant experimentation, seemed the premonitory places for trendy intellectuals to be. And so they were, though not in the expected sense. There is something of the hysteria of the death throes of the Weimar Republic in *The Orators*. There is also ambiguity, in more ways than one, in its intensely male atmosphere: its violence, its comradeship, what Auden himself has since called its 'Hero-worship' and its search for a faith to simplify and galvanise sick society.[23] Many—Cecil Day-Lewis for one—agreed with Julian Symons in detecting fascist undertones in the leftwing leanings of *The Orators*.[24] Auden, in his rather overzealously Christian latter-day fashion, now claims the author of such a work must have been only a couple of years off becoming a Nazi.[25] If so, his guardian angel must have been watching him closely, for he never made it. Perhaps the angel thought Auden's literary temptations were enough.

The sense of civilisation in travail leads to the most original element of *The Orators*, the one perhaps most fateful for Auden's later career. With its special mixture of psychology and politics, Auden the cultural-moralist takes a bow. As a psychologist and sociologist, aware of personal and cultural forces, he cannot moralise like Wordsworth or *The Edinburgh Review*: he knows he too is conditioned, perhaps even vitiated by his conditioning, and that in any case he can make no claim to be an objective party:

> Which was in need of help? Were they or he
> The physician, bridegroom and incendiary?[26]

He has to shift his ground from arguments of authority (which assume the critic's righteousness) to arguments of expediency (which embrace one and all, the critic included), from the thunder of good and evil to the perception of sickness and health. As Cecil Day-Lewis put it, Auden 'has done more perhaps than any other writer to replace in our minds the idea of the wickedness of society by the idea of the sickness of society'.[27] The result is verse dealing with the mental states of civilisation as a whole. Morality shades into psychiatry and psychiatry into anthropology. In this way the door is held open for subjective responses in an ostensibly objective world. It is in *The Orators* that one first comes across the painter of anthropological Edens so prominent in Auden's later verse. The Eden is ironically intended, but here they are all the same,

the tall white gods who landed from their open boat,
Skilled in the working of copper, appointing our feast-days,
Before the islands were submerged, when the weather was calm,
    The maned lion common,
An open wishing-well in every garden.[28]

Last but not least, the same twilit zone of subjective and objective responses produces the lunatic sermons so important to Auden's later art. The 'Address for a Prize-Day' is the embryo of the brilliant burlesque sermons for Marble Arch which are the star-turn of so many long Auden works. The atmosphere of these sermons is well described, by Cecil Day-Lewis again, when he objects that Auden's 'method of satire is apt to defeat its own ends. Spender has correctly called it "buffoon-poetry"; and in guying his victims Auden too often becomes identified with them, so that, instead of the relationship between satirist and victim which alone can give significance to satire we get a series of figures of fun into each of whom the satirist temporarily disappears.'[29] This gives a good idea of the farcical sermons of which the 'Address for a Prize-Day' is a primitive example. But because Day-Lewis stresses the 'satire'—understandably for the period, the early Thirties, when he was writing—he tends to miss, or rather dismiss, the subjective element which, in retrospect, seems the most meaningful part of Auden's 'satire' and the closely related light verse. Isherwood gave currency in *Lions and Shadows* to the idea that Auden adores playing the lunatic clergyman.[30] This again gives the impression, natural in the Thirties, that only the satirist is involved. Is it really an accident that, in later years, Auden has turned the Vicar's savage parody of establishment Christianity in *The Dog Beneath the Skin*, with a minimal change of words, into an apologia for the very beliefs attacked?[31] To judge by his writing, Auden is not so much a satirist playing the lunatic clergyman as a clergyman playing the lunatic satirist, which is quite another matter. In fact, in his own undoubtedly eccentric way, he has some unexpected claims to being the century's greatest writer of sermons in English. That these are loaded and overloaded with jokes and slapstick only proves what a showman Auden is and, perhaps given the culture, what dilemmas he faces. Because of innovations like this, *The Orators* is almost more of a source-book for Auden's later verse than the self-contained, though better disciplined, *Poems*.

The Orators, in its anarchic way, is a genuinely experimental piece of writing. Indeed, it is the last really experimental work in Auden's career. Henceforth, he will adapt many forms to his purpose, but his own innovations will be over. Immediately after *The Orators*, Auden's verse tones down into something less aggressive in its determination to be new. It is hard to know why, but there may well have been a political reason for this. *The Orators*, like many of the *Poems*, makes little sense without the expectation of imminent revolution. The myth on which it was built could hardly survive if this hope failed—as fail it did. In the very early Thirties, the prospect of revolution turned on Germany. Had Germany been taken over by the Communists, the whole of continental Europe might have followed suit. But Germany did not turn Communist. In January 1933, Hitler seized power, the German Left, or what remained of it, vanished into concentration camps and all hope of a Trotskyite miracle was killed stone dead. So far as one can tell from the publication dates of Auden's poems, the messianic tension seems to have abated in his poetry from that moment onwards. When Hitler came to power, Auden, like a traditional English liberal, found his poetry thrown back, as it were, on its protected island,

> This fortress perched on the edge of the Atlantic scarp,
> The mole between all Europe and the exile-crowded sea.[32]

It acquired the familiar English look of an undenominational radicalism, still angry to be sure, but less cosmopolitan, brittle and urgent. It is with this next phase that Auden's fame is most closely associated.

The slackening of tension can be seen in the two works which followed *The Orators*—the well-nigh negligible *Dance of Death*, and *The Dog Beneath the Skin*, the first and most interesting of the three plays Auden wrote with Isherwood. *The Dog Beneath the Skin* was produced by the Group Theatre in London in the autumn of 1935. A morality play, it has enough in common with 'Paid on Both Sides' and *The Orators* to point up the important differences between them. It is another vaguely expressionist work, dream sequences and scenes of symbolic import with no clear time and place treading briskly on one another's heels. Now, however, the atmosphere is not so much violent as high-spirited. Its surrealist abruptness owes less to anarchic depths than to the fact that its looseness of structure and freedom from the unities make it an ideal vehicle for dramatising moral abstractions. Auden, who helped found the Group Theatre in 1932 and dominated it as 'Uncle Wiz', believed that the avant-garde play should borrow the techniques of the modern musical comedy or pre-medieval folk-play.[33] The trouble with *The Dog Beneath the Skin* is that it succeeds too well in this. Its ostensible aim is to stage the rake's progress of a dying culture, the stations of the cross of the deathwish, in a series of tableaux—in a brothel, or in 'Paradise Park', or the Nineveh hotel—loosely connected and moralised by a chorus:

> We show you man caught in the trap of his terror, destroying himself.[34]

The best passages—half a dozen of the choruses, the Vicar's crazy sermon at the climax of the 'plot'—bear out this macabre programme. But as Julian Symons has pointed out, there is an incompatibility between the earnestness of the parable and the fairground buffoonery of the tableaux which occupy eighty per cent of the play: 'the picture of life and humanity created in the choruses was one thing, and the action of the play quite another. . . . (The action) did not merely employ the *technique* of "modern musical comedy", it *was* that musical comedy, or something so near to it that the edge of satire was indiscernible. One of the few passages of genuine satire, in which Destructive Desmond spits on and slashes a Rembrandt picture to the applause of the fashionable audience in the Nineveh Hotel, was removed from the stage version. The total effect was that the choruses and action seemed to belong to different plays.'[35] In the choruses Auden seemed to be writing for his muse, in the action writing down to his 'pre-medieval' audience. As there was far more action than choruses, the impression which sticks in the memory is of a superlative undergraduate romp and of the coming of age of Auden's music-hall style, lithe, brilliant and shallow.

The Dog has more bark than bite, its cheerfulness smothers all. Light verse of this kind, as Auden has written, is possible only when the poet and his audience 'are close together in interests and perceptions'.[36] His intimate relation to the audience sitting at his feet gave him the opportunity, in the mid-Thirties, to revamp triumphantly the tradition of light verse dealing with a broad range of life which almost died when the Victorians interred it in symbolic nonsense rhymes 'for children'. He was able to perform for the literary left much as Byron and Praed had performed for the Regency salons. The literary set on the fringes of the Left Book Club deluded itself that the accessibility of this verse made it 'popular poetry'. As Julian Symons implied, it was less political than society verse. Operating somewhere between the dream of a popular culture and the realities of box office and fashion, Auden produced reams and reams of light verse in the tone of:

> You were a great Cunarder, I
> Was only a fishing smack
> Once you passed across my bows
> And of course you did not look back
> It was only a single moment yet
> I watch the sea and sigh
> Because my heart can never forget
> The day you passed me by.[37]

The Dance of Death, from which the parody comes, finishes righteously with Karl Marx walking on accompanied by two Communists. That is not enough to turn a daisy-chain of cabaret turns into a politically significant art form. It turns politics into cabaret songs instead. By the time of the highly entertaining 'Letter to Lord Byron' (1936), much the longest and most sociable of all Auden's light poems, even the pretence of urgent political purpose has faded. The best passages are bravura pieces of autobiography or social and literary chit-chat:

> For now we've learnt we mustn't be so bumptious
>   We find the stars are one big family,
> And send out invitations for a scrumptious
>   Simple, old-fashioned, jolly romp with tea
>   To any natural objects we can see.

We can't, of course, invite a Jew or Red
But birds and nebulae will do instead.[38]

Auden has later remarked in one of his essays that 'satire and
comedy both make use of the comic contradiction, but their
aims are different. Satire would arouse in readers the desire to
act so that the contradictions disappear; comedy would per-
suade them to accept the contradictions with good humour as
facts of life against which it is useless to rebel.'[39] Auden's satire
is always being belied by the poet's irrepressible good humour.
At Oxford, 'he was outrageous, but he was not a rebel'.[40] In
any case, it is hard for a young man, even a rebellious one, who
has been promoted chief of the opposition by the young, and
even grumblingly endorsed by the not-so-young, to prevent an
insidious acceptance of his situation creeping over him. Byron
failed, so did Auden. To be a satirist, you must exude discom-
fort, and it is a help to feel some. It is difficult to remain really
indignant in such a cosy place as Britain. Auden, hired as early
as 1935 to be the script-writer of the official—if adventurously
official—GPO Documentary Film Unit (he wrote the scripts
for *Coalface* and *Night Mail*) was hard put to it to exude *saeva
indignatio*. There are inescapable ambiguities in being appro-
priated as Rebel Laureate—a status to which national pride
condemns the angriest young genius, whether he likes it or not.
Auden's abundant light verse, admirable as it is, stands as the
symbol of the increasingly conventional character of his poetry
in the early Thirties.

With Auden, always an idiosyncratic writer, 'conventional'
is a relative term. *The Orators* was so far above suspicion in this
regard as to cut him off from all but the most relentless in-
telligentsia. Auden's development towards a more traditional
manner made him accessible to a wider audience. Even in
retrospect, any losses his work suffered in concentration and
originality were made up—more, or less, according to taste—
by gains in clarity and spontaneity. It is significant that *Look,
Stranger!*, the volume which most tellingly illustrates the balance
he reached as a writer in the early Thirties, is in many ways the
most attractive of all his collections of verse.

Look, Stranger! brings together most of the short 'serious'

77

poems written between 1930 and 1935, and its themes are close to those of the early *Poems* and *The Orators*. In one way or another, all of its 32 pieces, on the condition of England or individual Englishmen, the coming revolution, and so on, can be placed along the familiar spectrum at one end of which stands Love, the creative principle, and at the other the Death-wish, the uncreative willingness to go under rather than change one's illusory or outdated assumptions. Not a single poem falls outside this range and each points a needle to fair, foul or variable on Auden's barometer of social weather. If this is a little too predictable, the fact that the readings are far more instantaneously explicit than in the earlier volumes adds to the immediate (though not necessarily lasting) impact of the pieces. Similarly, if there are signs of superficiality in *Look, Stranger!*, the volume has the qualities of its defects: it conveys a strong sense of surfaces and also of emotions. It is youthful not in its mastery, which is mature, but in its vigour: there is more *élan* in the writing of *Look, Stranger!* than in perhaps any other of Auden's collections.

Sometimes the *élan* overreaches itself and, like the light verse, verges on an excessive fluency. This fluency has something to do with the insensitivity to echoes of the man who has become too used to dominating the conversation. Reading a sonnet like 'A shilling life will give you all the facts', one cannot help feeling the mastery has become over-masterful. The supposed moral of the piece is that public success is no substitute for spiritual balance, but the tone is so assertive, so rapid, so self-assured, that every line identifies the author with the error he is ostensibly criticising: the tone saps the theme. In other poems, there is an uneasy hint of pre-fabrication. Images, even excellent ones, begin to look like spare parts for a mass-produced argument and the best poems are apt to suffer from a chromium-plated smartness:

> The sallow oval faces of the city
> Begot in passion or good-natured habit,
> Are caught by waiting coaches, or laid bare
> Beside the undiscriminating sea.
>
> Lulled by the light they live their dreams of freedom;
> May climb the old road twisting to the moors,

Play leap frog, enter cafés, wear
The tigerish blazer and the dove-like shoe.[41]

This is brilliant genre-painting, but the insect-watching of the social observer none the less guts the balnearic of much of its inner life.

For all its faults, *Look, Stranger!* leaves an impression of arresting and vivid spccch, cpigrammatic in detail and full in outline. The received term for Auden's manner at this period is 'conversational'. True enough as far as it goes, this hardly conveys the quality of a language, which is not so much relaxed and informal as dynamic. Auden has an ear which any dramatist might envy for turns of phrase conveying the energy of the moment. He does not merely say 'these years have seen a boom in sorrow', he fixes the human context by adding

For private reasons I must have the truth, remember
These years have seen a boom in sorrow,[42]

which is much more suggestive of an emotional context. The main line of a poem in *Look, Stranger!* is nearly always simple and strong, the metaphors in which it is couched varied, full of life and, for a modern poet, almost uniquely direct:

Pardon the studied taste that could refuse
The golf-house quick one and the rector's tea;
Pardon the nerves the thrushes could not soothe,
Yet answered promptly the no-subtler lure
To private joking in a panelled room,
The solitary vitality of tramps and madmen;
Believed the whisper in the double-bed:
Pardon for these and every flabby fancy.[43]

In *Look, Stranger!* Auden acquires the poetic equivalent of social poise. On the one hand, he has become familar enough with his own ideas to be able to take the structure of his thought for granted and not to torture his syntax to establish his certainties. On the other, he is still sufficiently involved in the detailed experiences which have led him to these convictions for them to excite him and throw up strong images. The result is a simple structure of beliefs still able to carry a multiplicity of judgements and observations tuned to vivid metaphor. There is an urgency which makes this much more than just a poetry 'of opinions'.

Still, *Look, Stranger!* would not be as memorable as it is were it not for the large number of its enchanting 'songs and other musical pieces'. Many of these deservedly became classics for the anthologies overnight. It is a curious fact that the lyrics which are probably Auden's finest achievement in the Thirties are also peculiarly an achievement *of* the Thirties, and the middle Thirties in particular. If one looks before 1933, say, to the pre-Hitler period, or after Spain in 1937, it is hard to say lyrics dominate Auden's art in quantity or that they stand apart from it very sharply in kind. It is arguable that 'What's in your mind, my dove, my coney' *is* a lyric, but it does not impose itself as one in contrast to any other of the early *Poems*. Similarly, later, 'Deftly, admiral, cast your fly' or the beautiful Lauds are only a nuance away from the 'non-lyrical' pieces of their periods. In *Look, Stranger!* the lyrics are not only numerous, they are also more distinctively songs. True, there is not the gap between them and the more obviously worldly poems there might be, say, in Byron, Auden is never an emphatically emotional poet. He writes lyrics of melancholy rather than of self-conscious passion; they are always reflective like his 'conversational' pieces. Nor is there a necessary separation in subject-matter between the lyrics and other pieces. In fact, the originality of one of the most remarkable of them, 'Our Hunting Fathers', put to music by Benjamin Britten, is that it makes a single movement of what might seem the most intractable material, a complex political despair. The crowning touch to it is that the last two lines, the dying fall—

> To hunger, work illegally,
> And be anonymous

—are a straight quotation from Lenin, whose prose, whatever its other virtues, has not usually lent itself to the felicities of lyrical writing.[44] Yet the fact remains that most of the lyrics exploit a vein of nostalgia or erotic melancholy which is 'lyrical' by the most traditional standards. When one comes to a poem like the title-piece of *Look, Stranger!*, one reaches the nearest thing to a straight Wordsworthian nature poem in respectable recent verse. This shining summer seascape attempts almost in the spirit of Debussy's *La Mer*, to create a lifeline between poetry and music, and between music and the movements of the sea. All that is left of objectivity is that the poet nowhere mentions himself. In terms of feeling he has made every effort to identify his subject with a human state, to fix the evanescent vision of a private Heaven. Though Auden condemns with unnecessary intensity 'Bysshe . . . the syllable-counting old cissy',[45] some of his own writing at the time has a breathless zeal for the incoming revolution which is positively Shelleyesque:

> Some possible dream, long coiled in the ammonite's slumber
> Is uncurling, prepared to lay on our talk and kindness
> Its military silence, its surgeon's idea of pain;
>
> And out of the Future into actual History,
> As when Merlin, tamer of horses, and his lords to whom
> Stonehenge was still a thought, the Pillars passed
>
> And into the undared ocean swung north their prow,
> Drives through the night and star-concealing dawn
> For the virgin roadsteads of our hearts an unwavering keel.[46]

This unexpected mixture of up-to-date interests and familiar cadences made Auden appeal to large numbers of people who might otherwise never have taken to his, or any other modern, poetry. Yet it is hard to imagine 'modern' poems with a more nineteenth century conception of what brings a poem to life. The lyrics in *Look, Stranger!* run to a linear flow, an essentially melodic line, which is far nearer Victorian conceptions than is comfortable for the twentieth century's vision of its purposes. Modern taste, like Auden's own at most periods of his life, leans to counterpoint and irony, which suggest the search for objective standards, not to the subjectivism of romantic verse. Melody, from this point of view, is facile and lines which are mainly mood pictures, like

> Certainty, fidelity
> On the stroke of midnight pass
> Like vibrations of a bell [47]

seem an almost mindless incantation. The fact that their music has compelling reverberations only makes them more suspect, a form of half-magic chanted out of the caves of what Grigson used to call 'Sheats's' sensual valley. Auden's contemporary tone, his slangy and superficially unromantic language, have disguised this resemblance. Nevertheless, superb as many of his lyrics are, they make a strange comment on the New Writing, on necessary impersonality and the proletarian revolution.

As such, they point up the paradox, even perhaps the mystery, of Auden's development in the early Thirties. Whatever happened to the highly controlled composer of the early *Poems*? The whole posture of Auden's art during these years is rather puzzling. In some ways, they marked the peak of Auden's powers. He wrote with an abundance and vitality, a wit and lyrical flair, that he has never matched before or since. He could, apparently without effort, produce memorable lines and any number of short anthology pieces. With all this brilliance and even promise of greatness, he did not produce anything laying claim to be a masterpiece. With all his creative vigour, the man who had experimented so fearlessly in his first years gave up being a radical in poetry well before he ceased to be a radical in politics. Why should the almost revolutionary poet of a few years back seem so traditional now? Why should explicitness, instead of adding a classic breadth to Auden's rather muscle-bound early style, add only attraction and seem somehow less weighty? Why, in short, should Auden have given up so abruptly the self-denying ordinance of the *Poems* and the future-facing irresolutions of *The Orators*? Even in retrospect, this remains an enigma. Could he not have kept more of his old concentration in the midst of his widening interests? Was it inevitable that he should become 'popular' in quite the loose-mouthed way he did? Was the shift after the *Poems* really motivated by political needs or was this only a rationalisation? It is noticeable that though Auden's politics changed again in the late Thirties, the outstanding poetic innovation of the immediately preceding years, the shift from the intensive to the extensive style, has proved permanent. The changes after the early *Poems* may not have been as political as they look.

Plainly, politics did play an important part in the process: 'these years have seen a boom in sorrow'. By 1932, output in most of the major capitalist countries had nearly halved. Britain had 3 million, Germany 6 million, America 14 million, unemployed. Only Russia, with its five-year plans, seemed immune to the general collapse of progressive government. 'Chartism and the Crimean war left many members of the community completely untouched, but the Great War and the Depression left their mark on every inch of the country. . . . Mass movements were in the air of the time, and quite explicably. Hunger Marchers were out in England. The militant unemployed were reading the *Daily Worker* (founded in 1930). There was a need and a clamour for social justice. It was easy, indeed, to see society in terms of a class war.'[48] It was natural in the confused and menacing Thirties, with civilised values under vicious attack, to make poetry 'a midwife to society'.[49] The spiritual condition behind the politics, which particularly concerned the artists, was almost more alarming than the politics themselves. In the spring of 1935, Cecil Day-Lewis, then a schoolmaster at Cheltenham, dared to speak on collective farming to the local branch of the Friends of the Soviet Union. This promptly produced a summons to appear before the chairman of the school governors, Lord Lee of Fareham.

> 'D'you realise what would have happened to you if you'd done that sort of thing in the Regiment?'
> I shook my head, dumbfounded by this extraordinary question. Regiment? What Regiment? It was impossible to associate Lord Lee of Fareham with the military life.
> 'The Colonel,' he went on, 'would have handed you over to the subalterns' mess; and when they'd finished with you, you'd have been asked to join some other Regiment . . .'
> That a public man of Lord Lee's eminence should allow himself to indulge in such crudities as this would have been shocking at any time; but the context of a period, when in Germany and Italy physical violence had become a commonplace of official policy, made it seem positively sinister. . . .
> I knew now what it felt like to be a family man whose job is threatened—how insecurity could fasten on the mind, setting up a corrosive anxiety; and I came thus to respect all the more sincerely those professional or working-class people who at this time of widespread unemployment risked victimisation for their political beliefs. . . .[50]

Such an incident helps one to understand many postures taken up by liberals in the Thirties which have since been attacked as preposterous, yet seem so now only because the preposterous, or sinister, attitudes which prompted them have declined and the critics view the results only as literature. It explains why men who were essentially moderates took so avidly to revolutionary movements and why even the subtle Auden, who was never as attracted to Communism as some of his contemporaries, and never stooped to identify art with propaganda, nevertheless wrote verse which some have regarded as near-Communist, and others, more damagingly, as near-propaganda. A radical style of poetry, hammering home its arguments to the crowd, is necessarily different from the private testing of emotional integrity, the laboratory experiments of *Poems*.

> Unable to endure ourselves, we sought relief
> In the insouciance of the soldier, the heroic sexual pose
> Playing at fathers to impress the little ladies,
>
> Call us not tragic; falseness made farcical our death:
> Nor brave; ours was the will of the insane to suffer
> By which since we could not live we gladly died:
> And now we have gone for ever to our foolish graves.[51]

Accordingly, critics tend to explain Auden's evolution in terms of his audience. Yet poets have private and unconscious motives for writing the way they do, as well as a sense of their public role or of audiences to satisfy. Auden testifies that 'all the poems I have written were written for love; naturally, when I have written one, I try to market it, but the prospect of a market played no role in its writing'.[52] He has also complained of people turning against authors they regarded as their spokesmen because these authors seem to have abandoned a role they were not truly pursuing.[53] If such reactions mean anything, it is that whatever his public purposes and their influence on his writing in the Thirties, these purposes must have been in harmony with what he felt to be his inner needs. They must have fitted in with what his instinct told him were the laws of growth of his art and cannot have been irrelevant to, still less have worked against, them. There was an inner as well as an outer compulsion for the poet's development in the 1930s.

Once the *Poems* had laid bare the bases of a modern mind and sensibility, the psychological context out of which Auden wrote was changed—both by what the *Poems* had achieved and by what they had left undone. He could now trust his own artistic strength and individuality and feel freer to be himself: there must have been something of this self-confidence in the relaxation of his style. So much the success of the *Poems* achieved. Other things they could not so easily satisfy. Their emotional titanism and their rationalist self-questioning, the one too rooted in adolescent feeling, the other too narrowly and privately based, were to be able to give Auden the answers to the questions he himself had posed. The *Poems* had enunciated the idea of search, of the Leader, without actually doing much to define, still less to pursue, the mysterious journey so insistently announced. The Leader could hardly delay his promised voyage any longer. Its discipline required him to take cognisance of his world. Auden lacked an inner certainty of values. It was precisely this sense of anxiety—

> insecure, he loves and love
> Is insecure, gives less than he expects[54]—

which drove him to much of his poetry. It was therefore hard to conceive without an attempt to embrace his society and his world. The political influences of the time, Nazism and the slump, probably gave the Leader only a final push in a direction he was taking anyway. Politics may have given a specific form to Auden's poetic journey, but in a larger sense it simply fitted in with the metaphysical search which had now begun to take over from the *Poems*' more static preoccupation with affirming identity.

There were special dangers for Auden in reaching out in this way beyond his own personal experience to embrace the world, however zestfully he did so. They were rooted in the nature of his talent. Being, as Isherwood has said, a ritualist, Auden is unfailingly inventive in building up clusters of instances round his basic thought, but his basic thought itself is abstract.[55] In an amusing snatch of autobiography, he says that:

> My first remark at school did all it could
> To shake a matron's monumental poise:
> 'I like to see the various types of boys'.[56]

85

It might be germs, or insects. Auden's cast of mind combines the scientist's detachment in scrutinising microbes and the intellectual's drive to the global view. This kind of approach, proper perhaps to the research laboratory, is fruitful to art only under rigorous conditions. Where strong personal feelings or convictions are involved, an air of detachment can actually increase one's power of expression: its inherent understatement canalises the emotional currents and enhances the pressure behind them. This was the case with many of the *Poems*. But when the poet, driven by his need to control his world moves out of the natural disciplines of his personal domain, the facts known multiply enormously and are in perpetual danger of overwhelming the facts felt. He is driven despite himself into a kind of poetic variant of exposition. The intellectual force of what he says may be considerable, but the emotional charge is connected too loosely to what he has to say to focus in sufficiently heightened language. This is certainly the impression *The Orators* and *The Dog Beneath the Skin* convey for long stretches. In *Poems*, Auden's compulsion to identify himself with the universe—or rather to select his own angle of vision on it — was not too dangerous. He was laying the careful foundations of his art, never moving far away from the matter in which it was rooted. From *The Orators* onward, when he was building a public edifice, commenting on the social condition at large, he lost part of this contact with personal roots. He made large gestures, he gathered whole societies within his embrace, but there was bound to be something thin and facile about such a relationship, rather like a tourist's to a panoramic view. The frequent 'the's' of the poetry of the Thirties symbolise this non-participation. It necessarily leaves the impression of a powerful but rather mechanical intelligence—and above all, of intelligence only—in the reader's mind. This tendency was aggravated, after *The Orators*, by the fact that Auden was no longer obsessed by the imminence of revolution or by the personal conflicts that the prospect of violent change engendered in himself. The reflexive quality in Auden's early verse, playing back on his own feelings, began to ebb away. Neither right in, nor completely out of, the burning social and political issues of the day, neither consumed by a collective cause nor obsessed by doubts about his person, Auden became the performer in 'popular' art or the social observer in the 'middle style'.[57] His detachment, though in itself only a stage in his gradual shift to apolitical, conservative humanism, reinforced the natural temptation of the intellectual to play the Unmoved Mover.

While this casts some light at least on the clinical end of Auden's poetic range in the Thirties, it does little or nothing to illumine the sharply contrasted lyrical one. Reading many lyrics and even light verses of the Thirties one might simply put them down to sex. Auden, now 25–30 years old, showed every sign of being in love. But Auden's previous poems are also much preoccupied with love (not only of the capitalised variety) and they do not go about it in this erotically melancholy way.* Moreover, there are lyrics of the Thirties which are not erotic but political or even, like 'May with its light behaving', philosophic, and these too have a wry or wistful tone. Something more than sex is required to explain this, particularly as one of the cardinal points of Auden's outlook in the *Poems* was the denial of the Wordworthian creed of unity with Nature (or with godhead through Nature) which had served most nineteenth-century artists as their secular religion. This denial implied the acceptance of Man's essential solitude. He could improve his situation, he could come to terms with it, he could rid society of specific ills. What he could not do was rid himself of the evolutionary dialectic of conflict. The *Poems* and *The Orators* are full of this sense of conflict. The poetry of the 1930s does not reflect it.

Here too the ebb of revolutionary drama—at least in Auden's mind—may have had some influence. When death and renewal, or the risk thereof, seemed imminent, Auden had to look to his own spiritual condition: the prospect of crisis wonderfully concentrated his mind. When revolution became more remote, the sense of personal responsibility began to fade; the millennium drifted away again into space, shining like a beautiful vision with no immediately personal implications. In a word, it became the guiding light long familiar to the

* Yet he writes that at Oxford 'I was more unhappy than I have ever been before or since' (*The Dyer's Hand*, p. 42).

millennial mind. This is quite clear in the attitude to Marx of
Auden and his friends:

> we waited for the day
> The State would wither clean away,
> Expecting the Millennium
> That theory promised us would come.[58]

This millennial influence is equally true, though not at all so
clear, of Freud's impact on the poet. This is more important
than Marx, in fact. The structure of thought which emerged as
the waves of Auden's first adolescent sense of fate, and then his
obsession with revolution, receded, was the Freudian psychology
which has always given backbone to his judgements of men and
affairs. Then, as in some texts of the New Left today, Freud
was still widely regarded if not as an honorary revolutionary,
at least as a thinker of value to the revolution. John Strachey,
then a Communist, might call him 'one of the last great theorists
of the European capitalist class'.[59] In a world of Lord Lees,
Freud's doctrine of repression still seemed an intellectual time-
bomb in the armoury of the underdogs. It helped them to give
inglorious and subversive explanations for the pomposities of
authority and to impale the powerful on Freud's fork: 'If you
agree with us, we are right; and if, as of course we know you do,
you angrily disagree, this proves we are right: you are visibly
repressing the unbearable knowledge that we have uncovered
your weaknesses.' When new, this line of attack, suitably
camouflaged, was very hard to parry.

> No wonder the ancient cultures of conceit
> In his technique of unsettlement foresaw
> The fall of princes.[60]

'Freud', Robin Skelton has written, 'was somehow a republican
and a socialist, toppling the princes and undermining the
capitalists. Thus any Freudian *exposé* of the way we are is a
Revolutionary document.'[61]

Had this been all, it might not have gone far. Even his most
enthusiastic followers could hardly see Freud as more than an
unconscious and *mild* revolutionary. But there was a millennial
kernel in the core of his teaching. Whatever the formalities of

his philosophic position (his emphasis on the Ego virtually revamped the doctrine of Original Sin), Freud's advice to the neurotic to rid himself of inhibitions on maturity, defined as the emotions' contract of enlightened self-interest with the world, is libertarian in appeal. Spender says that Auden at Oxford 'saw himself—as I then envisaged him'—

> with certain potentialities and talents, certain desires, certain attitudes of mind, living within a community governed by certain rules and traditions, and consisting also of people with different potentialities, desires and attitudes. His aims were to fulfil his potentialities, obtain satisfaction for his desires, and maintain his attitudes, without prejudice and without accepting any authority outside his own judgement.[62]

To someone with this outlook—the commonest today—the Freudian credo is a call to reasoned self-fulfilment. True, there are limits to such fulfilment: Freud offers emotional freedom through the acceptance of the human condition much as Marx offers political freedom through the acceptance of necessity. But, just as Marx offers the ultimate hope of anarchy, so, on Freud's logic, the only restraints on the fine flowering of the individual are the bounds set by lack of courage or imagination. The duty of the potentially mature adult is to free himself, and thereby help free others, from the unnecessary burdens of hate and denial. There is no essential conflict between men that reason cannot conquer:

> if we can trust we are free,
> Though alone among those
> Who within the earshot of the ungovernable sea
> Grow set in their ways.[63]

The *ultima ratio* of progress is the creative insight of the doctors of consciousness ushering in controlled, humane self-knowledge. The condition of England question, and the ripening of the individual mind, are really only the personal and collective aspects of a single hope, the liberation of humanity. By a devious route one has come back to the Rousseauistic stand that it is right to assume Man is good and *only* needs liberating. The old liberal tradition, emphasising moral regeneration and freedom is reasserting itself. It is not surprising perhaps that Auden's essential Englishness comes to the surface again during the middle 1930s in an undenominational radicalism.

Such radicalism is inherently millennial. It is astonishing how many of Auden's poems of the early Thirties build up on a teleological syntax whose implicit goal is either a climax or its mirror image, a dying fall. 'Our hunting fathers' with its prayerful 'thats' provides one example. The end of 'Out on the lawn I lie in bed' offers another:

> As through a child's rash happy cries
> The drowned parental voices rise
> In unlamenting song.[64]

In a third, the final invocation is:

> Let the hot sun
> Shine on, shine on, [65]

and even in a distant rejecting light one finds the trait inverted as:

> Cold, impossible, ahead
> Lifts the mountain's lovely head
> Whose white waterfall could bless
> Travellers in their last distress.[66]

The movement to a more or less concealed climax is one of the key mechanisms of Auden's lyrics at the time. Once one has recognised the tell-tale psychological lift, or fall, one finds it recurring again and again in Auden's poetry during these years. It is as if the verses were breathless for some epiphany, manifested in many forms but always on the same pattern: after the revolution the brotherhood of men, after the orgasm the kernel of fulfilment carried through life, after Love (social and outgoing to be sure) peace, after conflict unity.

The reason, then, for the sudden, temporary and almost paradoxical efflorescence of Auden as an outstanding lyrist in the mid-Thirties seems to be that he was at this time pursuing a Romantic notion of unity, whereas both the *Poems* and the later verses reflect a dialectical view of life in which conflict is inherent and cannot be resolved. The ideal which he had shown out of the front door in terms of Wordsworthian unity or the egotistic worship of experience had climbed back through the window in a political guise. However heavy the disguise, the poetry of the early Thirties is permeated with the Romantics' orgasmic view of final ends. No doubt it is because this transposed excitement surfaces too crudely in 'O love, the interest itself in thoughtless Heaven' that Auden blushes for it today. Such suspicions also help to explain the resentment of critics like Leavis at whole areas of experience being taken over by erotic analogies which provide more will o' the wisps than guiding light. In short, the doctrine in *Look, Stranger!* of a social Love different from erotic or greedy love is the sign of a tension in Auden's outlook, not of its resolution. The verse itself does not speak the language of resolution. There is a contradiction between the libertarianism which assumes Man needs to be released because he is basically good—the source of Romantic melody, egotism and assumptions of unity attainable on earth—and the dialectical view, call it Christian, Darwinian, even formally Freudian, which admits eternal conflicts and the need to define limits to contain them. The contradiction is suppressed not eliminated, in Auden's verse of the mid-Thirties. A man cannot be a Byronic radical in the twentieth century without begged questions creeping in. Hence, I think, a good deal of the superficiality and sense of a burking of issues which casts doubt on Auden's brilliant and abundant work at the time.

Although this sense of unease was the source of much of the reaction against Auden after the war, it has in terms of his own artistic development meant a gain as well as a loss. The traditional cadences to which Auden returned in the early 1930s point to an important difference between him and many of his near contemporaries. The majority of them have rebelled against Romantic aesthetics; he has not. While he has cultivated a deep mistrust of Romantic self-importance—which he never lost at any time and which in a number of others has vigorously survived—he has continued to be fascinated by the Romantics' outlook. His first published book of criticism, *The Enchafèd Flood*, published in 1951, was a spectrograph of their imagery. His emancipation from their assumptions has, then, been painful and slow but correspondingly deeper and more thorough.

It is the result not of an epidermic revulsion of taste but of a slow penetration of the shortcomings of Romantic values and an exploration of the insights he had, ahead of time as it were, in *Poems*.

3

ISOLATION

DURING the late 1930s, Auden's art was dominated by a reaction against his previous Romanticism. This was also, not surprisingly, the period when the poet began to lose touch with his followers and become less the leader of a movement and more the isolated artist like others before and after him. They were years of galloping change. In 1936 he was the centre of the younger literary movement; by 1939, he was — by choice —an exile in America. In 1936, he was still a vivid epigrammatic poet, painting a more brilliant picture of contemporary England than any of his peers; by 1940, much of his poetry was highly abstract, or spiritual if not religious. In 1936, Auden was still a Byronic radical of sorts; by 1941 at the latest, he was a Christian existentialist. The view of his work which both the critics and the lay public entertain has still not quite recovered from the shock to their preconceptions administered by the surprises of these years.

Auden himself has given much the most interesting account of his change of front in an untitled essay which appeared in 1956 in a book called *Modern Canterbury Pilgrims*. In this essay he discusses how his view of the world shifted from his early radicalism to his later Christianity:

> We assumed that there was only one outlook on life conceivable among civilised people, the liberal humanism in which all of us had been brought up, whether we came from Christian or agnostic homes (English liberalism had never been anti-clerical like its Continental brother).
>
> To this the theological question seemed irrelevant since such values as freedom of the person, equal justice for all, respect for the rights of others, etc., were self-evident truths. However, the liberal humanism of the past had failed to produce the universal peace and prosperity it promised, failed even to prevent a World War. What had it overlooked? The subconscious, said Freud; the means of production, said Marx.

Liberalism was not to be superseded; it was to be made effective instead of self-defeating.

Then the Nazis came to power in Germany. The Communists had said that one must hate and destroy some of one's neighbours now in order to create a world in which nobody would be able to help loving his neighbours to-morrow. They had attacked Christianity and all religions on the ground that, so long as people are taught to love a non-existent God, they will ignore the material obstacles to human brotherhood. The novelty and shock of the Nazis was that they made no pretence of believing in justice and liberty for all, and attacked Christianity on the grounds that to love one's neighbour as oneself was a command fit only for effeminate weaklings, not for the 'healthy blood of the master race'. Moreover, this utter denial of everything liberalism had ever stood for was arousing wild enthusiasm, not in some remote barbaric land outside the pale, but in one of the most highly educated countries in Europe, a country one knew well and where one had many friends. Confronted by such a phenomenon, it was impossible any longer to believe that the values of liberal humanism were self-evident. Unless one was prepared to take a relativist view that all values are a matter of personal taste, one could hardly avoid asking the question: 'If, as I am convinced, the Nazis are wrong and we are right, what is it that validates our values and invalidates theirs?'

With this and similar questions whispering at the back of my mind, I visited Spain during the Civil War. On arriving in Barcelona, I found as I walked through the city that all the churches were closed and there was not a priest to be seen. To my astonishment, this discovery left me profoundly shocked and disturbed. The feeling was far too intense to be the result of a mere liberal dislike of intolerance, the notion that it is wrong to stop people from doing what they like, even if it is something silly like going to church. I could not escape acknowledging that, however I had consciously ignored and rejected the Church for sixteen years, the existence of churches and what went on in them had all the time been very important to me. If that was the case, what then?

Shortly afterwards, in a publisher's office, I met an Anglican layman, and for the first time in my life felt myself in the presence of personal sanctity. I had met many good people before who made me feel ashamed of my own shortcomings, but in the presence of this man—we never discussed anything but literary business—I did not feel ashamed. I felt transformed into a person who was incapable of doing or thinking anything base or unloving. (I later discovered that he had had a similar effect on many other people.)

So, presently, I started to read some theological works, Kierkegaard in particular, and began going, in a tentative and experimental sort of way, to church. And then, providentially —for the occupational disease of poets is frivolity—I was forced to know in person what it is like to feel oneself the prey of demonic powers, in both the Greek and the Christian sense, stripped of self-control and self-respect, behaving like a ham actor in a Strindberg play.[1]

Clearly, then, the later 1930s were for Auden a period of both political and personal crisis. There is something typical of him that even in such an experience public and private elements were closely mixed. The Byronic radical, no more than the Christian, would dream of divorcing the two. To start with, it is plain from Auden's own testimony, that the challenge of the Nazis was a crucial factor in his change of mind. As a very young man, he had the then common notion of political progress, derived from Bloomsbury's cosy sense of the power of the higher intelligence: he expected the revolution to be the work of 'lucid' creators who would inject reason into a morbidly neurotic society. In the usual manner of the nineteen-twenties

> We expected the beautiful or the wise . . .
> Pleased to find nothing but stones and
> Able at once to create a garden.

Unfortunately, neither the 'beautiful' nor the 'wise' personified the Thirties as each year brought its burden of news more horrifying than the last.

> These pioneers have long adapted themselves
> To the night and the nightmare; they come equipped
> To reply to terror with terror,
> With lies to unmask the least deception.[2]

To find, as the last line puts it so tersely, the reformers themselves tainted, the long awaited Men of Good Will turning up as merciless haters, massacring Jews like the Nazis or, like

Stalin, purging Old Bolsheviks by the hundred thousand, killed the daydream of 'lucidity'. If the best indeed lacked all conviction while the worst were full of passionate intensity, the scheme of reason which underlay the social sciences was only a dream after all. Once this suspicion had wormed its way into Auden's rationalism, a number of attitudes always present in his view of society assumed a new force. A jaundiced view of 'our proletariat' was visible as early as *The Orators*:

> And see what they're at—our proletariat.
> O my, what peeps
> At disheartened sweeps—
> Fitters and moulders,
> Wielders and welders,
> Dyers and bakers
> And boiler-tube makers,
> Poofs and ponces,
> All of them dunces.[3]

Who, from Auden's reputation, would have imagined that this is what the prophet of the proletarian revolution really thought of his supposed protégés? Auden, of course, dutifully blamed the stunting of the working classes on a condition of society partly outside their control. This limited but did not change his estimate of the human quality of the masses on whom the brave new future was expected to rest. Nor was the estimate a quirk of rhetoric, Auden ironic or caught in the wind of his ranting and carried further than he had bargained. The same idea is repeated several times, as when he speaks of

> The little men and their mothers, not plain but
> Dreadfully ugly.[4]

There is little to separate this from the Walter Mitty of the 'Letter to Lord Byron' written in 1936:

> The bowler hat who strap-hangs in the tube,
> And kicks the tyrant only in his dreams,
> Trading on pathos, dreading all extremes;
> The little Mickey with the hidden grudge.[5]

When the masses are reduced to this, reduced to it by the forces of the industrial world their own aspirations impose upon

them, no theories for producing the more scientifically controlled state can heal the ills of urban man. Communism,
Fascism, even Liberalism, are all variants of

> mechanized societies
> Where natural intuition dies.[6]

Auden, exposed since 1939 to the American way of life, has
since foresworn the standards of the benevolent despot of social
science and preached anarchism and water:

> Thou shalt not worship projects nor
> Shalt thou or thine bow down before
> Administration.[7]

This is not really a denial of the old urges. Auden was, and is
still, looking for ways to cure, or palliate, the sickness of humanity. Only the optimistic view of the nineteenth-century liberals
that evil is ultimately powerless against conscious reason, the
optimistic view of the young Auden himself that Marx and
Freud are effective tentpoles for 'Love', has turned, by the end
of the 1930s, into a kind of bewilderment:

> Love like matter is much
> Odder than we thought.[8]

And even, 'we are lived by powers we pretend to understand'.[9]
The 'Look, Stranger' poem in 1935 speaks, in its vision of
felicity, of ships diverging 'on urgent voluntary errands'.[10]
A year or two later, 'Lay your sleeping head my love' already
speaks of the lover being 'fed by the involuntary powers'.[11]
During the late Thirties, confidence in masterful rationalism is
wearing thin.

From the first, Auden had never really displayed a political
turn of mind. He had little patience for the 'flat ephemeral
pamphlet and the boring meeting'.[12] In *The Orators*, he produced a brilliant burlesque of what later became the fifth
column method of subversive attack, but for this one surrealist
flash of insight, there were many glaring instances of obtuseness.
His dislike of the old order was at one time so inflamed that he
attacked the 'great malignant Cambridge ulcer' which did after
all produce Keynes.[13] (It is true that Spender claims this poem

'is an exercise in entering into a point of view not his own. It is his summing up of conversations with Communists rather like the ones I used to have with Chalmers in Berlin'.[14] But the Communist *persona* borrowed here by Auden is too close to his other roles at the time to be wholly dissociated from him.) Again, the pacifism of the 1938 play written with Isherwood, *On the Frontier*, blithely equates Hitler and his victims in its denunciations of European warmongering. Auden's political analysis was often only an allegory of the death-wish: habitually identifying external events with states of mind in a glorious psychosomatic jamboree, he hardly ever made a point which arose from a concrete political situation. Auden's political commitments were skin deep. They were only the fashions in which, for a few years, he dressed up his moral passion. It was natural that what was left from the ebb of the twin dreams of the socialist triumph over fascism and of reason's victory over ignorance should finally be the rock of individual conscience.

In the early Thirties, the individual conscience often figured in Auden's writing as a weak-kneed, liberal alibi for not facing up to necessary revolution. By the beginning of the war it had become the one real touchstone of value, even in discussing collective ills. The Leader-who-must-migrate of the *Poems* becomes, in the 'affirming flame' of September 1, 1939, the solitary individual bearing witness for a community morally at sea. The old reforming zeal turns into the conviction that 'there is no such thing as the State', only individual men;[15] and the former radical impatience with the 'old gang' into a liberal distaste for what the State is doing to the 'Unknown Citizen' holding 'the proper opinions for the time of year'.[16]

So far, Auden was only being fairly typical of his generation. The more intriguing question is why he went further and became a Christian. It was not inevitable that one should react against the threats of the Thirties in this way. Friends, like Spender and MacNeice, did not, even though Spender underwent a reaction against 'the God that failed' parallel to Auden's own. Why, almost alone of the Pink poets, should Auden have reacted into Christianity? Why should the leader alone be lost, from the point of view of his erstwhile flock, like Wordsworth long before? His reaction might seem characteristic of the conversions of eminent literary figures of the left in the nineteenth century. It is not at all typical of the changes of front of the literary left in the twentieth. Radicalism, receding, in most cases leaves behind a firm substratum of agnosticism; Auden alone has been washed by the baptismal tide.

Almost certainly one reason is that Auden, although emotionally a moderate, is intellectually more absolute than most of his contemporaries. His is the kind of intellectual nature which requires a global system covering all contingencies and doubts. He cannot be merely pragmatic (it is one source of his talent that he is always universal in his interests.) Giving up the scientific stance, he had to find some other system which offered a general answer to the problem troubling him. Moreover, as Auden's fragment of spiritual autobiography already cited shows, his own Anglo-Catholic childhood was never far below the surface of his mind. Isherwood, in 1937, regarded it as one of the three basic facts to tell a stranger about Auden that 'as a child he enjoyed a high Anglican upbringing, coupled with a sound musical education. The Anglicanism has evaporated leaving only the height: he is still much preoccupied with ritual in all its forms.'[17] Auden might have rediscovered the faith of his childhood, whatever the incidental circumstances of the route he took to return to it. In practice, the traumatic shock of Nazism undoubtedly speeded him on his journey. It is hard today to feel one's way back to the climate of the time. Today, one might perhaps argue that Nazism was a specific aberration, a nervous breakdown of liberal society peculiar to a period in which the spiritual values and material problems of the capitalist world were disastrously, but not inescapably, out of phase. One could, echoing Auden's own words, argue that liberalism is not to be superseded; it is to be made effective instead of self-defeating. This is optimistic, for one breakdown demonstrates the potential for another. Nevertheless, a relative optimism does not appear the mere whistling in the dark it certainly seemed to some of the best minds just before the war. In the late 1930s the economic failure of capitalism to raise or even maintain output and serve a social justice; and the political failure of the bourgeois democracies to proceed to internal reform and put up a brave front against Nazism's denial of civilised values;

suggested a basic flaw in the liberal heritage itself which could only be salvaged by a spiritual root-and-branch reform. Eliot's lectures on 'The Idea of a Christian Society', delivered in Cambridge in March 1939, assume this to such a degree that he does not even bother to discuss his assumption, and takes it as axiomatic that an élitist society pervaded by the Christian ethos is the only possible remedy against the disintegration of mercantile democracy into brute totalitarianism. In a similar vein, Auden's early wartime poem, 'Kairos and Logos', implies that the irruption of the 'savage' into the 'garden' is the direct consequence of the failure of liberalism to raise a spiritual wall against barbarism.[18] Freedom has no internal stabiliser: it is freedom to destroy as well as to create. Auden's assumption that civilisation 'must be based upon absolute and religious sanctions' is best expressed in 'A Note on Order' which he published in *The Nation* on February 1, 1941, and which Spears summarises in these words:

> Since the Renaissance, a third heresy . . . has arisen—an empiricism denying the necessity of metaphysics. This view, now dominant, is based on the scientific method of isolating the experimental field from the rest of nature; it assumes, by analogy, that this isolation is characteristic of nature. Therefore, it leads to an ignoring of the relations between different realms, and produces the atomistic view of society typical of liberal capitalistic democracy. This 'liberal' view, being relativistic, provides no basis for stability except force; and so has no ideological defence against fascism.[19]

Auden has such a habit of arguing in public terms that ideological motives have been taken as a sufficient as well as necessary cause of his evolution in the late Thirties. But Auden has himself pointed out that these years were a period of personal crisis. A love affair, certainly. Even that, though, does not tell one much, for what matters is the quality of mind Auden brought to the love affair, or disappointment in love, at this time of his life, and which he brought to his experiences in quite this way neither earlier nor later. Unhappy loves tend to come to those ripe for unhappiness, just as happy loves are too difficult to achieve by accident. There is every sign in Auden's poetry, in the later Thirties, of a psychological crisis.

On the surface, it is rather odd that Auden's early rationalism should have gone hand in hand, as it did, with the orgasmic *Weltanschauung* of his lyrics. The determined matter-of-factness of the scientific attitude is, in the British utilitarian—and anti-metaphysical—tradition, at the opposite pole from the absolute aspirations of Romantic enthusiasm. Nevertheless, opposite though the poles may seem, they share a common psychological tension: this is the sense, true to both, of the self-enclosed isolation of the individual. Neither has any conception of emotionally fertile relationships. Auden's idea of Love, though it carefully avoided the usual Romantic identifications with sex, offered little more than an aseptic notion of service. Though bloated by the mental associations with which the word 'Love' is soaked in the Christian inheritance of the West, it was never-theless, in the Auden canon, astonishingly devoid of commit-ment. Underneath the verbal trappings, his Love assumed a sovereign observer not subject to the temptations of ordinary humanity. It was the poker-faced Love of the Freudian psycho-analyst who must at all costs remain aloof from the patient on the couch who is trying to ensnare him in a private drama, a neurotic relationship, of his own. This may or may not be the right thing for a consulting room. As a philosophy of life, how-ever, it assumes that the psychoanalyst never goes home to his private life or, equally implausibly, that he is at all times master of it. That is notoriously beyond psychoanalysts and beyond poets too. Little by little, the objective stance of the observer was undermined by the evidence of what Auden could feel 'objectivity' was doing to the supposed observer in himself. As he expressed it a few years later, 'it is the Mover that is moved'.[20]

If the observer's duty is to be detached and see like an X-ray to the irreducible bone behind every worm-ridden feeling, there is no reason why humanity or Nature should not seem to reci-procate that detachment when he, as a feeling human being, no longer masterful, no longer controlling or detached, in his turn asks for some communion. 'The man who is not bound to anyone has no one bound to him; as he renounces his obligations to others, so he forfeits his claims upon them; his relationships being transitory, his alienation becomes permanent.'[21] Such is Auden's reputation for being a self-contained virtuoso, a devilishly clever manipulator, an intellectual whom emotions tickle without really touching, that the plain evidence of his own reactions to such stresses is ignored. Yet the signs of exactly the kind of response one would expect abound in his poems. The classic instance is 'Musée des Beaux-Arts', where Auden reflects in a mood of wry acceptance on Brueghel's *Icarus*:

> About suffering they were never wrong,
> The Old Masters . . .
> . . . the expensive delicate ship that must have seen
> Something amazing, a boy falling out of the sky,
> Had somewhere to get to and sailed calmly on.[22]

Here, one might say, speaks the man of sense. But so does the lonely man, isolated by the deep cleavage between his burden of feeling and the indifference to all save its own processes of the world in which he, or his borrowed logic, believes. As with Shelley, the suppressed doubts in Auden's optimism come out most clearly in the unmasked anguish of loneliness in many of the love lyrics of the Thirties.

The kind of feeling behind Auden's wary attitude to sex is displayed very clearly in a sonnet published in *New Verse* in October 1933 and never reprinted.

> Sleep on beside me though I wake for you:
> Stretch out your hands towards your harm and me,
> Lest, waking, you should feel the need I do
> To offer love's preposterous guarantee
> That the stars watch us, that there are no poor,
> No boyish weakness justifying scorn;
> To cancel off from the forgotten score
> The foiled caress from which thought was born.
>
> Yes, sleep: how easily may we do good
> To those we have no wish to see again.
> Love knows he argues with himself in vain;
> He means to do no mischief but he would:
> Love would content us. That is untrue.
> Turn not towards me lest I turn to you.

Sex cannot 'content us' because we want, through its 'preposterous guarantee' of communion and peace, to be released from all self-criticism. The usual supplications to the goddess of love to 'cancel off . . . the foiled caress' are false because the will to blind, thought-erasing unity can never by fulfilled in action. A man tramples on others in the attempt to capture it; and even then it will elude him. On that road, the tolls are high and when they have been paid the highway is found to lead no-where. Such is the conclusion. But, in the world of wishes, conclusions imply their exact opposite. The antiseptic quality of Auden's doctrine of Love reflects his attempt to sterilise his own desire to be lost in the infinite. In the sonnet, as in all Auden's early work, the conscious discipline to be exerted over unlimited desires wins the day. However, the need for total love has merely retired from the field. It has been brushed aside, but not eliminated. In retrospect, it is not surprising that love finally returned as the god from the machine. For, though in the early part of Auden's career his rationalism is brimful of confidence and holds the initiative, the suppressed part of the poet's nature begins to wage guerrilla war in the occupied territories behind the lines. Auden's lyrics show this most plainly. The most frequent personal note of his erotic verse in the Thirties is the fear of being left:

> For each love to its aim is true,
> And all kinds seek their own;
> You love your life and I love you,
> So I must lie alone.[23]

This could be due, simply, to an unhappy love affair—and no doubt it was—but the idea that 'each love to its aim is true' hints at hyper-awareness of necessary infidelity in the author himself. Auden strikes the note of fulfilment so seldom; and even his dreams echo daylight sorrows with almost obsessive images of desertion which surely suggest a predisposition:

> you, then, unabashed . . .
> Confessed another love;
> And I, submissive, felt
> Unwanted and went out.[24]

Could not the trouble be at least partly that Auden *expects* to be left because he is painfully, even obsessively, aware of the indifferent element in him which is itself quite ready to leave? One poem, 'As I walked out one evening', places love in the quite indifferent arms of time, and another 'Lay your sleeping head, my love', puts lover, love and Auden in the equally indifferent midnight of the poet's Id. The same sense of unloved and at heart unlovingly, desperately greedy solitude comes out of the more disingenuous world of Auden's generalisations about life, or even from his passing confessions:

> Such dreams are amorous; they are indeed:
> But no one but myself is loved in these.[25]

Auden's lonely men of action—the Leader, the Airman, Michael Ransom scaling F6—like his lack of instinct for drama, all show his concern for Soul and Self, his sense of a lack of commitment to others. (Once, in Berlin, in his most richly psychosomatic vein, he apologised to Christopher Isherwood for his myopia on the ground that it was the price he had to pay for being an introvert.)[26] Even on an apparently neutral topic, like novelists, his anxiety about self-regard makes him protest his praise too much at the expense of poets:

> The average poet by comparison
> Is unobservant, immature, and lazy.
> You must admit, when all is said and done,
> His sense of other people's very hazy.[27]

Throughout the Thirties, Auden had the nose of a bloodhound for self-love in himself and in others. This obsession is fairly normal, or at least common, with men in their twenties, for as Auden himself noted, 'every young man fears that he is not worth loving'.[28] It may be all the worse if, as a disciple, one has let Freud convince one the trouble is Narcissism. But it is also the result of an exercise in logic, or of the confusion of logic, because 'the destruction of error' offers little or no basis for confidence in the positive existence of Love. It affirms loving but does not even begin to suggest an object on which the will to love might latch. Without such a relationship, it remains pure abstraction. The clash of a naked sensibility and of a philosophy of indifference placed a well-nigh unbearable strain on the poet. It was begging the question for him to answer, as he did, that:

> Life remains a blessing
> Although you cannot bless.[29]

Such an unsatisfactory answer could only be temporary. Unremittingly, the 'low unflattering voice that rests not till it find a hearing' continued to plague the poet.[30] His art in the Thirties matured painfully on the lyric borders of despair.

It is, then, in character that consciousness, which Auden saw in his early days as the scalpel of Love, cutting out the gangrene of guilt from individual and society, itself began to seem a rusty instrument breeding the feared infection. The slow but steady evolution of the theme of the alienation of consciousness throughout the Thirties is a kind of fever-chart of Auden's growing sense of incarceration in self. Whether being self-conscious about one's own consciousness is a cause or an effect of the sense of isolation is hard to say, but that they are related is undeniable. An unconscious act is a simple extension of self. When the act starts to be conscious, it becomes a point in a process perceived from the outside. When, however, consciousness becomes obsessive, as in Auden, perception takes over and the sense of being *outside* one's acts and relationships is all-pervading. It forces one into a posture of seeing and magnifying one's own self-interest in every contact with others. I may then seize and possess something or someone else but I can never seem to be one with him or her. A person unconscious of the act cannot conceive of this problem. The person not obsessed by consciousness thinks it overwrought and unimportant. For the man obsessed by consciousness, it is crucial: his whole life is possession instead of belonging. As a result, all doing is threatened with meaninglessness, that is, with isolation in self. This process is clear in Auden as his early faith in consciousness turned into a febrile over-awareness of the process of consciousness itself. In the early *Poems*, the consciousness of Man is simply noted as setting him apart from the creatures around him. It does indeed load him with the burdens of free will and choice, but the responsibility is taken willingly, even with joy. Consciousness is urged as a corrective for erring nature-worshippers, the Wordsworthians at whom Auden is still scoffing in 'The Letter to Lord Byron'; it is a liberating force. However, by the time of the later poems of *Look, Stranger!*, the tone begins to change. On the surface, the problem is presented as a political one. In 'May with its light behaving' the alienation of the 'singular and sad' listlessly and shortly restored by the 'careless picnics' of the May, is related to the rotten state of public affairs:

> The unjust walk the earth.

But even at this relatively early stage, the political distemper has become only one aspect, almost one symptom, of the fact that ordinary pleasures have declined into mere stimulants. The cause of this is not primarily political, but a matter of the *awareness* of guilt:

> We stand with shaded eye,
> The dangerous apple taken

since our species

> From the vague woods have broken,
> Forests where children meet.

Consciousness itself bars us from direct or simple relationship with people or things. Now, to peeping and botanising minds, 'the real world lies before us' but it is no longer within us. Because our relationship to 'the real world' is that of the voyeur, obsessed but irremediably alien, everything has somehow become unreal. All that the 'animal motions of the young' produce is

> The common wish for death,
> The pleasured and the haunted;
> The dying master sinks tormented
> In the admirers' ring.[31]

The holidaymakers of the May require a new and redeeming marriage with their own processes, not a series of passing affairs with the life about them. Masterful knowledge cannot provide this salvation. The exercise of consciousness which automatically separates the observer from what he observes can only exacerbate the sense of isolation. Consciousness, then, in 'May with its light behaving', published in May 1935, has acquired a new emotional urgency. In the epilogue to *Look, Stranger!*, men are abruptly punned into despair as the 'cons*cious*-stricken'.[32] And in the famous chorus of *The Dog Beneath the Skin* the cry of anguish breaks right through the crust of the poet's official doctrines:

> But what shall man do, who can whistle tunes by heart,
> Knows to the bar when death shall cut him short like the cry
>   of the shearwater,
> What can he do but defend himself from his knowledge?[33]

Perhaps the audience at the time took this for a chic turn of intellectual style. In fact, there is precious little difference between the line of force of these verses and that of the religious symbolism of Auden's later years. It is no surprise, then, to find that in *Another Time*, the volume containing the shorter poems written during the latter half of the Thirties, the alienation of consciousness becomes ubiquitous. In the sonnet sequence from *Journey to a War*, written in 1938, it constitutes the distress itself, and the hint at the expulsion from Eden contained in 'May with its light behaving' is expanded into the key concept of the cycle:

> They wondered why the fruit had been forbidden;
> It taught them nothing new. They hid their pride. . . .

> The bird meant nothing: that was his projection
> Who named it as he hunted it for food . . .
> And shook with hate for things he'd never seen,
> And knew of love without love's proper object,
> And was oppressed as he had never been.[34]

Now, in short, the very fact that he is a witness sets the observer apart from everything to which he longs to be attached. He knows of love 'without love's proper object'. He is not involved, he is self-enclosed, self-hating and a slave to illusions which offer temporary and in the end self-disintegrating relief. Though Auden does not labour the point or draw the obvious conclusion, it is plain that by this time his view is essentially Christian. It is not that he has renounced his earlier view of Love. It is rather that, being compelled to become personally committed to it in order to make any living sense of his general-ised exhortations, he finds his whole attitude is necessarily trans-formed. Once he really strives to give content to the empty notion of Love he is bound to define it in terms which break out of the isolation, the lack of personal investment in feeling, of his earlier rationalism.

In the poems on Voltaire and Pascal he wrote in 1939, Auden treats Voltaire, the great rationalist, as a child, that is, as someone who is unawakened to the adult sense of loneliness: 'Only Pascal was a great enemy.' Why? Because

> he was born deserted
> And lonelier than any adult.[35]

In this opposition, Voltaire stands for Auden's earlier philosophy which set out from 'the *objects* of human knowledge, essences and relations'. Pascal stands for the new one arguing from 'man's immediate experience as a *subject*, i.e., as a being in *need*, an *interested* being whose existence is at stake'.[36] The sense of isolation at the core of the human experience of faith in objective reason has bred its opposite, a critique, rooted in subjectivity, of all human claims to a lien on perfection: 'we can only love whatever we possess'. An abstract Love which cannot attach itself to a real lover is not only too demanding for any lover to provide, it is also and above all greater than one's own powers to achieve peace in oneself. By definition, it demands something over and above whatever may be vouchsafed one. It is never sated, though it can be exhausted or even perverted into hate, not least of self. It is bound to issue, like any total freedom, in a desert of disappointment, resentment, thirst and perhaps self-destruction. The first step, then, is to renounce the impossible possession of the Absolute, the mirage of peace on earth lurking so paradoxically inside the rationalism which denies all absolutes:

> you should still be proud
> Just to peep at Atlantis
> In a poetic vision:
> Give thanks and lie down in peace.[37]

Once the Absolute is renounced in the here and now, it is possible to be relatively relaxed about the lover, the talents, the years, the children one possesses and even, within limits, the lover, the talents, the years, the children one does not possess.

> I believed for years that
> Love was the conjunction

Of two oppositions;
That was all untrue . . .
Bless you, darling, I have
Found myself in you.[38]

One can see this again in the contrasted conclusions of 'May with its light behaving' in 1935 and 'Perhaps I always knew what they were saying' in 1939. In the earlier poem, Auden concludes that love, which in a typically rapacious and erotic way, makes 'impatient the tortoise and the roe',

Urges upon our blood . . .
How insufficient is
The endearment and the look.[31]

The later poem takes up the echo and reverses its meaning:

now I have the answer from the face
That never will go back into a book
But asks for all my life, and is the Place
Where all I touch is moved to an embrace,
And there is no such thing as a vain look.[39]

In less than five years the Byronic radical of 1935, newly anxious about the alienating effects of consciousness, has turned into a man grateful for his relationships precisely because he has accepted that they are relative and recognises that the Absolute lives outside any immediate experience.

The upshot of all this is that Auden's transformation in the later Thirties is not at all an ideological near-caprice, a supple shift of hypotheses for purposes of intellectual convenience. It has deep roots in his own emotional development. He certainly changed in part for political, and therefore public or moral, reasons. But he also changed because he discovered in his own person that the notion of freeing man from the outside, assuming humanity can be released from conflict, breaks down on tensions in the very people who think themselves most free, the would-be scientific observer and the knowing poet himself. He found that his own need for contact was not compatible with his own detachment. Thereafter the Rousseauistic belief in Unity becomes impossible in any human future. Wherever Man's heaven lies, it is not on earth. In the new and more elaborate form of a Christian dialectic, the dualism of the early *Poems* is re-established. There is no peace, only a difficult struggle to evolve slowly to better things in which the will to love and the temptation to hate battle freely at every step. Under Christian trappings, Auden's evolutionary bias, the Darwinian myth, reasserts itself in terms of the individual's moral progress here and now.

As with all sudden breaks in continuity, there is something mysterious about Auden's emigration with Christopher Isherwood to the United States, on the eve of war, in January 1939. However, when he left England for America, he was clearly, among other things, shaking off the dust of his earlier Romanticism. His departure buried the messianic hopes he (and many of his disciples) had vested in direct action. The history of Auden in America is the history of a new poet, a middle-aged relativist who has come to terms with the merciless hungers of youth. For the followers whom Auden and Isherwood left behind them, their emigration was the end of an adventure, and almost— though it violated the pacifist principles of many even to think so—a betrayal. *New Verse*, established by Grigson to battle for the poetic revolution centring on Auden, folded up in May 1939 four months after his departure. The Group Theatre, the vehicle of Auden's and Isherwood's 'popular' drama, faded away at the beginning of the war, deprived, with their passing, of hope and sustenance. Editors like Cyril Connolly and John Lehmann saw their departure, rightly, as the formal burial of the Thirties movement and were left lamenting war-time Britain's loss, in Auden, of its pre-destined bard. Lesser lights assumed Auden and Isherwood were scared stiff of the coming war and that, once again in left-wing history, the leaders had deserted their troops: this resentment added a special impetus to the wartime and postwar decline of Auden's reputation in Britain. Yet, for Auden anyway, it is plain that the emigration to America really was a new beginning. It was a sign that the poet had sighted a New World in himself. His landing in the New World of fact was the opening move of a second artistic career. Brought up to a scientific, moral and largely supranational outlook, Auden had moved beyond the bounds of the narrowing island of his birth and the self-destroying conflicts of the Europe of his youth. Having in the early Thirties thought that external remedies could 'make simpler daily the beating of man's heart',[40] he had gradually come to realise that if men's hearts were anything like his, the problem for each individual was to come to terms with his own irremediable isolation. America, which was then still Roosevelt's America of the New Deal, was the pioneer of the voyage of discovery of twentieth century society. Man had to work out his own salvation on this new frontier of accepted loneliness.

> More even than in Europe, here
> The choice of patterns is made clear
> Which the machine imposes, what
> Is possible and what is not.[41]

Politically, it may not perhaps have been generous of Auden to put his artistic development over his obligation to his countrymen. Aesthetically, he was coming to terms with the central problem in himself, which is also a crucial problem in others, and obeying the laws of what he was best able to achieve. One may think that Auden's emigration to America eight months before the outbreak of the second world war was selfish. One cannot fairly call it a flight.

*　　*　　*

The last thing one would guess from the tone of Auden's verse in the later Thirties is that the poet was going through a crisis and, at its height, 'behaving like a ham actor in a Strindberg play'.[1] His poetry now reached an extreme of automatic detachment amounting almost to alienation. Though even in this period he wrote a number of remarkable poems it is, in retrospect, one of the least satisfactory of his career. The later Thirties are the first period during which it is plausible to speak of a falling off in Auden's powers. Sceptical observers noted his growing addiction to abstract words, a new opacity in his style—the last thing one would have expected on the record—and above all a dismayingly frequent dullness. Though it was, and is, common to see it written that Auden has a 'dazzling variety of styles', this was true in the later Thirties only in a technical sense.[42] In a deeper one, Alvarez's criticisms of Auden's monotony are far more apt.[43] A second-rate poem in *Look, Stranger!* is brightly epigrammatic. Its equivalent in *Another Time* is painfully pedestrian. 'In Memory of Sigmund Freud' is almost a routine obituary for the papers appearing the morning after the great man's death, on the outbreak of the second world war:

> When there are so many we shall have to mourn,
> When grief has been made so public, and exposed
> To the critique of a whole epoch
> The frailty of our conscience and anguish,
>
> Of whom shall we speak? For every day they die
> Among us, those who were doing us some good,
> And knew it was never enough but
> Hoped to improve a little by living.[44]

Is this verse at all? It is touching to witness the *désarroi* of John Lehmann, the editor of *New Writing* and then one of Auden's unflagging impresarios: 'I have been reading Wystan's *Another Time* which has just arrived for me from America' he noted in his diary on May 24, 1940, 'and find among many wonderful treasures (a large number of which appeared originally in *New Writing*) a terrible proportion of sententious, almost prosy stuff. And yet', he added, recovering himself, 'how superb some of the newest poems are.'[45]

The final note of hope was not, as it happened, purely pious. By 1939, Auden was beginning to find his voice again. But if one excludes these good later poems from *Another Time*, and a few others with roots in the early Thirties, there is very little in the volume displaying Auden at his best. Two kinds of piece predominate: either verbose descriptions of familiar Audenesque themes which, for the first time, fail to focus in plain or memorable speech; or poems which are neat, clean and original enough but apparently divorced from the feelings of the author. Neither is of a type to give great satisfaction. The verbose poems in particular strikingly lack the sense of shock which rivets the reader's attention to almost anything in *Look, Stranger!*. A poem like 'Oxford', apparently written as early as the summer of 1936, before Auden went off to Iceland, shows how soon the process began. One of Auden's many variations on the death wish of the 'old gang', it is painfully different from an earlier exercise on a related theme like, say, 'Hearing of harvests rotting in the valleys', written three or four years earlier. The older poem is simple with urgency. It describes a kind of purgatory:

> Hearing of harvests rotting in the valleys
> Seeing at end of street the barren mountains,
> Round corners coming suddenly on water,
> Knowing them shipwrecked who were launched for islands,
> We honour founders of these starving cities
> Whose honour is the image of our sorrow.

Its conclusion is clumsy with abrupt clutching after paradise:

> It is our sorrow. Shall it melt? Ah, water
> Would gush, flush, green these mountains and these valleys,
> And we rebuild our cities, not dream of islands.[46]

The images are short, sharp and vivid, a vision whose essential features have been burnt into the poet's imagination for the first time. Its movement is purposive. It does not actually call for action, but makes sense only in the light of such a call. 'Oxford' is not like that at all. The simplifying element is almost wholly missing. The beginning is floridly slow:

> Nature is so near: the rooks in the college garden
> Like agile babies still speak the language of feeling;
> By the tower the river still runs to the sea and will run,
>   And the stones in that tower are utterly
>   Satisfied still with their weight.

The ending is equally ornate:

> And over the talkative city like any other
> Weep the non-attached angels. Here too the knowledge of
>   death
> Is a consuming love: And the natural heart refuses
>   The low unflattering voice
>   That rests not till it find a hearing.[47]

This is not at all the old racy stuff shooting to an urgent conclusion. It offers no remedy, no fulfilment, nor really much relief: it describes a spiritual Limbo with a weariness which consigns the poem there. The sense of lifeless elaboration, of moving round in a meaningless routine while the sentence is served out, is increased by the fact that Auden's images no longer play on universally obvious goals, nor on the basic evidence of the five senses he shares with the common run of men. Understanding now calls for an easy and intimate familiarity with the special meanings Auden ascribes to key words and concepts. The opening stanzas of 'Oxford' make little impact on someone who does not know immediately that 'nature', 'rooks', 'agile babies' and 'stones' all stand, in Auden's world of mental associations, for the limited bliss of unconsciousness. Similarly, one needs to know that 'the talkative city' means the conscious, and therefore guilty, city and that 'the knowledge of death' really only means, in Freudian terms, the refusal to adapt. If one is familiar enough with Auden's doctrines and symbols the poem has warmth and feeling and a certain richness of texture. For the casual reader, though, or the person coming to Auden's private language for the first time, 'Oxford' is almost impenetrable.

It is always dangerous when an artist becomes used to his own categories to the point of losing touch with the force which originally bred them. What to Auden may seem urgent enough, is to others remote, obscure and not charged with any special verbal vitality. Even when 'Oxford' yields up its secrets, such as they are, one is bound to admit it is clotted and thick, and that there are moments when the rhythm frankly sags, as when the river 'still runs to the sea and will run': a very sluggish river. All too many pieces in *Another Time*, like 'Dover', 'Wrapped in a yielding air' or 'Underneath the leaves of life' have this same fatigue.

If the 'Oxford' type of poems creates one kind of unease, the second type, the neat, and clean, promotes another. In too many of them the guts of people and places are preserved like laboratory specimens and hung meticulously on their branch of the tree of knowledge. No less than 23 out of 37 'serious' pieces in *Another Time* have potted essay titles such as 'Voltaire at Ferney', 'Housman', 'Edward Lear', 'The Composer', 'The Novelist', 'Brussels in Winter', 'Spain', and so on. Many, perhaps the majority, of these are 'case histories' of famous writers or character types, sonnets beginning, in the Rilkean style, *in medias res*. Similarly, almost the whole of Auden's contribution to *Journey to a War*, the record of his and Isherwood's trip in 1938 to report on the Sino-Japanese struggle, is a cycle of such sonnets, vignettes of The Peasant, The Bard, The Merchant, etc., mounted in a historical, cultural and finally moral setting. This technique was to be used again in 1940 in another, and better, sonnet cycle full of psycho-portraits, 'The Quest'. These sonnets and case histories, though always well turned, often subtle and sometimes profound, read curiously like spiritual theorems with, as Henry Reed has complained, 'the word *explicit* written firmly at the end, the paper blotted, the pen returned sharply to the inkpot, and a severe glance cast round the class'.[48]

> Incredulous, he stared at the amused
> Official writing down his name among
> Those whose request to suffer was refused.
>
> The pen ceased scratching: though he came too late
> To join the martyrs, there was still a place
> Among the tempters for a caustic tongue
>
> To test the resolution of the young
> With tales of the small failings of the great,
> And shame the eager with ironic praise.[49]

The complaint is not at all that this is bad. On the contrary on its own terms, it is excellent—concentrated and perceptive. Yet how encapsulated and unchallenged by the shocks it so accurately analyses it seems to be! How neatly, and yet how excessively neatly, it trips off the tongue! It is in the verse itself, notably in the mechanical rhythms that something is missing: there is an insufficient sense of *resistance* in them, of the energy of the thing to be said overcoming the difficulty of saying it or of a conviction finding the exact tone it needs to convey not only its meaning but the weight of experience which led to the meaning's need to be formulated. Parable and allegory, as Auden's American champions have rightly pointed out, are old and valid poetic media which do not require romantic intensity. It is not the mode of writing which is at fault. The

charge against Auden is that his verses at this time only transmute a fraction of his imaginative potential. This is not so much
a question of energy as of quality of vision vested in the verbal
rhythms. Auden's poems at this time are usually interesting,
they are rarely compelling. They lack the imaginative force of
art based on the whole, she psychosomatic man. Intellectually
they often express greater depths of awareness than his early
works, but they lack the old sense of absorption in what they
say.

Sensing this, critics and reviewers began, around this time,
to praise Auden as a 'virtuoso', implying that the acrobat of
letters was taking over from the committed artist. There was a
circumstantial basis for this notion. In 1935, Auden gave up
teaching English at preparatory schools where, according to
Spender, he had been very happy, and became, as *de facto*
laureate of a rebel generation, the professional writer. He was
fashionable enough to command a market exceptional for a
poet. He was commissioned to write scripts for the GPO Documentary Film Unit (*Coalface, Night Mail*), plays for the Group
Theatre (*The Ascent of F6, On the Frontier*), travelogues for Faber
& Faber (*Letters from Iceland* with MacNeice, *Journey to a War*
with Isherwood) and to edit anthologies (*The Poet's Tongue, The
Oxford Book of Light Verse*) in addition to publishing articles,
book reviews and, of course, poetry (*Another Time, New Year
Letter*). From the production of *The Ascent of F6* and the publication of *Look, Stranger!* in the autumn of 1936 to the appearance
of *New Year Letter* in May 1941, that is in 56 months, Auden
produced or helped to produce seven volumes—an average of
one every eight months, excluding anthologies and articles.
This is prolific even by his own standards. Inevitably, some of
this work was journalistic and more than once the craftsman
must have come to the rescue of the artist *en mal de copie*. Auden
almost said as much a little later when he argued in the notes
to *New Year Letter* that:

> 'as Cyril Connolly has pointed out in his brilliant book,
> *Enemies of Promise*, the characteristic vice of the writer today is
> overproduction, and the major cause of overproduction is a
> need for money. Failing a private income or a complaisant
> patron, he must either take some non-literary employment and

write in his spare time or reduce his standard of living. The conditions of modern employment, however, are such that really his only choice lies between overproduction and living very simply indeed.'[50]

He underlined the autobiographical implications in the body of the poem by confessing that

> I relapse into my crimes:
> Time and again have slubbered through
> With slip and slapdash what I do.[51]

With such authority, a critic might be excused for ascribing any change in the later Auden of which he disapproves to a victory of the man of letters sticking to a job over the artist in love with his vocation. Suspicion of Auden's facile side is one of the elements in Auden's lowered postwar reputation.

Yet the marked improvement of his verse after 1939 casts doubt on such essentially moralising views of Auden's ups and downs. The internal evidence of the verse itself hints, in its very style, at some inner disorder rather than at a dereliction of duty. By 1936 or so, it begins to appear either over-ornamental or over-clear. These are apparently contradictory faults, but it is possible without, I think, overstraining the evidence, to detect a common cause behind them. Around 1936, Auden had apparently lost faith in the broadly political forms of salvation which engaged him earlier on, and in the poetry of social observation resulting from them. He no longer felt confident that goodwill can simply 'destroy error' that, in other words, there are no insurmountable contradictions in the *condition humaine*. Henceforward, he was instinctively looking for the individual self-discipline which would gradually, by effort, accomplish some of the improvements he had expected of a political miracle. But these reservations did not immediately focus in new convictions: for a time he had only half-suppressed doubts and half-formulated alternatives to suggest. There was no longer a clear pattern in his own mind. The anguish of confusion could reach the surface in more than one way. When the poet was in a mood to submit to his doubts, his dissatisfaction with his own categories led to a critique of the manner inherited from his own past conducted from within that manner itself, complicating, convoluting and even stifling it. It is not surprising that the poet's style should often be weighed down by unresolved conflicts. This goes a long way to explain the elaborate impotence of poems like 'Oxford'. At other times, though, Auden, essentially an activist, would try to shake off his dilemmas. It would be natural, in this mood, to rely on familiar political, psychological and therefore poetic remedies to reduce his new problems to a proper submission. However, since it was new, the instinctive search for self-discipline could not be encased in old notions suited to old beliefs. The social commentator's manner, kept up partly out of habit, partly in a desperate attempt to give clear contours to half-grasped issues, began to look increasingly habitual and dissociated from its subject-matter.

For, whatever the weaknesses of Auden's manner in the later Thirties, there is no doubt of the newness of his matter. In terms of the artist's preoccupations, they are a purposeful, perhaps *the* purposeful, period of change in his career. There are many signs of this. One is that the many different strands of Auden's poetry in the early Thirties get plaited together as the years wear on. His formerly diverse public roles as political commentator, nightclub wit and elegist lose their distinctness and fuse in a single character philosophising about life, men and affairs. If one leaves aside the earlier poems which have somehow strayed into *Another Time*, one finds that it contains few lyrics. Instead there are contemplative poems like 'Perhaps I always knew what they were saying'. Supposedly 'light' verse like 'Refugee Blues' or 'The Unknown Citizen' is much more like 'serious' work of the same period than like the light verse of the middle Thirties. By the early war years, a piece such as 'Many Happy Returns' is light metaphysical—different in tone but not in real weight from other contemporary pieces. It is not distinct in any obvious way as were the popular verse and love lyrics of the middle Thirties. In fact, the light verse declines in quantity and the love lyrics virtually disappear. This convergence on a single mode of expression hints at a growing, if only half-conscious, concentration on a single theme.

During these years, Auden moved slowly away from the provisional certainties of his messianic period to an increasingly personal and ethical relativism. Julian Symons says that by 1936 he was already, with Geoffrey Grigson and *New Verse*, on the humanist, relatively apolitical right of the literary left.[52] *Another Time* contains less political poetry than *Look, Stranger!* and above all the politics is treated differently. The poet's outlook is much more detached, even wary and critical. Vesting less faith in the future, he displays a much greater feeling for history. The sonnets of 'In Time of War' are the first example of the cultural history which becomes almost the trademark of Auden's work in the Forties and Fifties. Cultural history is really at the opposite pole from the radical political critique of contemporary society. It implicitly denies that blueprints can be applied to political situations by treating the whole of human history as a kind of collectively subjective development. This is far from fully worked out in the sonnet cycle of 'In Time of War'. Nevertheless, the present choice is placed in a historical context and the historical context presented in terms of characteristic types who have dominated phases of the past—the peasant, the knight, and so on. Whereas in *Look, Stranger!* Auden had a Freudian view of society as a whole, by 'In Time of War' he has subdivided, and somehow individualised, it into psychoportraits of social types.

The same shift can be mapped in what happens to the idea of the solitary journey of the man of free will, Auden's early myth of the man of action. The Leader on a field day or The Airman preparing for the fight with the Enemy had a public, imposed destiny; their values were political and they were judged by their social achievement or lack of it. By 1936, in *The Ascent of F6*, The Climber, Michael Ransom, leading the assault on a previously inviolate peak, is a much more ambiguous figure. The incongruous oedipoidal resolution of the play, when his mother appears on the summit to cradle her dying mountaineer, provides only one of the possible interpretations of the motives which precipitate the catastrophe. Whether Ransom's motives are public or private is ultimately enigmatic. In one sense he is the last of Auden's exceptional, Malrauxesque men of action. In another, the notion of The Journey begins, with Ransom, to modulate into that of the religious Quest. The Quest is the pilgrimage of any man, exceptional or ordinary—preferably ordinary, to underline the point—for his own reconciliation with self. Even the rather nasty ballads on grotesque failures—Miss Gee, James Honeyman and Victor—written in 1937, are about the destiny of isolated individuals. The case studies which dominate, and indeed almost monopolise, Auden's output for two or three years are the natural result of this changed preoccupation. At the time they seemed like Auden calling in Freud to the rescue of his fading inspiration. In retrospect, it is more convincing to see them as explorations of other men's destinies at a time when Auden was searching around for the destination in himself.

Even Auden's public history in the later Thirties illustrates the theme of the Quest. In 1936, he spent three months with MacNeice in Iceland. (His publishers no doubt thought it a good idea to send him to explore the birthplace of his family and his style.) In 1937, he spent six weeks in Spain. In 1938, he spent the whole of the first half of the year with Isherwood in America and the Far East; and much of the latter half with Isherwood in Brussels. Finally, in January 1939, he emigrated with Isherwood to the United States. The up-and-coming Auden of the early Thirties was almost parochially static compared with the professional man of letters turned Wandering Jew of the second half of the decade. The man who had almost personified the condition-of-England question in the early Thirties ended his private saga by going to America because, as he said, loneliness was the condition of modern man and America, as the home of loneliness, was the only place where a man could really explore and come to terms with it. He himself made a spiritual symbol of his self-imposed exile. In short, if the early Thirties marked the outward cycle of Auden's development, the later Thirties show him moving rapidly back into an inward phase. Whereas in the early Thirties all private events were measured against a public yardstick, in the later Thirties all public happenings are increasingly subjected to private tests.

The Quest is the image of this return to introversion. It was perhaps inevitable that The Quest should succeed poetically only when it was already in essence over, its passion spent, its conclusions drawn, its wisdom ready to be recorded in serenity.

The open echoes of Auden's personal crisis are caught only at the end of the period, emerging in the quietist, the almost-but-not-quite religious, poems of 1939. The prologue to them is the 'Musée des Beaux Arts', no doubt written during Auden's winter of discontent in Brussels in 1938–9. Its beautifully dispassionate treatment of suffering seems the first sign of the resolution of the crisis. In the next eighteen months it was followed by half a dozen or so deceptively calm pieces, 'Perhaps I always knew what they were saying', 'Not as that dream Napoleon', 'Law, say the gardeners, is the sun', 'Hell is neither here nor there', 'For us like any other fugitive' and 'The hourglass whispers to the lion's paw', all published in *Another Time*. There is a new and distilled limpidity, a quality of stillness, of truth apprehended calmly in the flesh, about these poems. They no longer have the slight air Auden's earlier verse had, of having been written by an engineer. For the first time they are aware of, and even celebrate, the 'shifting contours' of 'all real perception'.[53]

> But somewhere always, nowhere particularly unusual,
> Almost anywhere in the landscape of water and houses,
> His crying competing unsuccessfully with the cry
> Of the traffic or the birds, is always standing
> The one who needs you, that terrified
> Imaginative child who only knows you
> As what the uncles call a lie,
> But knows he has to be the future and that only
> The meek inherit the earth, and is neither
> Charming, successful, nor a crowd.[54]

These poems are abstract, if by that one means they have few starkly visual images or vivid verbal surprises. But their abstractions are beautifully organised and loaded with formerly warring feelings at last resolved. Complex mental states are fused in them till they give the illusion of purity which can only come of sustained inner coherence, a blessed aesthetic state which even good poets rarely achieve. It is around this time that Auden first defined poetry as 'the clear expression of mixed feelings'.[55] Just as 'Musée des Beaux Arts' seems the poem in which Auden just begins to come to terms with his emotional defeat, so 'Perhaps I always knew what they were saying' is the first in which he seems to draw a conclusion from it and crosses the divide from his early 'materialism' to his mature 'Christianity'. Collectively, these poems, most of them written in 1939, are the hinge on which the door between the early and later Auden opens and shuts.

It is intriguing, then, that in some ways these pieces resemble the *Poems* of his first days more than any other of his later poems. Like the *Poems*, they are detached in manner and often abstract in diction, yet personal in feeling; like them, they are vivid when concrete; like them, they have an uncanny power to give the music of poetry to analytic speech; like them too, they are strong because they are thoughtful but take no more thought on board than the precise occasion warrants. They work out the immediate meaning of the experience but no more. It is surely no accident that 'Law, say the gardeners, is the sun' is Auden's most notable reversion to Skeltonic verse after 1930. It is almost as if Auden's temperament required a scientific, or at least abstract, definition of his emotional and intellectual choice as a scaffolding for the more elaborate poetry which follows. The *Poems* laid foundations by being limited but solid— cornerstones; so do the pieces of 1939–40. The *Poems* stated in relatively naked terms the truths that were to be the building blocks of the future, and out of them a new phase slowly took shape; so it does from these. Just as Auden, once he had defined his intuitions in *Poems*, then gradually elaborated them into a system to which more and more ideas and illustrations accrued, so in the period immediately after 'Perhaps I always knew what they were saying', one sees the new vision taking on a growing richness and variety. The fine poems of the early war years, like 'Atlantis', are essentially ornamentations of the spare, structural poems of 1939.

In short, these pieces bear much the same relation to Auden's later work as the *Poems* themselves to his earlier; and, in an interesting way, have parallel literary virtues. Yet, when all is said and done, the differences between the poems of 1939 and those of a decade before are at least as instructive as the resemblances. Though many of the *Poems* propounded abstract concepts in quantity, their attitude to them was quite unlike the later one. If one takes a poem already quoted like 'Again in conversations' it is plain that though the manner is abstract, the occasion of it, the undergraduate confession, is concrete and individual and the mood of nostalgia vividly emotional as only youth can be.

> For every news
> Means pairing off in twos and twos,
> Another I, another You,
> Each knowing what to do
> But of no use.[56]

Auden's originality is that he is not, as youth often is, uncorrectedly emotional. At Oxford, the process of correction has (naturally) only just begun. Both the emotion and the correction are fresh, but whereas novelty gives the emotion the shock of a first encounter, it accords the corrective only the fragility of a coating which has not set. In early Auden, the correction of thought adds a style to the feeling and enhances it, but is not dominant. The young poet is still rooted imaginatively in the local particulars of his experience, even though his way of looking at them is already shaped by the universalist outlook of his education. The *Poems* normally move from the particular to the general. 'Since you are going to begin today/Let us consider what it is you do'; 'Watch any day his nonchalant pauses'; 'On Sunday walks/Past the shut gates of works'; 'Look there! The sunk road winding/To the fortified farm'—in almost every case the starting point is the clear image of a posture, landscape or dramatic situation. Even when one comes on an apparent (and slightly later) exception like 'Doom is dark and deeper than any sea-dingle', the verse immediately shifts to a dramatic picture of the wayfarer chosen by fate battering and battered 'Through place-keepers, through forest trees/A stranger to strangers over undried sea'. For all their trappings of thought, Auden's earlier *Poems* are very close to emotional bedrock. The ideas he enlarges into myths—the tension of Nature and the individual, the moment of private peace at the still centre of a turbulent world, the contrast of conscious guilt and ignorant bliss, the revolution and the leader—are powerful images precisely because they place a superficial coating of thought on turbid feelings.

123

When, however, one comes to 'Law, say the gardeners, is the sun', a subtle change has taken place. The gardener, judge, priest, crowd and idiot, though vividly painted, are all vignettes on the edge of the picture. They are not themselves, like the wayfarer in 'Doom is dark and deeper than any sea-dingle', the metaphor of the journey of life. They do not occupy the centre. The centre is unchallengeably held by an abstract principle, The Law. Even when Auden spoke in the early *Poems* as the Life Force, he held a dialogue of dramatically equal parts with the young man whose life was the instrument and perhaps victim of the process of evolution. Now the single abstract idea reigns supreme. This is not invariably the case. The quality which makes 'Musée de Beaux Arts' so outstanding is precisely that Brueghel's painting of the Fall of Icarus infuses the whole poem with a rich metaphor for the necessary indifference of the world to individual suffering. Yet even here and in 'Perhaps I always knew what they were saying', the drama and struggle disappear, replaced by a single presiding concept, an abstract unifying Idea, which reconciles and resolves all conflict. It is, in abstractions, the picture of God on his throne embracing the diversities of the universe. This shift, small in its surface appearance, is in fact of crucial importance to Auden's art. Compared with the past, it means that the element of coherent and disciplined thought, of correction of impulse, has reached maturity. Henceforth the impulse and the philosophy work on equal terms. This gives Auden's later poetry a counterpoint of ideas and a depth of judgement it often lacked in his youth. It also gives it a catholicity of insight, an ability to embrace the most divergent spheres of reality in a single vision, which gradually become the marks of his later poetry. Yet a price is paid. In becoming more coherent, and all-embracing, Auden loses much of the old immediacy and directness. Though his later style is at times majestic, he loses much of his former talent for gripping the reader's attention with a single phrase. The writing thickens and grows more opaque. Though it does revive in the following years, henceforth there is always a hint about it of middle-age spread. Little of this was immediately apparent in the careful and chaste poems of 1939. The potentialities still lay in the future. The poet still had to work them out, just as his philosophy still went on evolving for some time after his departure to America. Nevertheless, if there is a single moment at which it is possible to point and say: 'Here is the watershed', it must be 1939. The poems of this year are the turning point of Auden's career: quiet though they are, they mark the modulation between his youthful and mature work.

4

ISOLATION ACCEPTED

HAD Auden died at the beginning of the war, his achievement would have seemed a thing of fragments, remarkable but unresolved. He had to his credit a first volume with the promise of greatness and, in the following decade, many brilliant short poems and a huge literary influence amounting to a personal myth. For all that, he had produced no equivalent of *The Waste Land*, creating a world of its own. His verse in the Thirties seemed like snatches of brilliant dialogue between the poet and his muse from which the thread of continuity was lacking. It was symbolic that his one long poem, *The Orators*, should also be the least coherent. His work, though full of 'major' preoccupations and driving force, lacked the sense of firm design pointing towards inner necessity. It is evident when one looks at Auden's wartime poems that one of the resolutions for a new life he took with him to America was to correct this weakness or at least fill the gap. Whereas in the Thirties nearly all Auden's poems worth bothering about were brief, during the war years, that is, from the composition of the 'New Year Letter' at the beginning of the war to that of *The Age of Anxiety* at the end, his main efforts bore on four long works. The 'New Year Letter' (1940) is 65 pages long (152 pages with the notes, which are well worth reading in their own right); 'For the Time Being' (1941-2) is 64 pages long; 'The Sea and the Mirror' (1943-4) 54 pages; and *The Age of Anxiety* (half-finished by 1945) as much as 116 pages: in all, 299 ample Faber & Faber pages for four works. Auden managed to find time also for a fair number of shorter poems, some of which, like the 'Ode to Cecilia', 'Atlantis' or 'In Sickness and In Health,' are deservedly famous. But, collectively, these fade into the shadow of the larger works. Auden, after his arrival in America in 1939, was reaching for the *magnum opus*.

Indeed, the *magnum opus* is even larger than the sheer statistics of the bulk of the individual poems might suggest. 'For the Time Being', 'The Sea and the Mirror' and, to a lesser extent, *The Age of Anxiety*, are so convergent in style, form and content as to form a quasi-trilogy. If one treats them as a whole, they amount to one of the most massive poetic cycles of the twentieth century. The 'New Year Letter' alone seems markedly different, with its regular octosyllables and vaguely Augustan air; but this is partly illusion. Edward Callan has shown how its tripartite division is a formal analogue of its Kierkegaardian argument that 'the *Aesthetic* is dethroned and the *Ethical* fulfilled' in the *Religious* view.[1] The first part illustrates the shortcomings of the Aesthetic religion and the second of the Ethical one; the third part places both in the light of a Religious dialectic of free will. The three other works seem to illustrate the same Kierkegaardian triad as 'New Year Letter'. 'For the Time Being' interprets The Nativity in Kierkegaardian terms: its subject is the moment of revelation when the Ethical view changes into the Religious one. 'The Sea and the Mirror', marrying art and Kierkegaard, is about the illusion of the Aesthetic religion. *The Age of Anxiety* does not fit quite so neatly into the pattern. Concerned with the quest of four individuals typifying Jung's basic humours—the thinking, the intuitive, the sensationalist and the feeling—for reconciliation with self, it owes more, ideologically, to him than to Kierkegaard. Its publication separately from 'The Sea and the Mirror' and 'For the Time Being' underlines the difference. Nevertheless, its basic theme seems to be the impossibility of all human fulfilment accepted in the religious illumination. If that is the case, each of the three poems roughly corresponds to one of the three parts of the 'New Year Letter', and, by the same token, to one of the elements of Kierkegaard's triad. Nevertheless, each is an immense extension of the themes found succinctly stated in each part of the 'New Year Letter'. The 'New Year Letter' can be regarded as an introduction to what seems a virtual trilogy, even if it was not originally designed as such. It too is apparently part of the complex polyptych composed by Auden in praise of his new-found Christian humanism.

This spreading out may have been made possible, as Henry

Reed has suggested, by the relative leisure which teaching at American colleges now gave the poet almost for the first time since his Berlin days. This may be part of the story, but it cannot be all. It is surely no coincidence that the 'New Year Letter', in summing up Auden's experience of the Thirties, involves a critique of the outlook which drove him to emotional and philosophic crisis; and that the trilogy in setting up a vast basilica to Auden's newly acquired existentialism, draws the monumental consequences from that same central moment of vision. All four poems draw their inspiration from the same crisis, and all contribute to turn it into a cultural world. This is no doubt why all the wartime poems are long and systematic whereas most of the poems of the previous decade were as fragmentary as the poet's experience at the time. The war years mark the peak of Auden's ambition.

*   *   *

'New Year Letter' provides an unwontedly *pianissimo* opening to the coming grand climax. Given the traditions of English poetry, the very fact that it is written in octosyllabics—the unheroic couplets of *Hudibras* or *The Death of Dr. Swift*—advertises its lack of portentousness. The brash youthful genius is gone, gone the citizen broadcasting his plans for society, gone too the Leader. In tone, it is the quietest, even the most quietist, of all Auden's substantial works; verbally, it is the least vital and energetic. This was disappointing after the excitements of previous years, and Henry Reed duly found it dull—even a 'nadir of dulness'.[2] Indeed, after the liberating force on poetry of Auden's hungry universalism and conversational style in the Thirties, the apparently neat traditionalism of 'New Year Letter' must have seemed tame. Further, much of Auden's appeal in the Thirties was that he shamelessly raised the grand unanswerable questions, like the shortcomings of human love, while resolutely refusing to give the old traditional answers. That he should resort to them now seemed a renunciation of all that his old originality stood for. Such criticisms cannot be wholly discounted. 'New Year Letter' does lack something: its basic convention is a shade too flat, so that while the best passages have the crystalline neatness of an argument beautifully cut and mounted, at lesser moments one feels it could do with polishing. The self-deprecating style Auden has chosen to write in is dangerous and difficult. Nevertheless, its precision is greatly to be preferred to the looseness of some of Auden's later pronouncements on the state of The City, and its quietness is deceptive. Who would think from the simple octosyllabic surface that its formal structure is as complex as Edward Callan has shown it to be?[3] Who would have expected a poet famous as a brash virtuoso to deliver his first sermon on the crisis of his life—his longest sermon yet—in the most traditional and unassuming form he had ever adopted? These obvious questions warn us of depths in 'New Year Letter' that do not catch the eye and of its apparent colourlessness not being a guarantee that one sees clearly to the bottom of the pool. In fact, as with so many stances in Auden, its quietness is a dramatic posture. The world of the poem is situated somewhere between the famous statement in 'September 1st, 1939' that 'All I have is a voice to undo the folded lie' and the credo of the epigraph to a later volume, *Nones* (published in 1951) which pleads that 'we, too'

> would in the old grand manner
> Have sung from a resonant heart . . .
> No civil style survived
> That pandaemonium
> But the wry, the sotto-voce,
> Ironic and monochrome.[4]

The 'New Year Letter' is wry, sotto-voce, monochrome—and ironic, if irony is defined as a systematic awareness of the gap between conscious and unconscious drives, between desire and behaviour. Auden justifies this, as usual, by a public (that is, generalised) duty: the 'freedom', the 'form', of 'possible societies'

> Upon our sense of style depends.[5]

As usual too, though, there are elements in the poetry—a mood of meditative retreat, hints of contrition—which speak, as so often in Auden, of private reasons for ostensibly public attitudes.

Dear friend Elizabeth, dear friend
These days have brought me . . . may the truth
That no one marries lead my youth
Where you already are and bless
Me with your learned peacefulness.[6]

The same, almost convalescent, note of contrast between public
disaster and the momentary concord of right relationships in a
small group, is struck several times. It is easy to argue that
'New Year Letter' owes a great deal to Kierkegaard. Intellectually, and even formally, this may be correct, but with a
writer like Auden one is apt to get a very poor idea of the
emotional burden of a poem if one makes its motive force sound
as intellectual as its argument. The opening movement, on the
limits of art as a reason for living, shows that intellectual explanations do not take one very far. Emotionally, the 300 lines
or so of the first part draw on two plain and simple sources.
One is that Auden needs to plead with his own inner censor for
the right of the artist, as a virtual conscientious objector, to
follow his vocation at all:

No words men write can stop the war.[7]

This is clearly related to the difficult complex of emotions
around Auden's emigration to America. The nervous hangover
of his recent crisis and of exile is an obvious reason for his muted
tone. The answer given is that 'heart and intelligence' may, by a
closer commitment to the truth, lay the foundations of better
values in future. This implies that the artist's dedication to his
art should be at least as great as that of his fellow citizens to
combating Hitler. Hence the second *Leitmotiv* of 'New Year
Letter', the confession of the poet's past sins of overconfidence
and facility. In 'New Year Letter' Auden no longer poses as
the artist using emotions as a 'chemist' mixes colours from a
palette; he has

the rashness to
Believe that he is one of those
The greatest of vocations chose.[8]

Auden's revulsion from his own pre-war loudness, from his
'happiness ready made', the boisterous irresponsibility of his

youthful triumph, is an important factor in 'New Year Letter'. Rather histrionically—the self-conscious are irremediably condemned to be histrionic—it has a scrupulousness which probably stood in Auden's mind for the penitent's cleansing of old emotional and moral faults.

The same note is struck again, though with larger public implications, in the second part of the poem. Again, to say that this corresponds to Kierkegaard's Ethical sphere, though no doubt formally true, only scratches the surface of the matter and is finally misleading. Much more simply, this part is an analysis of the weaknesses of the romantic outlook Auden himself espoused in the Thirties. Here again the tone is confessional, because it amounts to an enquiry into the blindness to its own weaknesses of liberal humanism which failed to prevent two world wars in a single generation. Auden attacks the radical view, which sees only one side of the paradox of life, and assumes that 'one part is Good with absolute right to exist unchanged: the other is evil with no right to exist at all. Progress consists in a struggle between the two in which the Good is victorious, and salvation is only attained with the complete annihilation of Evil, and a completely Static and Monist universe.'[9] The 'Static Universe' is the famous peace after public and apocalyptic cleansing, the millennium after the revolution, when constraints are no longer required. This is clear from one of the notes to the poem: 'Who has ever met a left-wing intellectual . . . for whom the real attraction of Communism did not lie in its promise that, under it, the state should wither away?'[10] What Auden is rejecting in 'New Year Letter' is the chiliastic assumption behind his own best poetry of the Thirties. The conclusion of the second part, some 500 lines long, is that the only adult attitude is to accept the endless dialectic of living, the Augustinian free will, in which one is compelled to choose the better or worse at every step:

> There lies the gift of double focus,
> The magic lamp which looks so dull
> And utterly impractical
> Yet, if Aladdin use it right,
> Can be a sesame to light.[11]

The discovery of the limitations of secular millennialism, and the need for a less emptily confident view of the future is an essential element in the restraint of 'New Year Letter'.

The third and much the longest part of the work, over half the whole, brings these diverse elements together in a dedication of the poet to a new existence. The greater part of it elaborates the political theme, derived from the existentialist theologians, that Hitler's war is ultimately caused by the worship of the Ego which has flowered so variously since the Renaissance. But bit by bit, as he warms to his theme, Auden's views of the Ego modulate to something suspiciously like spiritual autobiography:

> our political distress
> Descends from her self-consciousness
> Her cold *concupiscence d'esprit*
> That looks upon her liberty
> . . . as the right to lead alone
> An attic life all on her own,
> Unhindered, unrebuked, unwatched,
> Self-known, self-praising, self-attached.
> All happens as she wishes till
> She asks herself why she should will
> This more than that, or who would care
> If she were dead or gone elsewhere,
> And on her own hypothesis
> Is powerless to answer this.[12]

It is impossible not to put this in parallel with the sense of isolation in 'Musée des Beaux Arts' eighteen months before and with the central theme of 'The Sea and the Mirror', two or three years later, that psychic loneliness is unbearable. The 'New Year Letter' also suggests the way out:

> Suppose we love, not friends or wives,
> But certain patterns in our lives,
> Effects that take the cause's name,
> Love cannot part them all the same.[13]

In other words, real relationships between people cannot be undermined by the thought that for each partner the approach is psychologically conditioned, because 'the patterns in our lives' can have no active existence outside those relationships. To deny the relationships is to deny the patterns too. The ultimate intuition of the 'New Year Letter' is the readiness to see life in terms of relationships between people which have to be cultivated and not of chance encounters between self-enclosed Egos. With it goes a gratitude for the relative, necessarily incomplete satisfactions granted one instead of the old insatiable, self-regarding hunger for more. From now on, Auden's slogan is no longer that revolution will usher in peace (or 'unity') — the Monist view — but that there must be 'diversity in unity'. 'There are not "good" and "evil" existences. All existences are good, i.e. they have an equal right and an equal obligation to be and become . . . Evil is not an existence but a state of disharmony between existences . . . Moral good is not an existence but an act, a rearrangement of existence which lessens or removes a disharmony.'[14] Utopia is renounced. Imperfection reigns. Short of perfection, one cannot stand still. Like Goethe, Auden denies Faust's ability to ask the flying minute to stop:

> once again let us set out
> Our faith well balanced by our doubt,
> Admitting every step we make
> Will certainly be a mistake,
> But still believing we can climb
> A little higher every time.[15]

In short, the formal art of the 'New Year Letter' melts so well into the substance of the work as to be invisible because the art is embedded in emotional truth. The Kierkegaardian ideas Auden has taken off the peg are only a rough styling for a custom-made suit based on the poet's own recent experience. The private tone of 'New Year Letter' is both a ritual cleansing and an act of dedication to the new life Auden means to lead after the personally noisy and publicly noisome Thirties.

All this is reflected in the style of 'New Year Letter' — that of civilised discourse. It looks like poetry of wit and has some of its formal glitter, but it also has the limitations of Augustanism falling short of Dryden's or Pope's heroic finish. It has few images which bowl one over, its music does not reach the compulsive ends of the register, nor is it riotously funny like the best in *Hudibras*. Though the argument is religious, it remains firmly rooted in a rationalist world of abstract definitions:

> there is neither good nor ill
> But free rejoicing energy.[16]

If this is Christian, it is Christian with a difference, like the

> quaker's quiet concern
> For the uncoercive law.[17]

Conversely, if concern for the 'law' is much like rationalism, it, too, is rationalism with a difference.

> How hard to stretch imagination
> To live according to our station.
> For we are all insulted by
> The mere suggestion that we die
> Each moment and that each great I
> Is but a process in a process
> Within a field that never closes;
> As proper people find it strange
> That we are changed by what we change,
> That no event can happen twice
> And that no two existences
> Can ever be alike; we'd rather
> Be perfect copies of our father,
> Prefer our *idées fixes* to be
> True of a fixed Reality.[18]

The mode of this verse may be that of Augustan discussion, but its inversion of the Augustan intellectual conventions could not belong to any philosophic style inherited from the eighteenth century. It claims to be a kind of 'Religio Laici' for the twentieth century, but Dryden's poem is for a university disputation, Auden's is addressed to the individual reading in his library. Dryden sets his flag firmly on revelation, which is pre-rationalist of him; Auden argues from the psychological failure of rationalism, which is post-materialist. For all its neat reminiscence of wit, 'New Year Letter' has a tell-tale flow, a renunciation of obvious antithesis in the single line (though the whole argument is in a sense one vast antithesis) which marks it as profoundly un-Augustan. It is not breaking down an old Unity at the end of its tether, like the eighteenth century, but trying to unify dualities at the end of theirs, in the style of the twentieth.

The result is that it is infinitely more complex than its un-assuming surface suggests. If it seems colourless on a first read-ing, like all good poems it gives increasingly the more one gives to it. One then notices how natural nearly all the language and imagery are, how appropriate to their position in the poem. The 'New Year Letter' appeals by its seriousness and epi-grammatic dexterity in handling concepts till they build up to a kind of ceremonial of argument. Lines which at first seem as square as didactic prose gradually become sinuous with patterns which belong only to poetry. 'New Year Letter' is not a great poem but it is a good one and deserves the praise Edmund Wilson has accorded it, perhaps excessively, more than the lack of regard, or even disregard, it has suffered in Britain.

'New Year Letter' is also—curiously, in view of the literary vitality unleashed by the inter-war years—the only long poem which openly, directly and systematically treats of the moral issues and lessons of the terrifying Thirties. Auden was well equipped to do this: much of the power of the work is in the calm finality with which it passes sentence on the poet's own experience of their torments. Its final residue is a profoundly troubled sense of their personal confusions and public cata-strophes. Though both in style and content it seems to look back, in the last resort it rounds off the observatory style of the decade with a remarkable synthesis of all the reasons why the poetry of observation cannot suffice. It closes the door on the Thirties and even before Auden has shut it, he is through and into another room. He had already achieved so much that it is hard to credit he was still only 33. If one forgot this, one might be led to read into the Letter the preoccupations of a much older man. In essence, however, it is simple—a farewell to youth and a welcome to maturity, the end of 'The world's great rage, the travel of young men'. This sense of transition is no doubt part of its tentative tone: anything less tentative than the baroque cathedral of the trilogy which follows would be hard to imagine.

*   *   *

Compared with the whispered ritual of persuasion in a private room of the 'New Year Letter', the trilogy is high mass in a metropolitan cathedral. In the 'New Year Letter', Auden sketched his new themes. In the trilogy he paints, and sometimes overpaints, them in the high baroque manner. 'For the Time Being'—*A Christmas Oratorio*—is a vast historico-cultural fresco of the Nativity in which by implication—and with a cheerful disregard of historical nuance—Auden treats the contemporary world as another Roman empire at its last spiritual gasp, thirsting for the Child. 'The Sea and the Mirror',— A Commentary on Shakespeare's *The Tempest*—probes the psychology of conversion in terms of the breakdown of self-love, disguised as the religion of art. *The Age of Anxiety* charts the rarely requited quest of the individual for self-harmony along tracks laid down by Jung. 'The Sea and the Mirror' corresponds to Kierkegaard's Aesthetic sphere; 'For the Time Being' to the Ethical; and *The Age of Anxiety* seemingly to the Religious. Together, the three works are a kind of modern literary equivalent of Hieronymus Bosch's holy-grotesque triptych of Heaven, Earth and the Underworld which, when closed, displays on the outer panel the universe's perfect sphere.

The ambition of this subject-matter is matched by the eclecticism of its form. All three works are built up as a series of chapters, subdivided into set speeches, dramatic monologues and lyrical pieces, some in verse, some prose, which complement one another in a kind of conceptual polyphony. All the technical stops are pulled out—between them, the three constitute a kind of encyclopaedia of the metrical, syllabic, alliterative, free verse and even prose-poetic inheritances of western rhetoric. Together, they erect a restless architecture of warring stresses—heavy, but in parts impressive because so precariously and stunningly balanced. Compared to the art of the Thirties, they are raised in antitheses and circles round a centre, instead of moving to their object as to a conclusion. Where Auden's earlier poems were on the move, passing views from a road leading ostensibly onward and upward, these poems raise a settled abode, they found an inwardly diverse city. Previously, Auden was for ever striving to escape from the past into a scientifically freed future. Now he is almost classically embedded in a sense of history, incorporating traditional wisdom into his sociological awareness of new circumstances. The result is a tremendous broadening and deepening of sympathies. Yet the trilogy also has the weaknesses of its strengths. Whereas in the Thirties it was justifiable to attack Auden for over-simplification and facility, all these poems are immensely complex in structure and subject-matter and, when they fail, it is by over-elaboration.

Many trilogies have been planned in the history of literature and none perhaps has been equally successful in all its parts. Wordsworth thought of 'The Prelude' as a mere *hors d'œuvre* to the great metaphysical *plats de résistance* of 'The Excursion' and 'The Recluse'. But 'The Excursion' is virtually unreadable and 'The Recluse' lasted the course for a single book. Of Auden's three poems only one really succeeds—'The Sea and the Mirror'. *The Age of Anxiety*, like 'The Excursion' a *magnum opus* that became a Rehoboam, outstays all but the specialist's welcome. 'For the Time Being', though many-sided and sometimes brilliant, is finally, as poetry, arbitrary. Only 'The Sea and the Mirror' marries form and content, emotional message and expression, outline and detail, in a satisfying way.

The earliest of the three works, 'For the Time Being', is intriguing because it is so nearly related to 'The Sea and the Mirror' that its failure illuminates the other's success. 'For the Time Being' broke new ground, appearing with all the characteristics of its two sister-works already fully fledged. Formally, this 'Christmas Oratorio' is the most complex work of the three. It is at once religious and historical, public and private, and it is filled with implied analogies between the eve of the birth of Christ and the second world war. The Roman empire, like the Third Reich, 'shall be secure for a thousand years'.[19] Behind these sham pretensions, men are adrift. Hercules cannot 'keep his extraordinary promise' to 'reinvigorate the Empire'.[20]

> What is real
> About us all is that each of us is waiting.[21]

Some, of course, are not at all content to wait:

> Outside the civil garden
> Of every day of love there
> Crouches a wild passion
>   To destroy and be destroyed.[22]

For the time being

> our true existence
> Is decided by no one and has no importance to love.

> That is why we despair . . . We are afraid
> Of pain but more afraid of silence . . .
> This is the Abomination. This is the Wrath of God.[23]

Auden displays a wealth of intellectual powers in conveying this message. He switches from one complex stanza to another (the climax being the 'Fugal Chorus' in ironical praise of Caesar and his works); from one mode of speech to another, with excellent commentaries and lyrical interludes; and even, with more than his usual finesse in ventriloquy, from one mask to another. He speaks convincingly for the Shepherds, for the Magi, for Joseph the religious hero, believing in the Absurd birth despite the suspicion he may be a cuckold, for old sweats in Herod's infanticidal army, for Herod himself, the would-be liberal about to be cornered by *raison d'état* into massacring the innocents, for Simeon the convert and even for Mary at the manger. But, though, on reflection, this many-sidedness appears as astonishing virtuosity, it is still lacking the final touch of vitality which breathes life into a poem. 'For the Time Being' is a very good poem struggling to be let out of a failure, and the more it aspires to freedom the more one is aware of its fetters. It is full of noble beginnings which fall just short of their appointed ends, lyrical asides which lose their music halfway through, choruses which start with a bang and whimper away into repetition and even subtle recitatives in the shadow of Eliot's 'East Coker' which almost succeed, only to collapse for lack of the Eliotic coil of anguish. The brilliant prose meditations alone, Simeon's soliloquy and Herod's comic tirade, really come off. The overall effect is of a would-be major work well and truly foiled by the lack an indefinable quality.

The next work, 'The Sea and the Mirror,' makes it clearer what this missing element might be. Though it resembles 'For the Time Being' in its rhetorical assumptions and discipline (to the point where Auden published them as siblings in a single volume), it has an emotional vividness that 'For the Time Being' hardly comes in sight of achieving. It is incomparably more alive. Not that it is free of the old faults. It is sometimes too wordy, with hints here and there of the habitual catalogues, the tendency to comment rather than transmute, to pile on instances rather than find the one all-embracing metaphor which conveys the whole experience; it has some jaunty whimsies and occasional jerry-built Freudianisms among other flaws; and the best moments are apt to come in abstractions rather than visual images. Yet, despite these familiar limitations and weaknesses, 'The Sea and the Mirror' has a ripeness and a glow which even Auden's vivid images rarely gave his verse in the Thirties. That this new quality is emotional can easily be gauged from the type of quotations which stick in the memory:

> Now, Ariel, I am that I am, your late and lonely master,
>   Who knows now what magic is;—the power to enchant
> That comes from disillusion.[24]

Again and again, lines like these lodge in the memory even before the reader has grasped their full intent. Again and again, they cast an aura round the literal meaning even when, as always with Auden, it is susceptible to the most scholastic definition. This new power to enchant comes, I think, from the acceptance of suffering: a feeling for it in the human condition, rooted in the conscious effort to absorb it in oneself. It would be quite wrong to suggest Auden was previously impervious to suffering. On the contrary, his early work seems quietly obsessed by it—or at least gnawed by a sense of insufficiency which came often to the same thing. He was always ready to throw off lines like 'heart of the heartless world' which have been forgotten in their original boisterous context but helped to found the literary fortunes of other poets who purloined them for a more conventional setting.[25] In 'Letter to a Wound' he even made neurosis the source of the creative faculty. A keen and critical awareness of frustration was one of the qualities which gave him an edge over his contemporaries. Nevertheless, the attempt to maintain an unsentimental control over feeling finally led him into a kind of puritanical inhibition about it. The clinical style, originally designed to repress false sentiment and self-indulgence, finally repressed feeling itself; in taking over clinical virtues, Auden was unable to immunise himself against clinical vices. There was an odd contrast, particularly in the later Thirties, between his mania for words connoting pain—tears, grief, sorrow, weep, and so on—and his refusal to treat them other than as specimens for a slide. Words rarely assumed their true proportions and were repeatedly shrunk to phrases like 'Eros Paidogogos/Weeps on his virginal bed' which hovered uneasily between insight and jeering, between the pain imprisoned deep in the poet and his determination not to let it out of its philosophic cage.[26] In the case of the Miss Gee ballads, this schizophrenia extended to whole poems at a time. The drawbacks of this apparent imperiousness were still apparent in 'For the Time Being'. In some ways, 'For the Time Being' comes to better terms with feeling than much of Auden's previous work. 'New Year Letter', which gave a cosmic setting to his new sense of the validity of subjective experience, at least did that much for him. It made him more confident of the context of his feelings and released him from the compulsion to burrow away at the roots of their honour. But the kind of crystallisation of the subjective view of the human condition that Auden was struggling to achieve in 'For the Time Being' could not easily be attained in the second or third persons, the 'You' and 'They' which had almost become an obsession with him. The upheaval of personality they implied required some hint at least of subjective depths. Auden needed a frame enabling him to be more personal in content, yet his horror of pure subjectivity, associated with lack of balance, made it inconceivable for him to be nakedly subjective. He had to remain ostensibly impersonal both in order to keep up the appearances allowing him to release his feelings and in order to retain his freedom of objective judgement.

'The Sea and the Mirror' provides the perfect compromise between these opposing (or rather complementary) needs. Its commentary on *The Tempest* is a series of monologues by all the characters in the play as they leave Shakespeare's island of reconciliation with self. Each member of the cast explains how he has found relative peace. This allows Auden to exploit the first person singular without committing himself since, formally, each 'I' is a dramatic mask. Such a compromise, on such a theme, at last liberates him from the apathetic fallacy. In 'The Sea and the Mirror', Auden suddenly finds subjective depth without giving up necessary impersonality.

Auden himself is perfectly aware of this: one might almost say knowledge of his liberation is the theme of the poem. From the very beginning Prospero, the artist, bidding farewell to Ariel, the spirit of art, admits that Ariel's 'magic' in his eyes was in fact a trance of self-absorption which isolated him from reality:

> at last I can really believe I shall die.
> For under your influence death is inconceivable:
>   On walks through winter woods, a bird's dry carcass
> Agitates the retina with novel images,
>   A stranger's quiet collapse in a noisy street
> Is the beginning of much lively speculation,
>   And every time some dear flesh disappears
> What is real is the arriving grief.[27]

The apparent objectivity of 'lively speculation' is identified as a pseudo-objectivity, a symptom of the narcissistic trance which is rooted in the refusal to admit the Ego's necessary limitations. The frightened Ego is instinctively aware of its real and relative position in the world, but can only accept this when its totalitarian self-esteem (the source of all the trouble) is protected and preserved. Ariel purges the forces which might break up the artist's narcissism; and by the acclaim he wins for his patron actually reinforces the spell whose bubble needs to be lanced. The hitherto invulnerable artist stumbles on a sense of the wealth of living only when he is compelled to acknowledge his vulnerability as a man. The contrast between the emotional poverty of the narcissistic trance and the rich feelings tapped when one accepts one's own self and one's real position in the world is the basic antithesis of the poem.

Auden sticks closely to the point throughout 'The Sea and the Mirror'. His subject is the impact of the transformation scene on the individual, not—for once—on its ideological repercussions. He focuses on it as an event in its own right, and not as an illustration of his Christianity. 'The Sea and the Mirror' is the only major modern poem to deal not with the faith to which there is conversion but with the psychology of conversion *per se*. The main theme is not the belief but the drama of the irruption of belief. By limiting the field of vision, with quasi-scientific precision, to the presumed fact, Auden exploits once again one of the more effective strategies of the early *Poems*. The deliberate circumscription of the enquiry concentrates both the poet's imagination and the reader's sympathy. It is here that 'The Sea and the Mirror' is so superior to 'For the Time Being' and later *The Age of Anxiety*. They make an ideology of conversion or the layman's religious life and fail largely because they seem generalised, or at least intellectualised. 'The Sea and the Mirror' succeeds because it gives the impression of being the faithful reflection of a particular experience and leaves the ideology as an overtone. They are to a great extent notions of what the world is, or ought to be. It is the parable of what appears to be the crucial moment in a man's life.

That this existential quality really is the source of 'The Sea and the Mirror's' special place in Auden's work tends to be confirmed by the last of the long wartime poems, *The Age of Anxiety*. Its subject is what Jung calls the process of 'individuation'. This is the evolution by which a person, if he is lucky and honest enough, gradually brings his conscious and unconscious selves into relative harmony with one another and becomes 'individual in the fullest sense of the word', tapping all the resources of his personality. This is plainly a step forward from 'The Sea and the Mirror'. Where 'The Sea and the Mirror' deals with the critical moment in itself, *The Age of Anxiety* places it in the context of a lifetime's growth. One would expect Auden to be peculiarly well equipped to turn this into poetry. Like Eliot, he is a subtle and even touching poet of the process of ageing, with a gift for spiritual biography and for the middle-aged graces of wry happiness. He does indeed say valuable things especially, as one might expect, when he speaks for the Thinker, Malin, the middle-aged homosexual, who has mastered his situation as well as one can.

Yet, on the whole, one can hardly deny that *The Age of Anxiety* fails. The key reason seems to be that Auden has tried too hard to be universal. Not content with describing the process of individuation in a single person, which would require insight enough, he tries to take a short cut to embracing the whole of humanity by having four characters, one for each of Jung's four humours. So, in theory at least, *The Age of Anxiety* provides a complete map of the psychic quest of all types of men and women from the cradle to the grave. Put in such terms, the wonder is not that it is so long but, at 116 pages, so short. Contrary to a common opinion, *The Age of Anxiety* is relatively condensed. There is little sheer padding in it; all its images add a point. Even so, its atmosphere of almost decadent over-ornamentation is no accident. It would need a Shakespearean imagination to enter into so many skins through each of the seven stages of their active and dream lives which Auden describes. But Auden is not Shakespearean. He may be intellectually eclectic and even all-embracing; imaginatively, primed primarily by self, he is far from that. His supposed universality, suggested by a universal range of reference, is, in imaginative terms, an illusion. The result is that *The Age of Anxiety* gives the impression of failing to connect Auden's ambition with the power points of his imagination. Too much of it is painted with the clotted brush of the epigone:

> down each dale industrious there ran
> A paternoster of ponds and mills,
> Came sweet waters, assembling quietly
> By a clear congress of accordant streams
> A mild river that moseyed at will
> Through parks and ploughland, purring southward
> In a wide valley.[28]

In parts brilliantly written, as a whole *The Age of Anxiety* thickens into the more ornate kind of late-eighteenth century aristocratic parkland poetry. Auden, who has always enjoyed charting psychic states as an 'inner atlas' and is encouraged to it by Jung's notion of the archetypes, systematically describes every phase of his four characters' journey through life, in terms of a natural landscape. This technique of writing a long poem in inscapes and psychoramas might constitute an original way of revitalising nature imagery. But the monotony of unrelieved psychological landscape-painting for 116 pages turns into the ruin of the countryside when Auden the poet loses his concentration and lets Auden the speculative builder of images have his way. Nor are matters improved by the alliterative monotony of the Anglo-Saxon and medieval Ur-metre—presumably archetypal—which Auden has adopted. The result is failure—honourable and interesting failure—but failure just the same. Though *The Age of Anxiety* is slow, complex and worth savouring, it can never be more than a special taste. It aims too manifestly to be encyclopaedic rather than poetically essential. It encourages the possibly mistaken impression that it has been written to round off a cycle of long poems according to programme, rather than that the poet is bursting with things he has to say. In short, it exhausts the impulse of the prewar crisis to which the wartime poems raise such an enormous monument. Auden himself seemed to have had enough. He has not written a long poem from that day to this.

*   *   *

The core, then, of what Auden was trying to work out in the wartime poems and, more important, of what, artistically, he achieved, is to be found in 'The Sea and the Mirror'. It is about one of the most important themes a writer can tackle: how a man finds himself, the acceptance of maturity.

> The extravagant children, who lately swaggered
> Out of the sea like gods, have, I think, been soundly hunted
> By their own devils into their human selves.[29]

'The Sea and the Mirror' is an extended gloss on this. Prospero's speech which introduces the main subject is one long declaration of independence from Ariel, 'the attendant spirit' of his imagination: 'Today I am free and no longer need your freedom'—the spurious freedom conferred by the magic of supposedly detached art which, in fact, buttresses one's self regard.[30] 'The supporting cast, Sotto voce' then play variations on the theme, each speech being the character's special nuance of reconciliation with himself, followed always by a five-line refrain spoken by Antonio, the spirit of negation surviving all acceptance. The argument finally comes to rest, if that is the right word for such an ebullient harangue, in the brilliant marsh of Caliban's immense prose-poetic speech, which covers over half the work. In practice, this means that apart from the prologue and Ariel's brief and haunting epilogue, 'The Sea and the Mirror' divides roughly into two contrasted halves. The first, in formal verse, celebrates the complex feelings of relief and gratitude of people who have accepted their place in life and find, by that very fact, the nearest possible site to the Good Place which has eluded them so long. Prospero's long initial speech is grave, informal, majestic and warm, sententious but one of the most rounded pieces of writing Auden has done. Prospero states the opposition between the broken past and reconciled present in terms of the classical humanist response. The supporting cast, following him, are briefer and more lyrical. Some of their soliloquies, such as Alonso's, paternally reminding his son Ferdinand to 'believe your pain', or Gonzalo's intensely musical adieu to past rhetoric whose

> self reflection made
> Consolation an offence,[31]

are very beautiful. They cast a golden renaissance glow over the whole work and establish the credentials of its theme of reconciliation. By Auden's standards, though, much of this verse, despite its conversational surface, seems strikingly traditional, with strong Elizabethan overtones. When Alonso asks Ferdinand to remember

> What griefs and convulsions startled Rome,
> Ecbatana, Babylon[32]

or Gonzalo finds romantic images for his relief—

> Even reminiscence can
> Comfort ambient troubles like
> Some ruined tower by the sea—[33]

one is entitled to assume Auden is trying to convey something by these borrowings. A born parodist, whether serious or with tongue in cheek, he is extremely sensitive to literary allusion and knows exactly what he is doing. The atmosphere of the first lyrical part of 'The Sea and the Mirror' is that of the central humanist tradition of European—and especially renaissance—art. The very echo suggests these poems are a coming to terms with life on the conscious, rational, level long accepted as orthodox by western culture.

It is only in the second part, with Caliban, that one comes back to Auden's familiar preoccupation with the unconscious, and by the same token back to his usual style of speech. Caliban's outburst is the argumentative core of 'The Sea and the Mirror'. Like so many of Auden's deeply didactic pronouncements, it is a sermon inverted into farce: the more the reader forgets traditional responses, the better he may swallow the traditional insights behind them. It is, in fact, the apotheosis of the surrealist sermon style which runs right through Auden's work from *The Orators* and the Vicar's sermon in *The Dog Beneath the Skin* onwards to 'Vespers' in *The Shield of Achilles* published in 1955. Auden's attempts at burlesque are often so far-fetched that they defeat his object, but in Caliban's speech the ebullience wells up so powerfully with the points he makes that the farce buoys up the morality instead of drowning it. Caliban is astonishing in that he pleads the Christian case in a *grand guignol* style which is also a grand manner and never once falls back on the stock-in-trade of apologetics, the biblical Elizabethanisms, which convey so little to the post-Freudian mind. Beginning as a parody of Henry James's last and most convoluted manner, Caliban's speech flows in a continuous current of vast and turbulent sentences, proliferating arms and reaches of subordinate clauses through a thick jungle of images and brilliantly plumed metaphors till finally it sweeps out to the sea of Auden's long postponed conclusion. Caliban provides the counterpoint to Prospero's classical humanism of acceptance. He displays the fury of 'all too solid flesh' forced to emerge from self-infatuation into the equal, objective light of the world. In Caliban, the unconscious comes into its own—or, rather, up to the surface—even though the clichés of psychoanalysis have, thankfully, been weeded out of the speech itself. The crucial moment comes at the point where the first honeymoon magic of shared infatuation between Caliban, the animal in Prospero, and Ariel, his ideal mirror image, has begun to evaporate.

> Collecting all your strength for the distasteful task, you (*the artist*)* finally manage to stammer or shout 'You are free. Goodbye', but to your dismay He (*Ariel*)* whose obedience

---

*My parentheses—F.D.

through all the enchanted years has never been less than perfect, now refuses to budge. Striding up to Him in fury, you glare into His unblinking eyes and stop dead, transfixed with horror at seeing reflected there, not what you had always expected to see, a conqueror smiling at a conqueror, both promising mountains and marvels, but a gibbering fist-clenched creature with which you are all too unfamiliar, for this is the first time indeed that you have met the only subject that you have, who is not a dream amenable to magic but the all too solid flesh you must acknowledge as your own; at last you have come face to face with me (*Caliban*), and are appalled to learn how far I am from being, in any sense, your dish; how completely lacking in that poise and calm and all-forgiving because all-understanding good nature which to the critical eye is so wonderfully and domestically present on every page of your published inventions . . . If I have had, as I consider, a good deal to put up with from you, I must own that, after all, I am not just the person I would have chosen for a life companion myself; so the only chance, which in any case is slim enough, of my getting a tolerably new master and you a tolerably new man, lies in our both learning, if possible and as soon as possible, to forgive and forget the past, and to keep our respective hopes for the future, within moderate, very moderate, limits.[34]

Just how moderate those limits are, the rest of the lecture proceeds relentlessly to demonstrate. It describes the rake's progress towards despair of people who cannot renounce the hope of finding salvation in themselves, 'a madness of which you can only be cured by some shock'.[35] Once that shock has shivered the rake's self-respect, his new acceptance of 'moderate limits' restores his lost capacity to rejoice.

Yet, at this very moment when we do at last see ourselves as we are, neither cosy nor playful, but swaying out on the ultimate wind-whipped cornice that overhangs the unabiding void— we have never stood anywhere else—When our reasons are silenced by the heavy huge derision—There is nothing to say. There never has been—, and our wills chuck in their hands— There is no way out. There never was—, it is at this moment that for the first time in our lives we hear, not the sounds which, as born actors, we have hitherto condescended to use as an excellent vehicle for displaying our personalities and our looks, but the real Word which is our only *raison d'être*. Not that we have improved; . . . our shame, our fear, our incorrigible staginess, all wish and no resolve, are still, and more intensely than ever, all we have: only now it is not in spite of them but with them that we are blessed by that Wholly Other Life from which we are separated by an essential emphatic gulf . . . it is just here, among the ruins and the bones, that we may rejoice in the perfected Work which is not ours.[36]

The moment we recognise we are not masters of our fate we can begin to give thanks for being alive.

At last Auden's secret is out. With a sure sense of dramatic timing, he has left his message to the ultimate reverberations of Caliban's eloquence. It is only here, at the dying gasp of 'The Sea and the Mirror', that he finally brings Kierkegaard out of hiding and exposes him triumphantly to his mesmerised audience. The cast of *The Tempest* are reconciled with themselves because they have given their allegiance to that 'Wholly Other Life' which is, of course, the existentialist surname of God. They are freed in the service of the 'perfected Work which is not ours', since they need an outward-looking worship they can never sate because they can never realise its object in themselves. Until they accept this, they are bound to be entranced in the narcissistic spell of their own unhappiness. Once they have accepted it, though, 'the sounded note is the restored relation' between them and the nature around, and more important within, them.[36] This is more than a personal matter, a question of growing out of the instinctive self-love of youth. It means renouncing the reasoned self-love of secular humanism. When men assume they can be indifferent, 'scientific', observers of the life around them, or conquerors of nature—so long as their outlook is tied to what is basically a dream of collective power—they are bound to act with an acquisitive logic which breaks down in the vicious circle of self-love, self-hate and acute distress. The abstracting habit of mind, seeking to stand outside nature and thus taking it—and all life—for granted, calls down on the unconscious felon the implacable nemesis of his own nature. It divorces him from himself as well as from the objects he proposes to control. The destructive solitude and undercurrents of violence of modern life lie not in peripheral moods but in the essence of liberal assumptions. Reason must be 'redeemed from incestuous fixation on her own Logic'.[37] Secular humanism can only be fulfilled in the Christian humanism of love of God. It must end in self-destruction when it stops short at love of Man.

From the point of view of the work of art, the vital point about this message is that the one place where it is delivered explicitly—and then in elaborately allusive terms—is the last paragraph of Caliban's speech: the climax of the work, but only two-thirds of a page out of 54. God is named directly only once in the whole poem, and then the words are not Auden's but Emily Brontë's in the epigraph when she refers to the 'God of Visions'. This reticence is stressed by the shape of 'The Sea and the Mirror'. It is odd, on the face of it, that a work about a mental crisis should start with the aftermath—the feelings of the actors once it is over—and only then describe the event itself. But the overwhelming advantage of it from Auden's point of view is that he can focus the poetry not on his new-found Christianity but on the psychological process of the transformation scene, discuss not ideas but feelings. As apologetics, 'The Sea and the Mirror' is infinitely more subtle than 'For the Time Being'. 'For the Time Being' asserts the universal thirst for a revelation which, on its own showing, the purblind majority persist in denying. The poet asks a suspension of disbelief from his audience which is automatically withdrawn, and turns against him, every time the verse fails to speak powerfully to common feeling. With the psychological approach of 'The Sea and the Mirror', no suspension of disbelief is required. Or, rather, it comes of itself, because the audience spontaneously take the experience on trust without an invisible curtain of controversy coming down between them and the poet. The manœuvre is plain: demonstrate the importance of the experience; when that is accepted, link it to God. It is the nub of the existentialist strategy; and as it appeals directly to human fellow-feeling, it is aesthetically a sound one. In short, 'The Sea and the Mirror' is adapted to a civilisation in which gods and revelations are no longer self-evident. Its Christianity is part of a natural order, a consummation to be argued from man's misery, not a faith to be asserted from the original revelation. It may emerge from human psychology, it does not unquestionably exist as part of the external universe. 'The Sea and the Mirror' is a religious poem, but a relativist one, picking its way carefully round a host of unspoken reservations. That is one of its main artistic strengths.

Whatever one's view of Christianity, the psychological process described in 'The Sea and the Mirror' is both important and fascinating. It begins with unease. As Alonso tells Ferdinand,

> How soon the lively trip is over
> From loose craving to sharp aversion.[38]

I read Sartre's *Age de Raison* and Simone de Beauvoir's *La Force de l'Age* at a time when the meaning of 'The Sea and the Mirror' was borne in upon me more vividly than before. Sartre and Simone de Beauvoir are both atheists, yet both of them have much the same change to record, at much the same time of life, round the middle thirties, as Auden in his poem. They suddenly had to admit to themselves that the exuberance of their expectant twenties was palling. She wept for the loss of the old exultations; he had a kind of nervous breakdown, and for something like a year was trailed by his now famous vision of lobsters. As one would expect, Simone de Beauvoir assumed that this was the nemesis of age and that the force was ebbing from her. It only gradually occurred to her the trouble might be that appetites could not indefinitely renew their effects and might be doomed more and more to disappoint her desperately rising expectations; and that finally a ceiling was bound to be reached, the ceiling of her own limits, with which closer acquaintance was henceforth unavoidable. Auden has described this condition as 'an infinite extension of the adolescent difficulty, a rising of the subjective and subjunctive to ever steeper, stormier heights'.[39] As for the resolution, bestial Caliban had much the same story to tell his master, Auden–Prospero: 'From now on we shall have, as we both know only too well, no company but each other's.'[40] For Sartre, it meant the bleak despair of his description of middle age as '*se boire sans soif*'.[41] For Prospero, it is the realisation for the first time that he is not invulnerable: 'at last I can really believe I shall die'.[42] Auden differs from Simone de Beauvoir at any rate, and can afford to be relatively optimistic where she undeniably felt let down, because he never had her naïve worship of experience. Like Ransom in *The Ascent of F6*, he never made the foolish assumption 'that it is fortunate to be alive'.[43] He always emphasised the need for precise thinking to control the impact of one's lusts and lingering childish cravings on one's view of life. He had another, more insidious temptation: the egotistical and ungrateful exploitation of his own gift. There is evidence that in youth Auden's real idol was artistic creativity. His self-dramatisation of the Leader, his concern with fame and the spiritual life, as in 'A shilling life will give you all the facts', his contempt for failures and mediocrities, the way he appointed his literary 'cabinet' at Oxford and named his 'ministers' in poems—these and many other small signs point in such a direction. There would be nothing strange or uncommon in this: to be 'creative' has been the true religion of most talented young men for at least two centuries and there is no reason why a prodigy like Auden should have been an exception. Certainly, all the central passages of 'The Sea and the Mirror' deal with conversion through a special preoccupation of his, the exhaustion of the enjoyment of one's talent as a reason for living. It is here that Auden's problem meets that of the French existentialist mandarins. Existentialism may or may not lead to faith in God; but it always registers the nervous breakdown of faith in the ultimate apotheosis of self.

If the thirties and the onset of middle age have no doubt always been as much of a challenge as adolescence, the shock they offer the heirs of liberalism is far greater than for their ancestors. The ages of poverty convinced a child of individual misery on his mother's knee. He had only to look around at material hardship everywhere and to grow old and toothless at forty to convince himself that fate was inescapable. Hell was a perfectly understandable experience because its grotesque, Brueghelian horrors were omnipresent. This rather bleak realism was not confined to the peasantry scratching the soil for an intermittently failing subsistence. It applied equally to the minority whose authority was concentrated, and therefore far more concrete, than today. They formed a small community of nobles, bureaucrats, clerics and merchants jockeying for power among themselves, from father to son. Each struggled for a place near the sun in direct competition with equals many of whom he knew in person. There was little room in such a world for seeing reality through a haze of abstractions and preconceived ideas. The highly practical outlook common to poor and powerful alike in an age of poverty was mirrored faithfully in the harsh fables of La Fontaine, where a courtly elegance and the detached pity of the observer alone temper the ruthless impact of the strong on the weak who always go to the wall.

Since the onrush of the industrial revolution, the Rousseauists have swept aside the mental and social hierarchies of the centuries. Science and the collective triumphs of mankind have cast a protective cocoon around the mental world of the young and powerless. They are encased in their security of comfort, their pride of education and their remoteness from affairs—all the characteristics of a world in which co-operation and the division of labour generate wealth and frustration. The perception of progress through the ages has created, in the classroom's secular view of the world, an optimism which masks the *condition humaine*. (It is not altogether accidental that the very phrase, with its hint of suppressed realism breaking through, comes from France where life, despite the myths of *la belle époque*, continued, until the last few years, to be a great deal harsher, or at least more down to earth, than in the truly industrial societies.) Our values and obsessions are derived from the mythology of material triumphs. They have no room for 'failure' or death, since they do not really refer to the individual face to face with his own inevitable limitations, but to society and the race which hope to overcome them. Thus the industrial mobile society which has exorcised so many tabus on sex and success has replaced them by a tabu on failure and death. Anything that does not bathe in a glow of optimism to the point of unreality is regarded as cowardly self-pity and life-destroying. It is significant that one of Sartre's discoveries in *La Nausée* is that '*on perd toujours. Il n'y a que les Salauds*'—his name for the successful bourgeois—'*qui croient gagner*'. [44]

Truths self-evident to our fathers and forefathers are a profound discovery for the normally aggressive, aspiring person who, at a certain age, finds himself brought up sharp against his natural frontiers. Clearly, he had suspected their existence; but everything in his upbringing had encouraged his expansionism and kept him from paying his respects sooner than he must to any immeasurable force. To him, the dream of love was religion enough, the loss of self in a trance of happiness where

> Simultaneous passions make
> One eternal chastity;[45]

and time was largely theatrical, the stage for hopes of fame and fears of failure, in the light not of death but of other men's judgements through the ages. It is only when he is forced to recognise the loneliness inherent in the adult state, the necessary obscurity of the individual, especially in a world of collective achievements, and the inexorable advance of life not to apotheosis but to personal oblivion, that he reaches what it is conventional to call 'middle age'. This is the time of life when the higher hedonism stops climbing mountain paths to ever taller and more rarefied excitements. Unless he moves away along the harder tracks of inner reconciliation the individual has reached a plateau whose sameness looks increasingly bleak. In Prospero's words,

> . . . I feel so peculiar . . . as if through the ages I had dreamed
> About some tremendous journey I was taking . . .
> And now, in my old age, I wake, and this journey really exists,
> And I have actually to take it, inch by inch,
> Alone and on foot.[46]

But to accept this is to stumble on a new wealth, forever renewed by the constant feeling of its precariousness. In this sense, the idea of death is the awakening to the difficult achievement of all that was previously taken for granted. The understanding of necessary personal weakness is at the root of a sense of the richness of life. This no doubt explains why both Eliot and Auden have talked at the age of forty, or in Auden's case even less, as 'old men'—Eliot with his 'agèd eagle' which so incensed Edmund Wilson, Auden with 'now, in my old age, I wake'. Conversely, Yeats's preoccupation, as a much older man, speaking far more in his own person, with lust (the mark, one would imagine, of vigorous youth) and with the permanence of mind against physical decay, seems to be a sign that while he was aware of the flimsiness of his self-confidence, he was not prepared to forswear it. His was an earlier and, in this, more Romantic generation: he was born more than 20 years before Eliot, more than 40 before Auden. When Yeats speaks of sex, he means religion; when Eliot and Auden speak of death, they mean the acceptance of life. Such acceptance implies the renunciation of the paradisiac hopes of the Ego; and awareness that in a world where relationships are necessary, absolutes are impossible. The reward is gratitude for what life has to give. This is, without doubt, conversion of a kind.

Yet the dominant feature of Auden's conversion is, paradoxically, its element of continuity with his 'secular' past. The whole process is very different from the popular notion of violent and sudden change, a Pauline stroke of lightning on the road to Damascus. Perhaps there always was an element of the fairy-tale in the belief that such breaks in continuity are possible. It is typical of popular myths which concentrate on dramatic externals and ignore the inner process. Nevertheless, it is striking that in terms both of his ideas and of his emotional attitudes, Auden's conversion suggests not a sudden break but a change of key in old ideas which, basically, live on. Even if one compares him with his fellow literary convert, Eliot, there is nothing at any point in his art like the personal anguish of Becket in *Murder in the Cathedral*. He seems to have come to his Christianity much more as a moralist, an exemplar of Kierkegaard's principle of Religion as the fulfilment of Ethics, than as a hermit of the dark night.

If James Warren Beech is right and Auden accepted original sin, revelation, the Incarnation and other Christian dogmas well after 1939, this would confirm the impression. Auden's crisis took place in 1939 at the latest, so that the crisis and the Christianity were markedly separate in time. There may, indeed must, have been a relation of cause and effect, but they were not simultaneous. Beech's view is supported by the change between 'New Year Letter' and 'The Sea and the Mirror'. In 'New Year Letter', Auden's view hovers ambiguously between seeing art as the 'greatest of vocations' and the curious little 'poet's prayer' he inserted into the notes: 'Lord,

teach me to write so well, that I shall no longer want to.'[47]
'The Sea and the Mirror' is firmly based on the idea that art
is 'magic' and that the free man must break its spell. There is
every sign that Auden's conversion was an evolution, not a
revolution: a transposition of what had always been there in
other clothing.

Almost every one of the young Auden's ideas are to be found
changed but not displaced in his later work. The familiar stress
on free will is merely reinforced by Christian orthodoxy. The
old notion of leadership grows into that of the Quest or Jung's
concept of self-discovery and 'individuation'. The old dissatisfaction with the insufficiencies of erotic love owns up to its
inherent logic and becomes the distinction between human and
divine love, Eros and Agape. The biological evolutionism of
the early *Poems*, seen from a great distance, across aeons and
light-years, turns into the slow dialectic of spiritual growth,
'still believing we can climb a little higher every time'.[48] Even
the early stress on guilt turns naturally and easily into the
doctrine of 'anxiety'. It was always hard to understand what
(outside politics) Auden really meant by 'guilt', except that
Freud had prescribed it, and that therefore it was. 'Anxiety' is
a far better term than 'guilt' for Man's inherent uncertainty
about his place in the cycle of life expressed in early pieces like
'Happy the hare at morning'. There are no revolutionary
changes here. Auden is still trying, now as before, to rationalise
the irrational. Some would say he does it at a deeper level,
others that the irrational has captured him. (I would say that,
in different ways, both are true). Religion does not greatly
change all this—nor for that matter the poet's emotional
habits. After all, his early poems were full of secular prayers,
and of the desire for 'unity'. Oddly enough the only notion on
which the change of key has the effect of a reversal seems to be
that of conversion itself. In the form of belief in the coming
Revolution, this was a concept of Auden's youth:

> No one will ever know
> For what conversion brilliant capital is waiting,
> What ugly feast may village band be celebrating.[49]

Now, Auden's imagination is no longer haunted by this idea.

The break with the past, far from being a break, is the realisation that no break may be possible, that the future can only arise gradually out of the processes observed in the past and the present. It is governed by the evolutionary laws of natural development which defy revolution. Revolution is, of course, a possible event. But would that necessarily hasten the real change, the creation of the New Man the Thirties so hankered after? Deep transformations can only be brought about by men's slow efforts to improve themselves individually. The faith in progress has been shifted along the spectrum from politics and science to ethics and religion, and even then only in part. Given this extraordinary continuity in basic perceptions, it is not surprising to learn that *The Tempest* fascinated Auden as far back as his Oxford days. I think it is plain that he was instinctively aware even then of the strains his beliefs created in him at the time, of their character as a conscious rebellion against his own unconscious drives, and that at some point consciousness and unconsciousness would need to be reconciled. When the reconciliation had already taken place, Auden was ready to use *The Tempest* for his own purposes; 'The Sea and the Mirror' is the result.

This continuity is equally remarkable in what one might call Auden's temperament or, more accurately perhaps, his predicament. There is less change in Auden's personality as an artist than one might expect. It is true that there is a conscious personal touch in Auden's poetry after 'The Sea and the Mirror' which is obviously a deliberate corrective to the 'Generalised Life', the pose of detachment, of his earlier work. But where his earlier work was detached despite itself, one sees little or no change. At one point in 'For the Time Being' he does say of the Christmas story that

> for once in our lives
> Everything became a You and nothing was an It,[50]

but there is not much sign of this in his own poetry. All four wartime works are vast monologues or collections of monologues: at no point in any of them does anyone speak *to* anyone else. The only players addressed are *alter egos* like Ariel, mere emanations of the self. Nor can one say that Auden displays much of that sense of belonging which is usually thought the mark of the recent convert. True, Alonso offers his son Ferdinand, the blessing of

> your father, once King
> Of Naples, now ready to welcome
> Death, but rejoicing in a new love,
> A new peace, having heard the solemn
> Music strike and seen the statue move
> To forgive our illusion.[51]

But, though acceptant, this stops short of belonging. And the last words of Prospero to Ariel the 'unanxious one', convey the exact opposite:

> sing
> To man, meaning me,
> As now, meaning always,
> In love or out,
> Whatever that mean,
> Trembling he takes
> The silent passage
> Into discomfort.[52]

There is little or no evidence of real relationships in the poems. On the other hand, they are one long testimony to the fact that, isolated though Auden remains, he has now found a way of placing himself and his feelings in an acceptable relationship to the universe as he sees it. He has integrated himself into his cosmology, which he had signally failed to do in the Thirties. He has come to terms with his isolation and is able to live with it. Most of the best pieces in 'The Sea and the Mirror' are variations on the theme of the acceptance of loneliness. The most vital parts of Caliban's curtain speech are about the gradual palling of the artist's talent and success as reasons for living. Prospero the introvert creator, Gonzalo the orator, Alonso the father-figure, Trinculo the joker, The Master and Boatswain, the sociable gossips, even Stephano in love with his belly, are all recognisable aspects of Auden's constant poetic self. Much of the beauty of 'The Sea and the Mirror' comes from its capacity to accept, and make a world of, loneliness.

* * *

In terms of Auden's psychological development and his ideas, the long wartime poems are without question a climax. They fulfil the drive of his youth to formulate an exact and all-embracing notion of his world: they are the logical conclusion to the Thirties. If one thinks in stylistic terms, however, one becomes aware that in the wartime poems themselves, from 'New Year Letter' to *The Age of Anxiety*, Auden the composer travels a long way. Stylistically, they cannot be seen as a unity but as steps along a road: they introduce the future as well as close the past.

'New Year Letter' is still near to the quietist poems of 1939. It moves one step away from their personal record of Auden's reconciliation with himself by defining its social and moral context. But, like them, it is still preoccupied with definitions: it states the basic antithesis of Romantic yearnings and religious discipline in the abstract manner. It is still influenced by the verbal habits of the Thirties: Auden writes like a latter-day moralist of the *esprit de géometrie* which Pascal attacked, even though his formal position is now close to Pascal's own.

With 'For the Time Being' and 'The Sea and the Mirror' he moves a long stride beyond this. In these two poems he goes beyond definition: he grapples with his experience in more existential, or emotional, terms. The antithesis acquires vitality from the energies of commitment which go into it. The various elements of thought and feeling are brought into much more confident focus and the warring instincts, brilliantly related among themselves, develop into a baroque humanist style. It is the culmination of that intense and not always successful search for a landscaping of the Good Place which animated Auden's thoughts throughout the Thirties. The old contrast between an inflating awe and constricting reason which created the tension of the early *Poems*, and no doubt also the effortful compression of their language, has been resolved. The more conventional excitements of the discovery of self through sex and politics, the energy of the rebellious 1930s, have also been as it were absorbed and transmuted. All these hidden reserves of power have been brought from the unconscious to the surface. The result is a mastery of all the tones of expression, a tension of balanced opposites, a structured sense of the rich diversities of life and feeling, which give Auden's art for the first time a classic air. As he moves closer and closer to a grasp of the conscious disciplines necessary to poise civilised values on the knife-edge of contentment, so his style moves away from the taciturn and vatic, or youthfully excited, cadences of his early work to the urbane expansiveness of maturity. The disappointments of the later Thirties usher in a discursive variant of the grand style.

Yet this fulness contains warning signs of flatulence; and in *The Age of Anxiety* it becomes over-ripe. 'For the Time Being' and 'The Sea and the Mirror' both give the impression of a creative artist still in search of his ideal form of expression, still making discoveries. *The Age of Anxiety* seems to take the baroque humanist style for granted as a settled convention out of which to write. The conscious reconciliation of conflicting stresses becomes a habit of consciousness turning every instinct into a domesticated psychic state, baroque tension becomes ornament and generates its own clichés. G. S. Fraser forgivably writes of 'decadent classicism'. Take a matter of language like the use of obscure—indeed obsolete—words. A budding affection for them appears in 'New Year Letter' with 'webster' (old English for a weaver) and 'orgulous' (middle English borrowing from the French *orgueilleux* meaning 'proud'). They disappear in 'For the Time Being' and 'The Sea and the Mirror'. Then, in *The Age of Anxiety*, they gush up again in force, with 'watchet', 'deisal', 'indagation', 'fumerole', 'acquisities', and so on. They are obviously very learned, but are they still alive? In a way, one is led to ask the same question of the metaphors. Little is left of the awesome horrors of a nuclear explosion in

> colossal bangs and
> Their sequential quiets[53]

or of drowning in

> They swallowed and sank, ceased thereafter
> To appear in public[54]

or of the agony of the Jews in

> bruised or broiled our bodies are chucked
> Like cracked crocks onto kitchen middens
> In the time He takes.[55]

If the deliberate reduction of violent events to psychic states in these images is designed to stress the isolation of the unregenerate Ego, they succeed to the point of shutting out the reader. They extract the *virtù* from psychic states in the very act of apparently particularising them. They do not even truly relate to a dreamworld, for dreams are emotionally enormous while these images are intellectually precise and emotionally almost non-existent. Sucking the blood out of mental associations is a form of parasitism which weakens the poetry itself. It becomes a kind of catalogue, or dictionary, of mental states in allegorical form but communicates none of the supposed impact of these states. This goes further perhaps in *The Age of Anxiety* than in any of Auden's other poems. But the tendency is important and needs to be noted: *The Age of Anxiety* is in many ways the last link in the chain between Auden's early and later poetry. It ushers in his postwar style.

With all these differences between them, the long wartime poems still have an overwhelming family likeness: their themes, their complex shapes, their style, set the seal on their close parentage. Whether this was deliberate or not, the three—or the four—of them have a unity not to be denied. In this, as in other ways, they hold in Auden's work a place surprisingly like that of the *Four Quartets* in Eliot's. Auden and Eliot are so different that the comparison seems more obvious in their intentions than their achievement. Yet there is more in common between the poems than meets the eye. They come alike at the very end of the high tide of early twentieth century verse and alike summarise many or most of the impulses that went before: it is as if the turbid feelings of the interwar period had here, at last, reached the balanced and systematic conclusions most of the poets were unconsciously looking for, and having found them, lost the stimulus to further major creation. Both are in supreme degree meditative monologues; both combine the surface freedom of a conversational style with an elaborate underlying formalism. This almost certainly reflects a commanding need—the surface ease, a burning desire for precise truth, renouncing the inflations of self-importance; the contrapuntal forms, a compulsion to contain the destructive spiritual undertow of a confused era.

Beyond that, if one sticks to conventional estimates, it is presumptuous to set Auden's work on a par with Eliot's. Eliot rises
in parts of the *Four Quartets* to almost unattainable rarefactions
of sensibility and phrasing which warrant the musical analogies
of his title. Auden is relatively coarse-grained, even as a craftsman; his paragraphs do not built up palatial façades of sound
in Yeats's aristocratic style, nor do they follow a feeling almost
unbearably along the nerve like Eliot's: in conveying emotion
or even in the poetical economy of words, Auden cannot rival
either. There is less inner cohesion to his writing, it seems less
carefully worked. Doubts have been expressed about Auden's
capacity to write successful long works. Spender has said that
'Auden's long poems are singularly weak in construction'.
Certainly, not one of his long works, from 'Paid on Both Sides'
to *The Age of Anxiety*, has the formal unity of Eliot's major
productions: 'only a unified personality can hold a long poem
together'.⁵⁶ All Auden's long poems shift between didacticism
when speaking of the world and lyricism in speaking about the
self, with little middle ground where the inward and outward
approaches meet. (This may be why farce is so important in
Auden's writing; it is a kind of fusion from which the poet
partly dissociates himself.) The result is that there is no consistent certainty of tone informing a single work. The one exception is 'The Sea and the Mirror' where Auden juxtaposes
the lyrical and didactic parts of his genius and leaves Shakespeare's theme itself to provide an off-stage unity. Because his
form allows him, in this poem, or series of poems, to finesse his
weakness, it is the one work where it is not apparent and where
the poet can express his talent without half-conscious fears in-
hibiting him from doing so to the full. It is not so much that he
has found a form to shape his art as that he has found one which
conceals what his art cannot do. 'The Sea and the Mirror' is,
in short, a compendium of what Auden can achieve and therein
lies its superiority to all his other long works and in particular
'For the Time Being' and *The Age of Anxiety* which are object
lessons in what he cannot achieve. It alone can hold the torch,
within its own conventions, to Eliot's greater works.

Indeed, with its author freed from his limitations, or rather
operating freely within them, 'The Sea and the Mirror' is in

some ways superior to the *Four Quartets*. It is more of a natural force than they can claim to be. Its relaxed rhythms of speech exude an impressive kind of emotional obviousness, an 'extravagant sanity'.[57] 'The Sea and the Mirror' is a rationalist's experience of religion and the difficulty of living. This gives a positive meaning to its renunciation of the more obvious effects of the poetry of extremes of sensibility or passion. The power of 'The Sea and the Mirror' is not primarily in the originality of its ideas (though they are far from stale) nor in its formal art (though it contains a high proportion of Auden's finest verse), but in the massive strength and solidity of its occupation of the middle ground of sense and balance. Indeed, by comparison with 'The Sea and the Mirror', the *Four Quartets*, though in flashes possibly the best writing of the century, are flawed by a built-in spiritual hypochondria forever trembling between transfiguration and senescence. One feels the beginnings of creative fatigue in them. 'The Sea and the Mirror', taking one thing with another, marks the summit of Auden's vitality. It is, along with the *Four Quartets* and *The Waste Land*, one of the very few longer masterpieces to issue from the rich and ambitious thirty-year season of poetry from Yeats's *Responsibilities* of 1914 to Dylan Thomas's *Deaths and Entrances* of 1945. It is, in Spender's words, 'difficult to think that future generations will not discover new and ever deeper meanings in it'.[58] 'The Sea and the Mirror' is, for Auden, the central achievement giving meaning to a corpus of poetry which would otherwise be strangely lacking in organic shape.

5

ECLOGUES FOR AN URBAN
CULTURE

'BETWEEN the ages of twenty and forty', Auden has written, 'we are engaged in the process of discovering who we are'.[1] At the age of twenty, in 1927, he was composing the first of his published poems. By the age of forty, in 1947, he had completed *The Age of Anxiety*. Throughout those years, he figured as a system-builder. His passion to know the world, to embrace it all, made him potentially a major poet even when he was least satisfactory. It was because everyone sensed this that his personality so dominated the Thirties despite the fragmentary nature of the verse he actually wrote. But, for Auden, poetry is a 'game' of self-knowledge.[2] Once the large works of the war years had suitably enshrined that self-knowledge, he no longer needed to be systematic to be whole. As the rambling failure of *The Age of Anxiety* showed, the synthesis had satisfied, but also exhausted, that impulse. A new poetry, if any, had to be based on a different approach. Auden was quick to sense this. Since *The Age of Anxiety*, his art has become consciously personal and, in a word, he applies to some of his poems, 'bucolic'.[3] There are no more long works, though these short ones are of a kind that only a major poet could write. As Walter Allen said of the earliest of Auden's postwar volumes, *Nones*, they are 'written in the margin of great themes', limited in themselves, but with the hinterland of Auden's completed world filling the horizon.[4]

The constant contrast between past and present—as Auden sees it, between old illusion and new understanding—leads to a poetry of great complexity. Auden's early poems, for all their evident ambition, lacked the double power of the later ones, at their best, in patently concealing more than the others ever knew. In their urbane and relaxed good talk, lyricism spreads out into an all-embracing but restrained enjoyment, sex is replaced by a sense of the ironies of love and desire, drama emerges mainly in reflection on its consequences. It is the language of balance, of the constraints of reality upon ambition; and every stimulus—a couple of lovers at a country house party, the dawning consciousness of waking up, or shuddering at the thought of living in a plain—moves the poet to post-prandial musings on the dangerous laws of the good life. This is poetry middle-aged almost to the point of caricature, consciously quiet, studiedly private, a mosaic of flat statements and throwaway lines. The sweet and sour of Auden's later poetry—the wisdom, the irony, the catty benevolence, the virtuosity, the old hand's aggression in shocking the *enfants terribles* by owning up to the one quality they cannot admit, banal weakness, in the one way they cannot stomach, flat familiarity—add up to one of the most idiosyncratic styles of the century, When Auden begins a poem

> I know a retired dentist who only paints mountains,
>> But the Masters rarely care
> That much

he offends not only nineteenth-century Byron but seventeenth-century Amaryllis as well: this looks middle-class and middle-powered as well as middle-aged.[5] Pose for pose, both would prefer a touch of theatre. Auden's renunciation conveys a whole world of subtly changed assumptions in its ostentatious quietudes.

There is little poetry so aggressive—sometimes with blatant bathos, as when Auden interjects 'I wish I weren't so silly', or 'Just reeling off their names is ever so comfy'—in dramatising its modesty.[6] This comes out through incongruous parentheses, in abrupt changes of tone, through constant irruptions of cultural reminiscence in passages of feeling which convention demands should be self-forgetting. Auden himself points out what this is driving at:

> All, all, have rights to declare,
> Not one is man enough
> To be, simply, publicly, there
> With no private emphasis.[7]

As in the *Four Quartets*, the flatness of Auden's later diction claims to be not the cold common sense of middle age, but its reverent refusal to be entangled in youth's false airs and graces. Naturally, the lyrical and dramatic renunciations of middle age imply the loss of a certain ebullience. They bring compensating advantages, not least a capacity for subtly disguised depths. Most of Auden's later poetry expresses the search for a conception of human dignity neither heroic nor exceptional, but vested in the ordinary continuity of daily life. Hence, no doubt, its heightened stress on play. Play may express perfection of a sort, but makes no claims for its own seriousness and is therefore a morality of gratitude, a 'reverent frivolity'.[8] Similarly, dignity can come of giving thanks for the precarious moments of success snatched or created from a sense of oblivion, a thankfulness foreign to hungry assumptions of a right to self-fulfilment:

> To be sitting in privacy, like a cat
> On the warm roof of a loft
> . . . . would keep me happy for
> What? Five minutes? For an uncatlike
> Creature who has gone wrong,
> Five minutes on even the nicest mountain
> Are awfully long.[9]

There could hardly be a more deflationary way of expressing what a Victorian as matter-of-fact as Browning would have, indeed did, put as

> Infinite passion and the pain
> Of finite hearts that yearn.[10]

Auden celebrates another kind of dignity still, that which is obtained from losing oneself in service:

> You need not see what someone is doing
> to know if it is his vocation,
>
> you have only to watch his eyes:
> a cook mixing a sauce, a surgeon
>
> making a primary incision,
> a clerk completing a bill of lading,
>
> wear the same rapt expression,
> forgetting themselves in a function.[11]

Beneath the disclamatory surface, the low key of Auden's later poetry implies a conscious rejection of 'rights' and a celebration

of the honest wages of the spiritual life. Its very language de-
plores all the things which belong to man's self-approving
difference from the animals rather than to life itself, all self-
congratulation on achievement rather than gratitude for powers
conferred in the cradle. The very flatness of this poetry is a
mark of dedication to the life which owes us nothing but to
which we ourselves owe everything.

The basis of Auden's later poetry is the sense of reconciliation
with self achieved during the war. The result is a culmination
of his progress towards a style of consciousness in which all the
elements of the situation are explicit in the scenic surface of the
poem. This is striking when one compares two poems like 'This
lunar beauty' and 'The More Loving One', which treat the
same subject thirty years apart. Both are meditations on the
separation of Man and Nature prompted by the night sky. 'This
lunar beauty', written in the late twenties has an air of mystery
about it, an aura of ambiguities, while 'The More Loving One'
is almost metaphysical in its integrated wit. As one looks into
these first impressions, one finds that they are based, in the one
case on tentativeness and in the other on certainty. The earlier
poem may not look tentative, but it merely states its theme,
the illusion of communion and prudently draws no conclusion
from it, least of all a personal one. The later poem, for all its
airs of being an amusing trifle, is a manifest credo and its playfulness has the effortless poise of long-confirmed certainties.
The very title seems doctrinal compared to the refusal of the
earlier piece to have a doctrine. The language too has changed:
'This lunar beauty' is compressed, to the point where the full
meaning of the key concepts, like the 'lover' or 'daytime',
cannot be conveyed without clues from other sources. Though
its method is precise enough, its effect is enigmatic. The music
too has something of this indefinition. It has no formal rhythm,
and its informal rhythm seems to arise out of the thought itself:
it is organically related to the effort of divining and defining a
position. 'The More Loving One', by contrast, is not only
doctrinally clear and personally committed, it is also classical
in form, regular and orthodox. Both are fine poems, but the
first is unfulfilled and searching, dominated in a curious way by
the unconscious; the second is fulfilled and as conscious as

humanity can make it. It is by far the riper and formally more satisfactory poem, but in its very ripeness and fulfilment there is something already completed and closed.

From fulfilment to contentment and sclerosis is only a few short steps. The danger of the poetry of reconciliation is personal complacency, political conformism and creative sterility. Auden, as usual, is still more conscious of this than are his critics. He has reacted to it, as in *The Age of Anxiety*, by giving his service to all that is impulsive in human nature. In the battle he celebrates in many poems between the impulsive forces of 'Hermes' and the organising ones of 'Apollo', he comes out enthusiastically on the side of the 'Hermetics'.

> Thou shalt not answer questionnaires
> Or quizzes upon World-Affairs.
> Nor with compliance
> Take any test. Thou shalt not sit
> With statisticians nor commit
> A social science.[12]

The comic war of Hermes and Apollo is the final form taken by Auden's familiar doctrine of the alienation of consciousness. If Auden, recognising in one of the finest of his poems, 'Vespers', that Hermes and Apollo are necessary to each other, nevertheless sides with Hermes, this is not only because of temperament. Certainly, he was, as one sonnet began, already 'fleeing the short-haired mad executives' in his most nearly Apollonian period, in the early Thirties. But there was more to his final choice than that. He now follows Jung in believing that the fulfilled man must be in touch with the dark gods he has inherited through the 'collective unconscious' of the race.[13] This conviction gives systematic justification to Auden's bent for anthropological poetry, concerned with the analogies of modern behaviour going back before philosophy. Auden cannot, for instance, begin a 'Thanksgiving for a Habitat', his poem of praise for the new house he acquired in Kirchstetten in Lower Austria in 1957, without insisting that

> Nobody I know would like to be buried
> with a silver cocktail shaker,
> a transistor radio and a strangled
> daily help, or keep his word because

of a great-great-grandmother who got laid
by a sacred beast.[14]

This constant harping on the ritual analogies of modern behaviour is probably the dominant feature of Auden's later
verse. By bringing together his scientific and irrational interests,
his psychology and history, it is the apotheosis of the tendency
already visible in *The Orators* with 'the tall white gods who
landed from their open boat'.[15]

Auden's later poetry is full of solemnly innocent creatures
and creations like Bellini's music or museum pieces like over-
shot waterwheels—happy freaks of an indulgent providence
which dispose the mind to privacy and inner harmony—but
from which anything smacking of an imposed, vacuum-making
order has been barred. Auden's view of sex has been governed
by the same principles. One would expect an English Protestant,
even an Anglo-Catholic, to place a quite excessively high-
minded emphasis on sin. But not at all. In 'Vespers', Auden is
blandly irreverent about the Christian sermon on sex.

In my Eden each observes his compulsive rituals and super-
stitious tabus but we have no morals.[16]

In fact, Auden's relativism about Christianity is based on the
the same conviction as his scepticism about liberal Reason and
the New Jerusalem where 'the temples will be empty but all
will practise the rational virtues'.[16] Auden's Eden, where the
religion sports 'lots of local saints' and public statues are 'confined to famous defunct chefs',[17] is littered with friendly descendants of the dark forces which always haunted the fetichist
recesses of his verse and psychoanalysis.

It is not
To the Cross or to *Clarté* or to Common Sense
Our passions pray but to primitive totems
As absurd as they are savage.[18]

These dark forces of the mind must be dredged up into consciousness to be domesticated. White magic pays homage to
the unknown, unsung and unloved but irrepressible forces in
each human being which must be wooed, sung and loved
(within limits) to exorcise the lurking blackness in their spirits.

The result is a poetry which is almost dutiful in its constant ritualism and encyclopaedic cultural memories. One has an impression of almost endless reminiscence in this Alexandrian style of verse—the feeling of walking through a *Musée Imaginaire* of cultural impressions.

In 'Vespers', Auden at least implicitly identifies himself as an 'Arcadian'. His Arcadia is not to be taken literally, of course. Auden is no countryman. In fact, it would be hard to think of a single major poet since Pope, except possibly Byron, who was a more confirmed townee. True to his own past and to present realities, he is not much concerned with country matters, nor with spinning daydreams of the individual happy life in the hellenistic and renaissance manners. His pastorals remind one little of the classical sporting with Amaryllis in the shade. They are urban and intellectual, dealing as ever with public ethics, standards and values. Even celebrating Vespers, Auden, one is hardly surprised to find, considers that the twilight hour has much to do with 'what a citizen really thinks of his citizenship'.[19] The link between Auden's eclogues and those of the central tradition is less in the landscapes which provide him with metaphors, than in the appeased attitudes expressed. They are cultural and ethical, not rustic, eclogues.

Auden's Arcadia, in common with its ancestor of the Peloponnesian valleys, is the happy abode where men live in amity because they understand their own natures. It re-embodies the ideal of what Greeks called the 'scientific' and we would call the 'humanistic', or perhaps rankly amateur, adaptation to environment. It is the attitude, for instance, of Polybius commending Arcadia: 'The cultivation of music . . . is beneficial for all human beings, but for Arcadians it is absolutely indispensable.' To the Greek mind, the very violence of its mountain climate compelled Arcadia, in compensation, to stress musical training more than other communities. 'The Arcadians made music a compulsory subject in the education not only of children but of youths from puberty to the age of thirty, whereas in other spheres they were extremely puritanical in their habits.'[20] Arcadia is, in short, a kind of ritual paradise, spanning the abyss between the polytheism of the unconscious and the concern for a natural order of the rational man. It makes sense primarily as the symbol of the rediscovery of—or perhaps only desire for—a natural order encompassing both the conscious and unconscious levels of the mind.

As if to underline this, the values of Arcadia turn round the typically modern assumption that self-fulfilment is desirable. As full as possible of amiable eccentricities, Arcadia is rather like a renaissance picture of paradise, a *foison* of animals and plants lying around in picturesque profusion without any urge to act consequentially or to justify their existence by good works. Far from being an instrument for the repression of sin, the moral order symbolised by these harmless eccentricities is essentially libertarian. But they are not beyond good and evil. The very fact that the eccentricities *are* harmless reveals Auden's stress on the relative character of liberty, that it can only exist in a framework, that the dream of fulfilment is possible only in self-discipline. A price, even a high price, has to be paid for Arcadia. The accent is not on fulfilment, but the highest *possible* fulfilment, which is in turn the fruit of an effort that must be both individual and collective. Intellectually, at least, Arcadia is the very reverse of Eden or the Golden Age: it is the definition of the character required to inhabit the Good Place and not, like Eden or the Good Place, a release from the limitations of character. As in the hellenic Arcadia, peace is the result of government designed to induce every Arcadian to make himself in the full sense self-governing. Arcadia is the home of the mind helped by a gymnastic of external harmonies to an apprehension of harmony within itself. Auden's later poetry is really about the true democracy of individual and spiritual self-government.

This vision is simple enough to provide clear standards of judgement and sufficiently rich and subtle to offer endless opportunities for irony and compassion. It plays an appreciable part in making Auden's later poetry in some ways actually superior to his early writing. The combination of assured standards and of a supple feeling for their inner complexity helps Auden to bring the highly formal poem, of satirical wit, or psychological analysis or simply of technical elaboration (as in the villanelle) to a pitch of ritualistic elegance which is new in his art. The same crystalline dialectic serves the cunning old gnomic in larger poems covering greater doctrinal ground. Perhaps his two most brilliant and important late pieces, 'Under Which Lyre' in the light vein and 'Vespers' in the grave (though far from solemn) one, both of them dealing with the combat of Hermes and Apollo for man's soul, are based on the same dualism. In 'Vespers', Auden rises above his own chosen battlefield to a sense of the necessary interdependence of the two gods, each reminding

> the other (do both, at bottom,
> desire truth?) of that half of their secret which he would
> most like to forget,
>
> forcing us both, for a fraction of a second, to remember our
> victim (but for him I could forget the blood, but for me he
> could forget the innocence)
>
> on whose immolation (call him Abel, Remus, whom you will,
> it is one Sin Offering) arcadias, utopias, our dear old bag
> of a democracy, are alike founded:
>
> For without a cement of blood (it must be human, it must be
> innocent) no secular wall will safely stand.[21]

In this subtle ascent of a ladder of opposites to a higher balance, the key mechanism is the contrast in Auden's outlook between the simplicity of his general scheme and the inner wealth of its insights. The reconciliation with himself on which they are based now allows Auden to respond more accurately to the inner mood of an event than he did in the intellectual hustling of his activist youth. He has a new sense of the specific gravity of an occasion which, in his youth, he would simply have set down in its appropriate circle of heaven or hell. This can even take on a tragic tone, as in the funereal rhythms of 'The Shield of Achilles':

> A crowd of ordinary decent folk
> Watched from without and neither moved nor spoke
> As three pale figures were led forth and bound
> To three posts driven upright in the ground.
>
> The mass and majesty of this world, all
> That carries weight and always weighs the same

> Lay in the hands of others; they were small
> And could not hope for help and no help came:
> What their foes liked to do was done, their shame
> Was all the worst could wish; they lost their pride
> And died as men before their bodies died.[22]

These allowances for a world of pain on either side of the narrow beam of light enhance much of the later poetry. Far from contradicting its dominant note of happiness, they are a crucial part of it. Contentment has no power to renew itself without tension and contrast. It is no accident that in the same volume as 'The Shield of Achilles' one finds 'Lauds', that rarest of poems, the successful lyric of mental peace. In this beautiful poem, Auden does find a symbol for his vision of happiness. It shows once again that when he is situating himself or mankind at some defined spot on the map of the Good Place, or describing its delights, the later Auden is, if anything, better than he ever was.

Despite this, the bulk of Auden's later poetry suffers from an inherent internal contradiction in the very idea of a conscious ritual of irrationality. The ritual is supposed to conjure up the dark gods; but the self-consciousness sucks the blood out of them. The ritual seems willed and, except when it is used as a set of metaphors for the traditionally Audenesque activity of defining a point of view, in the last resort unspontaneous. This can be seen quite dramatically in the changing role of some of Auden's favourite imagery, such as the debris of industry. In the early *Poems*, ironworks, gears, 'equipment rusting in unweeded lanes', 'snatches of tramline running to the wood/An industry already comatose', 'Pylons fallen or subsiding, trailing dead high tension wires', are assimilated not only to failing love but to a natural cycle of death and renewal, 'the last of shunting in the Autumn'. The 'disaster stammered over wires' echoes the geological menace of the 'ice-sheet moving down'. Impregnated with the awe of childhood, their imaginative enormousness permeates whole landscapes. Later on, when one comes to the poems of Auden's mental change of life, in 1939, these images, though less numinous, have the benign authority of the beloved tutors of one's first awareness of the world:

Those beautiful machines that never talked
But let the small boy worship them and learn
All their long names whose hardness made him proud.[23]

The abandoned lead-mines may not loom physically in the
old way, but they do have the aura of memory: they are essential to the poet's sense of his past and present. When, however,
the same images reappear in *The Shield of Achilles*, they have
become a species of cherub:

> In my Eden we have a few beam-engines, saddle-tank loco-
> motives, overshot water wheels and other beautiful pieces of
> obsolete machinery to play with: In his New Jerusalem even
> the chefs will be cucumber-cool machine minders.[24]

This is charming. Yet the very way in which Auden flirts
with his cherubs, his insistence on associating them with
Rossini's music or a meal by Carême, with croquet tourna-
ments and mild dionysiac dreams shows that the 'obsolete
machinery' has shed the last traces of Sacred Awe about which
Auden theorises so eloquently in *The Dyer's Hand*. Ritual, the
stylisation of impulse, should be the lifeline to the dark gods,
the greenwood service to the destructive power of creation.
But what is the symbolic value of Auden's rituals? They are
there because he does love his cherubs; because he is waging
comic war on the Apollonians; and because Jung has convinced him that no man is truly 'individuated' without his
attendant spirits. For all that, the poet's attitude is a patronising
indulgence, as the village elder joins the children in their games
for a few unbending moments. Auden is careful to tell one
Eden is not the real thing. It is a dream paradise 'which your
memory necessarily but falsely conceives of as the ultimately
liberal condition' or 'a magic Eden without clocks'.[25] The
poet's own failure to suspend disbelief not only deprives his
images of literal meaning; it undermines their symbolic one as
well. They are domesticated, tame, perhaps not live at all:
plaster deities. The naming of gods who, unnamed, dominated
Auden's early work has somehow emasculated their powers.
They are a notion of ancestors which it tickles Auden's fancy
to entertain, they are no longer presences haunting his

imagination. They are not even used as emotive ritual, in the way Eliot, Joyce or David Jones have used them. The landscape which was once so numinous has become a suburban rockery of polychrome dwarfs.

In fact, the irrationality of Auden's later poetry is largely doctrinaire. He was at his least allegorical and least fantastic when producing his earlier, more urgent and, for the most part probably more necessary, poetry. Spender's testimony in his autobiography about a visit to Auden in 1948 bears minding:

> I found the manner of Auden's own changes disconcerting. When, after his travels to Germany he returned to England in 1929, he held the doctrine that 'the poet' must not leave his own country. Now, in America, he had published an essay arguing that the modern creative writer must be international, and probably, celibate; and implying that the literary pilgrimage of Henry James to Europe was now reversed, for today the European writer should come to America. Dogmas grew in this way out of Auden's own actions, tastes and prejudices. I can remember a time when he held it against a friend of mine that he liked the novels of Firbank: that he should do so, he said, was 'symptomatic' of some vital defect in his character. Now Firbank had become for him a saintly innocent of literature, somehow mixed up in the theological pattern.[26]

Firbank is just the kind of fantast who suits Auden's later attitude to art. Auden says as early as 'The Letter to Lord Byron', in 1936, that he would like to write 'like Firbank, Potter, Carroll, Lear'.[27] But in the earlier Thirties he disliked Firbank precisely because he did not at that time believe in allegories or in domesticated little gods. He may have written in parables and peddled portents:

> Last night at Hammergill
> A boy was born fanged like a weasel,[28]

but he also poured contempt on 'Graffiti-writers, moss-grown with whimsies,/Loquacious when the watercourse is dry'. However, the last section of *Homage to Clio*, published in 1960, entitled 'Academic Graffiti' is a collection of clerihews, limericks and whimsies. In youth, he was far too much taken up with what he thought the literal truth of the rationalist salvation he was promoting at the time for his poetry to be allegorical or fantastic except in the sense that all poetry is to some extent both. It is only in his later verse when his psychological self-consciousness has become even greater that the allegorist, the fantast, becomes his dominant image of himself as artist. I suspect, from its very exaggeration, that the later Auden's stress on Unreason may well express fear for what his own Reason may be doing to his artistic gift. Fantasy can be an outstandingly clever man's way of bowing to the Unreason his whole career shows he is determined to control but which, if he ever succeeds, he is in danger of suppressing. To stress it so much is a form of compensation. A highly conscious artist like Auden tends almost automatically to correct in theory the weakness he divines in his own practice. In Auden's youth, his imaginative values were at least partly Romantic, but he posed as the objective and detached surgeon. In middle age, his work is almost at an extreme of conscious control, the turbulent elements in his gift at last ordered in a pattern which covers their contradictions, yet he praises ritual and the Old Man's Road. In fact, the rituals and the namings of Sacred Objects remain firmly within the ideological frame: they have all been brought into the New Order. The cunning of Auden's counterfeit unconscious cannot prevent them from mourning the old freedom and *imprévu* of the real one.

Auden tries to be ripe and controlled, witty and grave, an acceptant Prospero, a philosopher at play, who has learnt to savour the minor pleasures of life in a way which accords them their rightful, major importance. Too often, the result is this:

> As Shaw said—Music is the brandy
> Of the damned. It was from the good old grand
> Composers the progressive kind of
> Tyrant learned how to melt the legal mind
> With a visceral A-ha; fill a
> Dwarf's ears with sforzandos and the dwarf will
> Believe he's a giant; the orchestral
> Metaphor bamboozles the most oppressed
> —As a trombone the clerk will bravely
> Go oompah-oompah to his minor grave—
> So that today one recognises
> The Machiavel by the hair in his eyes,
> His conductor's hands.[29]

This overdined and overwined crawl through sententiousness is testimony to a sad loss of impetus. This loss is not due to the convention of speech which, in itself, is willed and perhaps justified. Nor can we blame the formlessness of the poem by traditional standards (in fact it is far from formless: the penultimate syllable of one line rhymes with the last one of the next); this too is plainly deliberate and even careful. In any case, this is not the kind of poetry to be judged by familiar standards of line, stanza, metre or even rhythm. The effective unit is not the stanza but the mental association. The rhythm is not in the music of what is said but in that, unspoken, unheard, made by the patterns of the mental associations themselves. If the mental associations produce a pattern the poem succeeds. If not, it fails. This is an interesting and genuine mode of poetry and, though difficult, there is no reason why it should not succeed. The trouble is that the mental associations do not produce a pattern. For some reason, they obstinately refuse to latch together. Nothing shows this better than comparison with Auden's early poetry. Contrary to appearances, the later manner is in direct line of descent from the poet's early florid manner, which was equally artificial and elaborate, and dependent (whatever the formal stanza) on an inner pattern nearer to surrealist prose than to metrical poetry. This becomes evident if one actually *transproses* the poetry (to borrow Dryden's pun), a proceeding which may be unpardonable in itself, but helps to bring out the underlying structure of the writing.

> Came summer like a flood, did never greediest gardener make blossoms flusher: Sunday meant lakes for many, a browner body beauty from burning: far out in the water two heads discussed the position, out of the reeds like a fowl jumped the undressed German, and Stephen signalled from the sand dunes like a wooden madman 'Destroy this temple'.
>
> (*The Orators*, Ode I)[30]

It was from the good old grand composers the progressive kind of tyrant learned how to melt the legal mind with a visceral A-ha; fill a dwarf's ears with sforzandos and the dwarf will believe he's a giant; the orchestral metaphor bamboozles the most oppressed—as the trombone the clerk will bravely go

oompah-oompah to his minor grave—so that today one recognises the Machiavel by the hair in his eyes, his conductor's
hands.

(*Nones*, 'Music is international')

The difference in energy between the two passages, the first
written around 1930, the other probably in 1947, leaps to ear
and eye. Both are loosely co-ordinated. In fact the one long
sentence of the first is only a quirk of punctuation; it could
easily have been written as five separate sentences. Nevertheless, the whole stanza is clear and purposive and homes straight
to its target—the camp hysteria of Stephen signalling like a
wooden madman from the sand-dunes. This is partly because
the separate clauses are quick and businesslike and lead with
a brisk action to the conclusive last sentence: this makes an
easy and natural vocal line for the reader's inner orator to
voice. But it is also because the images, though individually
so energetic and apparently self-contained, nevertheless form a
picture and converge, as it were spontaneously, on the final
gesture. The stanza, though parts of it are inverted gram-
matically and perhaps over-compressed, seems inwardly
bristling with animal spirits and exhortatory life. Not so the
later passage. The mental units of the pattern are themselves
thoughts rather than visual images—one can assent to them,
but they make no particular impact on ear or eye. They are
allusive rather than arresting. More important still, there are
imaginative gaps between the associations, so that though one
can work out the argument well enough, there are no natural
bridges between the separate impressions. This is a sin which
pattern poetry, so dependent on imaginative leaps, cannot
forgive. This—and not the convention of speech—is why
the poem seems prosy. The formlessness of the verse is a criticism of its lack of imaginative energy, not of the way in which
it has been written.

Very few of the many later poems of this kind—'The
Model', 'In Praise of Limestone', 'Hammerfest' perhaps—
seem to preserve an inner shape and not merely to ramble on.
Auden has failed, in short, to make syllabic verse formal, as
Marianne Moore has done. The decline in his capacity to keep
an imaginative grip on his more elaborate style, which begins

to be evident in the mid-Thirties in poems like 'Oxford', 'Dover' or 'In Memory of Sigmund Freud', invalidates far too much of his later writing. It even makes his informality seem oddly artificial. It is often said that to be conversational is a tone of voice. Let one read the ordinary run of late Auden poems and what one hears is the ripe plum of an elite voice, soaked in civilisation, aping informality: the tone of voice is cultural, not conversational. In fact, a great deal of Auden's later verse, not all of it by any means, but enough to give the tone to the later volumes, verges perilously on cultural chat.

There is an inner contradiction in the very notion of poetry as cultural chat. Poetry is a way of conceiving; two impulses combine and beget a third—a *Gestalt*. Culture is a form of knowing—a record. Poetry has to be re-invented every time, words, as Valéry wanted them, 'so well expressed that they could not possibly have been thought before—a creation of language that is necessarily also a creation of thought'.[31] Culture need only be acquired. *Si jeunesse savait, si vieillesse pouvait*: poetry declines with *pouvoir*, culture with *savoir*. When poetry seems primarily cultural, this is because it has lacked a certain fusing power at source. There is a dutiful air of heaviness about the subtle and accomplished *ars poetica* of Auden's later verse. In fact, as one looks over the whole range of Auden's later verse one begins to suspect that though there should be no limits to the range of poetry, the natural home for cultural talk is the essay, not the poem. It is appropriate that Auden's two volumes of criticism have both been published since *The Age of Anxiety*. *The Enchaféd Flood*, 'The Romantic Iconography of the Sea' (which appeared in 1950) and above all *The Dyer's Hand* (1963), have established him as the most richly original critic of the mid-century. Auden's mythopoeic imagination heightens the allusions of the cultural essay, whereas its suggestion that everything is only a symbol of everything else tends to suck the life out of a poem. Despite the respectable number of beautiful poems Auden has written since the war, *The Dyer's Hand* has claims to being the work which most extends the range of his later vision. It is in any case typical of his latter-day personality as one of the panjandrums of western culture, ambitious in a typically disclamatory way to be 'a minor atlantic Goethe'.[32]

Since he became an American citizen in 1946, Auden has divided his time busily between New York and Europe. He has, with Lionel Trilling and Jacques Barzun, founded two book clubs in America, edited a large number of books and written innumerable reviews. He was professor of poetry at Oxford from 1956 to 1961, was elected a fellow of his old college, Christ Church, in 1962, and in 1968 was lecturing in Canterbury at the University of Kent. He has become the leading librettist in modern opera, playing Hofmannsthal first to Stravinsky in *The Rake's Progress* (1951), then to Hans Werner Henze in *Elegy for Young Lovers* (1961) and *The Barmecides* (1967) as well as writing *Delia* (1952) and making new English versions of the libretti of *The Magic Flute* (1956) and *Don Giovanni* (1961). This has put him in the international musical set as well as the literary one and placed him on the central European as well as Anglo-American circuits. (Auden has always found Germany more congenial than France, presumably because it is a more impulsive culture). From 1946 to 1957 he regularly spent his summers in Italy, on the island of Ischia—which has a lot of local saints. So has Austria; and he transferred his summer residence, in 1958, to a house he bought at Kirchstetten in Lower Austria, which figures prominently in his 1966 volume, *About the House*. Yet, for all his cosmopolitan activity and catholic interests he has, in his attitudes, seemed more and more a caricature of an Edwardian upper-middle-class Englishman of his year of birth. His clerihews, his whimsy, his faintly stiff-upper-lip emphasis on the decencies—

> Even a limerick
> ought to be something a man of
> honour, awaiting death from cancer or a firing squad,
> could read without contempt[33]

—his nonsense rhymes, his daydreams of lawns and rain-gauges, his dislike of ash in teacups or his assumption that a *nurse* will first point out the moon to the infant poet-to-be, have vanishing English privilege written all over them. To emerge as a posthumous Victorian is a curious consummation for the marxist *enfant terrible* of the Thirties and naturalised postwar American. It is a distinguished and well-earned retirement, but a kind of retirement all the same.

*   *   *

One may take two views of this epilogue to Auden's career. One is that no poet, as poet, has a long life and that Auden has simply lost his creative power. The other, which does not deny the assumption of a certain decline, explains it by more specific causes, a shrinkage of the area in which his poetry could be cultivated.

That Auden has less to say is suggested in the crudest and most measurable terms by the reduced quantity of his work. There is no comparison, in sheer bulk, between the fifteen ebullient verse collections and plays of the first twenty years of his career and the four shortish ones, eked out by two remarkable works of literary criticism, of the next twenty. Between *Poems 1928* and *The Age of Anxiety*, Auden (if one includes the choruses and songs of the plays) published not far short of a thousand pages of verse or prose poetry. If one takes the four volumes since *The Age of Anxiety*—*Nones* (published in 1951), *The Shield of Achilles* (1955), *Homage to Clio* (1960) and *About the House* (1965)—he has produced barely 250 pages. Even this is still abundance by the standards of many poets; Baudelaire published little more than 250 pages in a lifetime. By the standards of Auden's almost Victorian prolixity, this is little enough. He has himself pointed out the implication in the endearing epigraph of *Homage to Clio*:

> Bull-roarers cannot keep up the annual rain,
> The water-table of a once green champaign
> Sinks, will keep on sinking: but why complain? Against odds
> Methods of dry farming shall still produce grain.[34]

In a sense, this quatrain belies its own message by the vigour of its metaphor. But poets conscious of drying up—Coleridge in the 'Ode to Dejection' is the classic case—are apt to be at their best on sterility. Auden's later poetry does not, like his earlier, push its way out as if nothing could stop it. Its scope too is reduced; and the style shows signs of failing vitality. The early poems were sharp because they presented the poet's primary reactions to himself, to life and to the world. The later poems are much further away from this primitive inspiration. They are more and more corrections of the primary impulse in which the ash of facts grows thicker and thicker on the fire of wishes. Auden has embraced the world until his style is crushed beneath the weight. Moreover, the process seems to be progressive. The short wartime poems published for the first time in the *Collected Shorter Poems* (1930-44) —which appeared only in 1950— are still preoccupied with Auden's religious problems. The immediate postwar pieces in *Nones* (though like all the later ones essentially personal) are relatively political, or at least civic: titles like 'The Fall of Rome' or 'Memorial for the City' make this in some ways Auden's cold war volume. The angle of vision is still wide. In *The Shield of Achilles*, with its pastoral air, the scope narrows, though form and content are so beautifully matched that this is probably Auden's classic later volume and one of the finest in his whole output. However, by *Homage to Clio* and still more in *About the House*, the shrinkage of interest, or perhaps simply of energy, has become unmistakable. Quality, in these volumes, tends to vary in inverse proportion to the claims of a poem, so that the best pieces are usually found among the neatest and least pretentious. On this view, the neo-Theocritan epilogue to Auden's career is the burnt-out residue of a consumed major art.

Yet such a simple conclusion is not borne out by the quality of the best later poems. They may be different from the earlier ones, riper, less dynamic, but it is impossible to say they are less good. Some poems like 'Vespers', 'Under Which Lyre', 'Woods', 'The Willow-wren and The Stare', 'In Praise of Limestone' and a sizable number of others are as fine as anything Auden has done. But when one looks at the poems which surprise one into immediate assent, or even phrases like

Thousands have lived without love, not one without water,[35]

one finds they usually have a gnomic ring, at least a gnomic framework, as Auden's pieces always had. Some of the good poems are almost purely personal impressions, such as the charming 'Not in Baedeker'. But even many of the poems which are personal impressions, like 'At the Party', are striking because their definitions are diamond-like in their precision. Most of the good poems, when one looks carefully at them, do not so much relive an incident as make a well-defined point. 'Vespers' and 'Under Which Lyre' discuss the antithesis of Hermes and Apollo. 'Woods' explains how

> A culture is no better than its woods.[36]

'An Island Cemetery' praises the bones that are all that's left of men in the end—

> This underlying thing in us
> Which never at any time made a fuss.[37]

The song says of the lover serenading his mistress

> *Did he know what he meant?* said the willow-wren—
> *God only knows*, said the stare.[38]

Even the poems of wit, like 'The Love Feast', or the highly formal poems, the villanelles such as 'Lauds' or 'Nursery Rhyme', seem good as they are by an antithetical brilliance of ironies. In short, again and again, one sees that Auden is at his best when, as in his earlier days, he has a clear purposive point to make. One also sees that many of his poems no longer seem to have a clear point to make; in a word, that the poetry of intellectual digestion is far rarer than it was. This, surely, is a clue to the limitations of Auden's later work.

The fact is that the reconciliation with himself recorded in the wartime poems raised a major problem for the poet. During the fifteen years of Auden's search for peace of mind, his verse, with all its faults, conveyed a sense of rapid and continual discovery. Whatever the drawbacks of such mutability might be, it was hard to deny the driving force behind it, the energy of the quest for the Good Place. But once the poet had accepted his personal situation, the poetry of mobility ceased to be relevant. Verse of the old kind, of images organised round a clear thematic structure—a one-night stop on a mental journey —would begin to appear repetitive, definitions within definitions settled in their outlines long ago. They could no longer have their former urgency. Auden could no longer rely on his old methods and his old subject-matter. This, no doubt, is why his poems of definition, though they have continued to appear, are so much reduced in quantity and in scope.

Faced with this dilemma, the poet could either choose silence or seek an alternative field for his imagination. Silence certainly crossed his mind: Christianity pleaded for it. But, although Prospero allegedly no longer needs Ariel's freedom; although Auden has conceived that one should write so well one would no longer want to; although he now believes that 'a Christian ought to write in prose';[39] he has nevertheless steadily gone on writing poetry: 'Make me chaste, Lord, but not yet.'[40] That left the other course, to find an alternative field of operations. Auden has sought this in a poetry celebrating the subtle laws of the good life. Unfortunately, it must be admitted that, by the standards of his own talent, Auden lacks something as a celebrant. He has taught himself to hold a sacramental view, but he does not display a sacramental quality of the imagination. This is not exactly surprising, for the greedy universalist who made his earlier work what it was now stands in the way of sacrament. His habit is to possess, not to belong, to situate rather than to dedicate himself, to define rather than to praise. The very desire to know and control which has carried him so far, bars the way to success on the same scale in the new role. In the very act of offering up praises, Auden remains obstinately the eternal critic. His intelligence is rarely, if ever, fused into the invocation, its self-conscious spirit breaking up the concentration on the service. Auden has been trapped in an impasse. He can no longer pursue a mobile art, where his powers are displayed to their best effect. Compared with the *Sturm and Drang* of the Thirties the evolution of his later poetry seems minimal; that it can be dealt with under a single heading is evidence enough of that. But when it comes to static poetry, Auden is a man divided against himself. His sacramental poetry instead of being ritualistic becomes too often flabby for having acquired 'the blander motions of the approved state'.[41] Why a poet displays a burst of talent is ultimately a mystery; and so is the question of why his gift seems to fade. But, on the evidence, it is at least as plausible to argue that Auden's subject has failed him as that his creative fire has gone. Auden is neither a

Hermetic nor an Apollonian, he is Faust; and Faust had succeeded all too well by the end of the war. He had fulfilled his passion to possess the world to the point where he had largely worked himself out of his vocation.

Epilogue

FORWARD FROM ROMANTICISM

ONE of the dominant characteristics of Auden's poetry is the broad range of its development. This power of growth has usually been discounted because it has been seen as a predominantly intellectual and ideological affair with shallow roots. There has been a tendency to emphasise the constants, especially the constant limitations, in his art. This reaction was perhaps natural after Auden's over-exposure, and to some extent false exposure, in the nineteen-thirties. Nevertheless, the poetry rejects such simplifications. The gap between his youthful Norse Saga writing and his late ironically cultural one is wide by any standards. There are striking contrasts between the sculptural verse of his early period of self-identification when he was carving out a public and artistic personality for himself; the poetry of the early Thirties when he was relying on the millennium for peace of mind; and the complex antithetical manner of the later years where wish and reality, assertion and acceptance, are constantly juxtaposed, contrasted and occasionally fused. The very shrinkage in his output since he became reconciled to himself is evidence of how much the process of development has contributed to his creative *élan vital*, his poetic necessity. The same point is urged in the opposite way by the evidence that, like most poets, Auden tends to be at his best when the major experiences of his life mobilise his talents. On the whole, the early *Poems*, the lyrics of the Thirties and 'The Sea and the Mirror' are more successful than, say, *The Orators*, that 'fair notion fatally injured' or *The Age of Anxiety* and most of the later poetry.[1] What are the *Poems*, the lyrics of the Thirties and 'The Sea and the Mirror' if not poetic definitions of crucial stages in their creator's career? The *Poems* mark the phase when Auden is piecing together the main features of his *Weltanschauung* and situating himself in relation to them. This is the adolescent discovery of self, when the young man is becoming conscious of his ambitions as artist and citizen and formulating a creed of salvation through consciousness. A few years later, in the lyrics of the Thirties, this view of the world and of the self is brought up sharp against the politics, as it were, of Auden's own emotional life. His dream of relationships fulfilled by reason is confronted in these lyrics with a painful and exactly contrary reality—his personal exploration of non-involvement and non-fulfilment. Mainly through the insufficiencies of erotic love, they chart the discovery of loneliness in intimate contact with others. They are elegies of the consciousness which isolates a man from his fellows. When, finally, after the crisis to which this leads, Auden accepts his isolation and learns to live with it, the result is 'The Sea and the Mirror' which, in many ways sums up his emotional life. It absorbs the suffering of isolation in a larger harmony. In short, Auden's development has been a constant dialectic between his awareness of isolation and the need of contact with others which no human being can forego. His poetry is the record of a life spent struggling to bring these two opposing realities into some kind of balance so that the poet can feel more or less at ease with himself. His creative imagination is raised by the crucial moments in this struggle to its most sustained levels of performance; and when the struggle ceases, so does the larger incentive to his writing. The strength Auden's abundant talent has acquired from this painful, constant and consistent dialogue between the isolated self and the human condition at large elevates his poetry, to my mind, to the level of a major art. As Gerhard Masur has written of another anxious and invert liberal, Gide, 'he is a writer whose chief concerns [are] moral problems, not a moralist who [tries] to express his ideas through the medium of literature'.[2]

Auden's impasse, for such it has been, also makes him a touchstone of the great changes the twentieth century has operated in its nineteenth-century Romantic inheritance. It is sometimes argued against Auden, as if it were a sign of modishness, that his intellectual development was typical of many of his generation. This could on the contrary be seen as a sign of the necessity of his art. *Some* of Auden's curious impersonality at least must be due to the way in which modern self-consciousness divides the personality. It contrasts sharply with the Romantics' attempt to sidestep the discomforts of admitting this by stressing immanent inspiration. The old strategy led, in many cases, to a rather mindless assertion of unity with Nature which, in retrospect, only underlines the opposite. Now, in the dissociated world of contemporary emotional logic where

> every time some dear flesh disappears
> What is real is the arriving grief

(this again has been held against Auden whereas it merely states a tragic opposition), any commitment necessarily carries with it its own critical dissolvent.[3] It is impossible to be 'rapt' (that is, unselfconscious) or 'sincere' (that is, not self-seeking) in anything, since the critic goes along with every act re-interpreting it in terms of self. Should one try to meet the critic by committing oneself not to a person but a principle, like Love, he moves with one on to the far side of the fresh commit-ment, and from his new vantage point casts an eye as glassy as it ever was. It is like sitting in a hall of mirrors or one of those *art nouveau* restaurants in Paris where the diners' faces are multiplied to infinity in mutually reflecting mirrors. This kind of self-consciousness emphasises the gap of detachment to the point where the only reality defying scepticism is the self that starts it all. No wonder that

> far from your being led by [the artist] to contrition and sur-render, the regarding of your defects in his mirror, your dialogue, using his words, with yourself about yourself, becomes the one activity which never, like devouring or collecting or spending, lets you down, the one game which can be guaran-teed, whatever the company, to catch on. . . .[4]

Auden implies in 'The Sea and the Mirror' that he has escaped from this condition, as the existentialist does, by leaping from the logic of doubt to the commitment of faith. Yet, in some ways the most striking examples of detachment are provided pre-cisely by Auden's later poetry. Although the love of that 'Wholly Other Life', which is one's only chance of release from self-love, requires, by definition, literal faith (attachment with minimal mental reservations), all Auden's writing gives the impression of a series of notes towards a Supreme Fiction. As the poet himself would probably be the first to admit, his own language is soaked in 'duality'—that is, the language of science which collates, relates and analyses, the language of observer and observed, of mind the conqueror and conquered fact. In 'The Sea and the Mirror', Ferdinand, serenading Miranda in the most orthodox (and unloverlike) existentialist terms as 'Dear Other at all times'—that is, dear release from my self-regard—is nevertheless looking for

The Right Required Time, The Real Right Place, O Light.

This is not at all the language of the faithful, with that literal eye-on-the-object look Auden so reveres, but the 'Heaven of the Really General Case', where 'Life turns into Light', which he regards, only a few pages further on, in Caliban's speech, as the fools' paradise of the high-minded self-regarder.[5] This sort of thing gives a special significance to the fact that in Auden the case for *agape*, the outward-going and ideally self-forgetting Christian love which was once only a Greek dialectical shadow of the Judaic Passion, now overshadows the passion instead. The Passion, on these terms, becomes misted over with ambiguities, diluted with reservations.

> Since the analogies are rot
> Our senses based belief upon,
> We have no means of learning what
>   Is really going on,
>
> And must put up with having learned
> All proofs or disproofs that we tender
> Of His existence are returned
>   Unopened to the sender.
>
> Now, did He really break the seal
> And rise again? We dare not say;
> But conscious unbelievers feel
>   Quite sure of Judgement Day.
>
> Meanwhile, a silence on the cross,
> As dead as we shall ever be,
> Speaks of some total gain or loss. . . .[6]

Now the analogies 'our senses based belief upon' are acknowledged 'rot', there is no basis on which to affirm anything of

God. As *pater familias* speaking to an adoring people through the lawgiver Moses or the crucified Christ, God made sense. But what is a notion of 'some total gain or loss'? The intuition of Judgement Day (based on the *non sequitur* that because most people instinctively fear that misdirected ambition leads to retribution they must also believe in divinity rather than process) may itself be only one of the sensual analogies taken from family relationships with the Deity now lost. Auden criticises post-Renaissance culture for destroying the older 'unity':

> The Middle Ages believed that an ultimate and intelligible unity embraced all the diversity of experience . . . Faith in this unity, or rather faith in its intelligibility, was shattered in the sixteenth century . . . Luther denied any intelligible relation between Faith and Works, Macchiavelli any intelligible relation between public and private morality and Descartes any intelligible relation between Matter and Mind. . . . The dualism inaugurated by Luther, Macchiavelli and Descartes has brought us to the end of our tether and we know that either we must discover a unity which can repair the fissures that separate the individual from society, feeling from intellect, and conscience from both, or we shall surely die by spiritual despair and physical annihilation.[7]

Those are urgent, even desperate, words. But what 'intelligible relationship' does Auden offer between God and the contemporary knowledge of the nature of the universe? A world which long believed in miracles and whose cosmology (until 1859) failed to bridge the gaps between man with a soul and the animals without, or (until very recently indeed) between the plants with life and the minerals without, could regard the Passion, the arbitrary irruption of the Deity among His works, as one more quasi-natural event. The psychology was that of Auden's own note to 'New Year Letter': 'Miracles are not supernatural interferences with natural laws, for truth cannot be divided against itself. . . . Miracles are events which occur contrary to our prediction. . . . The special value of miracles is that they reveal the imperfection of our knowledge and stimulate us to search further.'[8] The miracle itself, then, was in some sense normal, that is, within the accepted range of expectations.

But now that the geologists and Darwin, the physicists and biochemists, have filled in so many conceptually missing links in the chain of being from man to the gases of outer space, or at least suggested a likely continuum of creation, the Incarnation has to be Absurd, inexplicable. The resurrection no longer demands assent of pragmatically doubting Thomases who want to lay a finger on the event, it strains the belief of people brought up by all they regard as truth to think that, however mysterious life's ultimate energy may be, there is nothing on which hands could ever be laid. Auden himself is not ready to lay Pascalian bets within the meaning of the Acts. Short of such a commitment, he is left with a universe centred on the Law.

> It is a purely human illusion to imagine that the laws of the spiritual life are, like our legislation, imposed laws which we can break. We may defy them, either by accident, i.e., out of ignorance, or by choice, but we can no more break them than we can break the laws of human physiology by getting drunk.[9]

Auden always writes impressively about the law, and nowhere more impressively than in this imposing maxim. But, though this view is plain Anglican orthodoxy, it requires more than a gloss on Christian symbolism to regard the law as a mistaken identity for God. Spiritually profound though it may be, the remark conveys little in terms of faith. It stops short inside the world of science and the language of science. For all Auden's revulsion from the psychological inadequacies of militant rationalism, one sees in it, as always in his verse, the deeper rationalist 'dualism' that he himself saw in renaissance mercantile man:

> One notices, if one will trust one's eyes,
> The shadow cast by language upon truth:
> He saw his role as father to an earth
> Whose speechless, separate, and ambiguous things
> Married at his decision; he was there
> To show a lucid passion for their fate.[10]

Auden affirms unity in the old style: each of us should seek to *know* as the religious man or the lover hopes to do, not as Faust the voyeur or the pseudo-detached observer. But his poetry speaks of duality in the new style. The conflict between the two takes a grotesque form in a fancy of which Auden seems rather fond, since he has used it more than once: 'One can conceive of Heaven having a Telephone Directory, but it would have to be gigantic, for it would include the Proper Name and address of every electron in the Universe.'[11] The obvious continuity of diction with Auden's secular past, the reticence of his terms when confronted by the key concepts of Christianity, his acceptance of the categories of science and its jargon of laws and forces independent of, or abstracted from, the human will, suggest that even when he is paying homage to the unity of faith, science or duality irradiates his every phrase.

In the circumstances, it is not surprising that very different people who have come near Auden, especially in later years, have noted a strange arbitrariness in his creeds. Auden worked in 1947 with Stravinsky on the libretto for *The Rake's Progress* and Stravinsky was deeply impressed. Nevertheless,

> I was puzzled at first by what I took to be contradictions in his personality. He would sail on steady rudders of reason and logic, yet profess to curious, if not superstitious beliefs—in graphology, for instance . . . , in astrology, in the telepathic power of cats, in black magic (as it is described in Charles Williams's novels), in categories of temperament . . . , in pre-ordination, in fate.[12]

Stephen Spender, who knows Auden well, though he is not by temperament fully in sympathy with him, marvels at his

> disconcerting facility in allowing his intellect to lead him where it will. . . . When, early in 1950, Auden together with other intellectuals answered a questionnaire about his religious beliefs, he alone of all those who answered seemed to experience no difficulty in accepting the strictest dogmas of the Christian faith. Reading his answers, I had the impression that he could so easily believe things that are almost incredible to many people because the Christian faith was to him the premise of a hypothesis explaining human behaviour—just as, at another time, Freud's theories had been.[13]

Logically, no doubt, this is incompatible with Auden's doubts, already quoted, about the Passion, but it confirms the rather narrowly intellectual quality of his 'commitment'. The final impression is that for all Auden's claims, he is a great deal nearer than he would like to be to the condition of the high-minded whom he sees hesitating on the brink of the great Leap:

> Religion and culture seem to be represented by a catholic belief that something is lacking which must be found, but as to what that something is, the keys of heaven, the missing heir, genius, the smells of childhood, or a sense of humour, why it is lacking, whether it has been deliberately stolen, or accidentally lost or just hidden for a lark, and who is responsible, our ancestors, ourselves, the social structure, or mysterious wicked powers, there are as many faiths as there are searchers, and clues can be found behind every clock, under every stone, and in every hollow tree to support all of them.[14]

Eden is a symbol of the rich life which cannot be apprehended without religious standards, but in itself is only magic. Religious belief cannot be expressed in any literal or communicable terms: Auden specifically states that it is not a subject for art. Nor like the religion of Thomas à Becket in *Murder in the Cathedral* nor Roquentin's discovery, in *La Nausée*, of the Absurd, the monstrous all-inflating life of the tree root under the bench where he sits, does it refer to the absolute of one's own emotion. In Auden, there is always a need to *prove*. It is only natural, then, that his images do not always convince one, for one fails to detect in them the still point where they are *totally* self-evident to the poet himself. If anything, they convince one rather less in the last phase, when he has supposedly reached solid and balanced convictions than they did in the Thirties when, whatever his possible doubts about Love or the millennium, Auden gave the impression of believing quite literally in the saving powers of consciousness. Now, although Auden calls for 'absolute religious sanctions', his poetry itself fails to proffer these ultimate terms of reference. There is a relativism built into it which marks it off from the work of other converts.

He is equally hard to pigeon-hole in the other classic category to which his conversion points, that of the lost leader. Superficially, Auden's political history might seem an almost classic case of the Romantic change of life: radical and secular in youth, he has become conservative and religious in middle age. At first sight, nothing could be more familiar. Yet, on further inspection, it becomes apparent that Auden wears his conformity with a marked difference. Wordsworth embracing the Anglican establishment and Claudel the Vatican, like many others, have all accepted authority because they assumed that sanctions had to be imposed. Their pessimism about human nature, sometimes though not always, nor even usually, rooted in their own early experience as liberals, led them to the conviction that discipline was needed to check the self-destructive folly of the erring flock. Auden's way is different, not that of authority but of individual enlightenment. Though convinced, like any Christian, that civilisation cannot survive without the 'absolute' sanctions already mentioned, he remains very cagey about any attempt to impose them. Society, that is the individuals who compose it, must become convinced of the need of such sanctions for themselves. Auden's conversion differs from the literary conversions of the past two centuries because he remains a democrat. All his statements show he places himself at the end of the liberal genealogical tree even though he is filled with dismay by more frangible branches of his spiritual family. In the conclusion to *The Enchaféd Flood*, he says of the Romantics:

> Our temptations are not theirs. We are less likely to be tempted by solitude into Promethean pride: we are far more likely to become cowards in the face of the tyrant who would compel us to lie in the service of the False City. It is not madness we need to flee but prostitution.[15]

In much the same spirit, he also writes, in the introduction to his selection of the works of Sydney Smith:

> unattractive and shallow as one may feel so many liberals to be, how rarely on any concrete social issue does one find the liberal position the wrong one. Again, how often, alas, do those very philosophers and writers who have most astounded us by their profound insights into the human heart and human experience, dismay us by the folly and worse of their judgements on the issues of everyday life.[16]

In Auden's later poetry, the young men saunter down the cliff path, 'at times arm in arm, but never, thank God, in step'.[17] However little they have in common, Auden's poet and peasant agree in their hearty suspicion of all bureaucrats.[18] The outstanding feature of *agape*, the Christian love on which Auden harps so much, is free will, the individual's responsibility for readjusting his outward-going love to ever new moments and situations. In short, Auden insists on the one hand that self-criticism and self-control are essential and on the other that the individual remains the yardstick. He offers a synthesis to delight Hegelians, of the revolutionary and conservative poles of nineteenth-century tensions—of democratic aspirations on the one hand and the need for standards on the other. The fact is that Auden, early and late, has always been at heart a bohemian anarchist. He was a radical political anarchist in youth, now he is a conservative religious anarchist. In practice, today, this makes him very much a conservative, since it commits him to resist revolutions and exalt the evolutionary process (taking the risk of its slowing to a stop in many places). In terms of feeling, it nevertheless puts him nearer the students who suddenly swept away a hundred years of Marx in anarchist revolt in 1968 than to their elders who thought that since they were incoherent they made no sense. Much though Auden's conversion may resemble those of the recent past, it is not *ancien régime* so much as 'post-industrial'.

Since Auden is neither a religious poet nor a lost leader in the familiar sense, some people have doubted that his conversion adds up to much and have treated it as an intellectual affair, almost a mental exercise. I do not believe the poetry bears this out. It is plain that it does record a genuine crisis; only the upheaval has been fitted out with a doctrine rather than allowed to produce a parable of its own. When one looks at the emotional content of 'The Sea and the Mirror', one finds a number of recognisable experiences: the discovery that total fulfilment of oneself on ever 'steeper stormier heights' is quite impossible and leads to emotional breakdown; the acceptance of the limitations of the self, that what one is, is all one has; from which follows at first a tentative and then grateful investment in relationships with other people or things (like nature)—in short, a reconciliation with self and by extension with others. This coming to terms with one's own life is undoubtedly a conversion of sorts. The Romantic afflatus, or at least hope vested in infinite expansion, leads to total alienation; there is a breakdown; and out of the breakdown comes a new peace in living with what is rather than what would be. This is traditionally associated with religious conversion to a specific faith and Auden follows the traditional route in asserting that a man can only be redeemed from narcissism by the love of an external and unpossessible God. Yet, doctrines apart, one finds exactly the same experience in the early masterpiece of the atheist Sartre, *La Nausée*.

La Nausée, too, in some ways exactly parallels the traditional path of conversion. In *La Nausée*, the nausea, or nervous depression itself, would, in Bunyan's day, have been called the Dark Night. Roquentin's overwhelming experience of the tumescence of life in the tree-root ('I was the root of the chestnut tree') would have been seen as the Revelation. His conviction of its power, its daemon, though Sartre calls it existentially the Absurd, would have been his Faith. The acceptance of solitude which Roquentin finally reaches would have been his Joy. Roquentin even has his kind of Salvation, heard behind the recurring jazz tune to which he listens as he lunches by himself in the café: *'sans jamais l'approcher, une petite mélodie s'est mise à danser, à chanter: "C'est comme moi qu'il faut être: il faut souffrir en mesure"*. . . . *une espèce de joie'*.[19] Nothing is missing from the traditional pattern. There is the Holy Innocent, the *Autodidacte*, deprived of his vision by his ignorance (this is the one modern touch); the Pharisees, the hated *'salauds'*, the successful *bourgeois*; the false Eden, the hope of 'perfect moments', typified by a former mistress, which has to be sloughed off; the temptation of the flesh taken on the side with the nice proprietress of the café (who needs a man a night); and above all, original sin, *'le péché d'exister'*, the sin in effect of being born at all. Nothing is missing, except the central turning point of the whole experience which is reduced to a powerful emotional moment dependent on the psychological evolution of the individual, not on faith or revelation of the deity. In *La Nausée*, the period of alienation, or rather of nervous breakdown, reaches an extreme of desertion and aimlessness where the artist has only two choices: either to accept the extinction of the personality, or else to reassert it on a much narrower but emotionally more convincing basis. The issue is quite simply a spiritual to-be-or-not-to-be and Sartre's anti-hero, Roquentin, reaches a moment where from the very failure to commit suicide, his need *to be* has to reassert itself at a level below intellectual conviction. Sitting gloomily on a bench in a municipal park, Roquentin suddenly becomes aware of the mammoth, almost obscenely tumescent, life-force of the great root of the chestnut tree passing between his feet. The awareness is so intense and concentrated that it becomes a conviction, a revelation in itself. It is not a revelation of deity—or only in a special sense—but it *is* vested in something both inside and outside, because rooted in but also reaching beyond, the ego of Roquentin himself. It is an external point of reference, even if self-created, to which his convalescing spirit can attach itself. Though the awareness seems sick and even repulsive at the time—neither beautiful nor consoling nor, certainly, 'happy' —nevertheless it does begin to mend the broken umbilical cord between Roquentin and all the life around him; it creates a kind of relationship, an attachment, and brings relief at last from the narcissistic trance of meaninglessness even though he remains alone. The period of alienation is over, though it is not replaced by the traditional religious 'joy'. There is simply a form of rededication to living, without enthusiasm, but accep-tant, even 'committed' and with a hard core of respect verging, but only verging, on gratitude, for being alive. So of the jazz tune: '*derrière ces sons qui, de jour en jour, se décomposent, s'écaillent et glissent vers la mort, la mélodie reste la même, jeune et ferme, comme un témoin sans pitié.*'[20] This is religion in a way, but natural religion, consecrating a perfectly conscious psychological process and extending it as a philosophy of relationships, of 'dialogue'. To put it at its simplest, this implies the discovery of reverence for life rather than self, that is, for life manifested in others as well as in self. Though Auden argues, like a good apologist, that such natural piety requires faith in the Christian God, the discovery of it is dissociated in Sartre from Christian beliefs (if not emo-tions: his background is Protestant, an important fact in the French context). Even in Auden, it appears to have *preceded* his reconversion to Anglicanism, which thus becomes an extension of the experience rather than an integral part of it.

There is literary evidence of this. It is revealing that 'The Sea and the Mirror' contains only lyrics about what it feels like to be reconciled after conversion and a harangue as to why the conversion was necessary. There is no artistic expression of the act of conversion itself. This is quite unlike *La Nausée* which is shaped from start to finish by the great event and moves, in the classically French way, hardly a step to left or right (though two great set pieces, *la cérémonie des chapeaux* in the main streets of Le Havre on Sunday mornings and the wet afternoon in the municipal art gallery are to some degree self-contained satires). To that extent, Sartre, in *La Nausée*, seems artistically more solidly anchored in his experience than Auden, both in language and in structure. There is a clear relationship between the nature of Sartre's awareness of the event and the conclusions he draws from it, so that his language is full, simple, strong and specific. Much the same is true of the structure of the parable. In Auden's case, the relationship is not so clear, so that the shape of 'The Sea and the Mirror' is looser and the exact weight of the language more difficult to determine. Though both are major works, *La Nausée* is more closely attached to its theme and so more powerful than 'The Sea and the Mirror'. Nevertheless, both express the same experience of the ego broken by its own demands upon itself and the discovery, in the broken shell, of an idea of the sanctity of life not simply confined to the all-demanding self. One could argue that this is simply another way of saying that both Sartre and Auden are existentialists, one as an innovator, the other as a borrower. This, though, puts a much too narrowly intellectual gloss upon the matter. The truth seems to be that the experience of both is, in a literary and a biographical sense, a reaction to, and in some ways a growth out of, the Romantic culture of the past two hundred years. In many ways, the most interesting question about Auden is his complex relationship with that culture to which the lyrist in him and the man isolated in self both obviously belong, while the objective and self-deprecatory classicist just as clearly does not.

*　　*　　*

Romanticism, which has too often been analysed in aesthetic terms, in fact expressed a sensibility with roots deep in great social and intellectual changes. Romanticism was the first cultural movement marked by the surfacing of the previously submerged nine-tenths of society, the 'subjects' of agricultural civilisation formerly tied to the narrow horizons of the soil, the village and the 'great house'. It was also the first cultural movement launched out of a context of incipient atheism and a secularised sense of man's place in the process of the universe. The great cultural effect of the explosion of the agricultural nature-dominated civilisation into the technical man-made one has been to make men aware of their importance in society at the same time as their lack of importance in the universe. This paradox conduces to the characteristic 'materialism' of the past two centuries, which is not quite the utilitarian affair it seems. As E. F. Schumacher has written

> the essence of materialism is not its concern with material wants, but the total absence of any idea of Limit or Measure. The materialist's idea of progress is an idea of *progress without limits*.[21]

Limitlessness is the hallmark of Romantic aspirations.

At the social and political level, this limitlessness has been associated with a heady sense of liberation from the old personal allegiance of the subject to his social superiors, to the hierarchy of family, church and state, and beyond them to the tyranny of natural scarcity. The Romantic movement has above all brought an immense enrichment of hope and interests, a sense of personal and intellectual expansion. For the first time the individual has dared to be self-aware as an individual: he is no longer an addition of a soul in the religious sphere on Sundays and feast-days and of an economic and social function, often at the lowest level, at all other times. From Hobbes to Chamfort, European literature and art thought in moral theorems which took all men as mathematically equal. The great achievement of the Romantic period was to begin to regard men as infinitely various. The very fact of seeing the individual as of interest outside society, as a prime mover in his own right and not as the most valuable property of the Prince, gives the artist vast new areas to explore. One is the unending subject of the individual himself: the cult of Byron symbolises the fascinating obsession with oneself which has dominated Romanticism and led to real advances in consciousness and values. That is not all. Once the individual and society are separated, society too becomes an entity. It is not just a collection of individuals. It has collective characteristics and ways of behaving of its own. It is more, and sometimes arguably less, than the sum of the individuals who compose it. The sense of society as an organism, alive almost like a human being, seizes hold of history, literature and the arts and gives the essential impulse to the growth of sociology. Last but not least, once the individual and society have been identified each in their own spheres, and not as a seamless continuum, one becomes aware of the relation of the individual, or rather each individual, to society: this, summing up and binding all the new preoccupations in a new approach, no doubt explains why the long-despised novel suddenly, in the Romantic period, became the dominant literary form. All this was immensely enriching: nothing less than the birth-pangs of a new, universal civilisation freed from restraints of poverty and famine. Yet one sees the limitations as well as the immense force of this sudden self-discovery in the leading literary figures themselves. Compared to their eighteenth-century predecessors, men like Balzac, Hugo or Dickens are astonishing for their encyclopaedic gusto, their vulgar self-dramatisation and their amateurish efforts at universality. They seem to have unbounded ambition and no genuine knowledge of the world: they are the *nouveaux riches* of literature. No doubt dolphins of genius, first poking their snouts above the waters to look at vast new horizons would be afflicted with similar excesses of confidence and egotism and would overgeneralise their competence in the same way. Here they were, discovering for the first time vast new landscapes offered them by culture, whereas their own personal experience had been extremely limited. All these men were, after all, products of the *petite bourgeoisie*; and the characteristics they displayed can be sensed in the outlook of the age, even in politics. When the *petit bourgeois* Rousseau told all the other *petits bourgeois* that the trouble was They, not We, he stilled self-criticism and opened the dykes to the moral infantilism of the citizen. The infantile, or at best adolescent, hope of the Millennium-without-self-criticism is at the heart of the politics of the nineteenth and early twentieth centuries. Popular good conscience is the one constant behind such diverse movements as revolutionary socialism, *fin-de-siècle* militaristic nationalism, Fascism, even Mariolatry. The conservatives, with some inkling of this, fought for more realistic values, but were deservedly discredited because they were, above all, fighting for their privileges inherited from the old civilisation and as a result in their conceptions, at least in the continental countries, static and authoritarian. Conservatives were in office everywhere most of the time, but ideologically they were constantly on the defensive. The revolution of rising expectations, and their own shortcomings, were too much for the heirs of the eighteenth century. For the previous two centuries or more, there had been cause, in one or other of the leading areas of Europe, to appeal from privilege to the increasingly radical and scientific reason which treats men as equals and, on the other side, socially rooted interests to be defended tooth and nail against the constant encroachments of New Men. Now, as change accelerated in the nineteenth century into the industrial revolution, it seemed that the intellectual appetite, the creative powers, of Europe, had gathered momentum on a diet of opposition continually renewed against *anciens régimes* of effete privilege and power. Romanticism carried the sense of emancipation to a paroxysm. The new civilisation, emerging from the chrysalis, began to worship its own sudden ability to fly. No wonder science, equality, truth, freedom, the good life and the future all seemed wedded to one another for ever and ever, amen.

The political and social forces behind this expansionism were matched by the inner dynamic of an outlook increasingly divorced from the intellectual beliefs, but not the emotional attitudes, of the old religion. All the major Romantics tried to fill the emotional gap left by the weakening of faith, and some to rejuvenate the faith itself, by asserting Man's unity with Nature. The purpose which holds together the bewildering variety of intellectual and aesthetic postures of Romanticism is the belief that by soulfulness or, in the later and more extreme stages, by a systematic *dérèglement* of the senses, it might be possible to achieve oneness with the Universal Spirit. As Balzac wrote of the French Romantic school: '*Celle-ci est Divine en ce sens qu'elle tend à s'élever par le sentiment vers l'âme même de la Création.*'[22]

This attitude, baptised 'spilt religion' by T. E. Hulme, is true of Wordsworth's nature worship, of Shelley's panting neo-Platonism or of Hugo's megalomaniac *têtes-à-têtes* with the Almighty over the shadowy traffic of the abyss. It is equally true, later, of Rimbaud's volcanic anarchy, of Dostoievski's nihilists and of the would-be automatic writing of the Surrealists. This search for unity with the universe was a transposition of the attitudes inherited from more literal forms of religion: it affirmed the old family relationship with God the *pater familias*, however vague and depersonalised the God himself had become. But, plainly, the abstract Romantic God could no longer manifest himself in the explicit, externalised way of the baroque God who topped the vertical chain of being rather as the monarch of Divine Right topped the social and political pyramid. The Romantic God is no father like the authoritarian God of Laud or Bossuet. He can only be apprehended as an immanent spirit working through the artist himself; and the artist hopes, by breaking up his own personality, to enter into purer and purer —and closer and closer—intimacy with Him. The consequence, with time, was that the individual through whom the immanence was manifested became the only earnest of the spirit blowing through him. Shelley *was* Shelley's West Wind. The artist's self-projection and the immanent godhead became identified. By an inner logic of the emotions, spiritual egotism became the single most important element in the Romantics' unconscious, and by the *fin-de-siècle* conscious, code. It influenced their ideal of the soul, seen as a kind of infinity coequal with the Universe and God; of solitude in Nature as the unique passport to the universal spirit; of freedom which put one in touch with Nature; of innocence which was the mark of this intimacy; of society which should aim at a saintly congregation of solitudes; and of love, which incarnated heaven at first chastely in Woman and later frankly in the orgasm (no mere body can be effective spirit). At first this was identified with the general progress of mankind; but the loss of faith in progress, which afflicted many Romantics in the second half of the nineteenth century, did not slow up the basic impetus. The Voyage, the image of perpetual extension towards godhead, came to be pursued for its own sake. When even this fails him, Baudelaire can only sail beyond sense and sensibility into death:

> *O Mort, vieux capitaine, il est temps! levons l'ancre!*
> *Ce pays nous ennuie, ô Mort! Appareillons!* . . .
>
> *Nous voulons, tant ce feu nous brûle le cerveau,*
> *Plonger au fond du gouffre, Enfer ou Ciel, qu'importe?*
> *Au fond de l'Inconnu pour trouver du* nouveau![23]

Passion, movement, even suicide, become ends in themselves, for they alone put one in touch with the universal spirit. The final logic of this worship is total formlessness, deliberate indefinition, dissolving chaos. Even today, its aftermath still gives a kind of holy status to hippies and drug addicts. Significantly, except in Rimbaud, where communion turns to brutal assault upon the laws of nature without doctrinal disguises, it is precisely the belief in 'oneness' which now seems the most old-fashioned, even embarrassing and jejune side of Romantic art. It spoils the conclusion of a great and calm poem like 'Tintern Abbey' just as, at the other end of the Romantic period, it flaws the hymns of Yeats, in his Fifth Symphony period, during the nineteen-twenties, when he seemed to think he could trumpet-blast his way into eternity.

No wonder Romanticism has been primarily an orgasmic culture obsessed with the climax-that-passeth-understanding followed by an eternal post-coital peace: for some, the achievement of wealth which would wipe out all conflicts between men; for others, the revolution instituting the anarchist Eden; for many, sex, releasing the ego for communion with the universal spirit; for those with the hope of talent, the achievements of genius followed by fame defying time. Today, the new left's ideal of 'participation' as described by Edward Shils is on the same pattern of a constantly expanding universe:

> 'Participation' is a situation in which the individual's desires are fully realised in the complete self-determination of the individual and which is simultaneously the complete self-determination of each institution and of society as a whole. In the good community, the common will harmonises individual wills . . . Participation is the transformation of expanding sentiments and desires into reality in a community in which

all members realise their sentiments simultaneously. Anything less is repressive.[24]

These are almost the terms in which the high priests of *laisser-faire* spoke of competition and free trade in the early nineteenth century or Ranke of the balance of power:

> The definite and positive predominance of a single state would encompass the downfall of all the rest. The amalgamation of all, on the other hand, would destroy the substance of the individual state. True harmony will emerge if each nation pursues in isolation the cultivation of its own pure fulfilment.[25]

The results of each nation pursuing 'in isolation the cultivation of its own pure fulfilment' have been demonstrated rather crudely in the early twentieth century. The results of each individual doing so are not so easy to demonstrate, yet the evidence of frustration has been steadily mounting.

The sense of being 'manipulated', voiced by the New Left, is one sign. It is rooted in the existence of a vast middle-class far from the constraints of poverty and power. Its very *mass* tends to hem one in. The division of labour which has freed the individual from the personal bonds of the old society is increasingly coming to limit his freedom of action in impersonal ways. Vast numbers of people crowd into the middle stations of society where the natural pride of awakened hopes of personal self-determination is frustrated and insulted by the mediocrity of one's responsibility and power. A crowd of people all seeking the same objectives may, and often do, produce results that more or less frustrate the objectives of each individual in the crowd. This is obvious on the roads or in the suburbs. It operates less spectacularly but just as powerfully in the intellectual life. There is an 'achievement gap' in the modern city which is particularly insidious since it makes it hard for the individual to come to terms with himself. This is the contrast between his sense of potency, standing high up on the giant shoulders of the culture and a half-conscious vertigo about his own personal performance at such heights. Television, radio, universities, travel, books, records and all the other paraphernalia of modern mass culture give more people than ever before an apparent view of the commanding heights of the present, past and future, of politics, art and science, of macro-cosm and microcosm, the inner mind and outer space. In fancy it has never been easier to imagine oneself into any experience or to embrace reality from a great height as Auden himself so typically did in his youthful poetry. It has been said of this 'Protean style' of the modern mind that 'one can, in a sense, be anyone and no one' and shift from experience to experience 'with relatively diminished psychological cost'.[26] But this is only true locally; for the personality as a whole, there is a considerable cost to pay. The visions are borrowed: 'the one thing' Proteus 'had great difficulty in doing . . . was to carry out his own authentic function'. Authenticity has little prestige in a self-consciously mobile society where it is identified with the traditional 'static' mind. Nevertheless, it counts. The individual who has been bred to world-spanning ambitions which have no relationship to his personal experience of competition with others (except in so far as they draw energy from his frustrations) is liable to find his personal challenge—in an office, say—both trivial and daunting. In this way, the culture of self-awareness democratises both self-dramatisation and the secret fear of failure. It also raises acute doubts about one's own personal identity. As Pierre Emmanuel has said: 'We tend to accept more and more the idea that man is not a person looking for his unity, his oneness, but is a succession, or even a simultaneity, of fragmentary perceptions in a fragmented surrounding. And at the same time we accept the idea of "scientific" control of this fragmented individual.'[27] It is time to begin to redefine human limits.

Auden's art records just that—one man's discovery of the limits of romantic limitlessness. No doubt part of this experience has been public and external: Auden's prewar encounter with fascism has been crucial to his vision of the nihilism inside western culture. This encounter can hardly be over-rated, so long as it does not lead one to under-rate the other, and much more discreet, because more personal, encounter with himself, which his poetry shows to have been at least equally potent. The poetry expresses the painful discovery that the religion of life without limits does not merely complicate, and ultimately negate, life in society; also, and more cogently, it destroys any standards by which a man can live with himself. This is true of Romanticism in both its guises, that of the scientific observer and that of the dionysiac celebrant who serves as the mirror-image in art. The scientific appeal to 'objective' consciousness creates an admirable and unprecedented culture of detachment, but starves the equally strong human need for attachment. So does the orgasmic religion of sex. Such a cult is natural in a highly expansionary age of quantitative assessments even of qualitative values: sex is the only source of unquantifiable satisfactions which is physically and materially undeniable. In itself, though, it is viable only as a temporary expression of youth; it is inherently corrosive as a permanent value. It is not surprising then that a large number of the literary masterpieces of this century—*Heartbreak House*, *The Four Quartets*, even in a negative way *Waiting for Godot*, tend, like *La Nausée* and 'The Sea and the Mirror', to demonstrate the frontiers of the ego, or at least uncover a world in which the cultivation of the ego appears infantile. Such works replace the worship of the ego by a sense of contract, of the restraints of life and relationships. This is less a Christian revival than a spiritual complication of the materialist doctrines, in Schumacher's sense of materialism, which have run their race, less a reaction against the new insights of Romanticism than an attempt to correct the illusions of a new civilisation where, for the first time, every human being thinks of himself as a citizen with rights. Itself born of a new civilisation, it tries to initiate that civilisation into the mysteries, that is, the code of self-restraints, of manhood. This is true even of Eliot and Auden, whose Christianity might be thought to hark back to an older, more static and authoritarian world of family, church and state. The strength of their best poetry is that it stands up, as an argument about experience, and specifically modern experience, without their faith having to be accepted. The key notion in all such works, is that of dialogue, of relationship. It is, interestingly enough, the same concept some philosophers of the computer have been reaching, and have been forced to reach for, to distinguish humanity, or man working with the computer, from the man-like computer able to react *objectively* like a human being. The Romantic culture of energy has foundered in the twentieth century in private dead ends as well as public disasters. In place of the culture of energy, the new outlook proposes, in effect, the ideal of a culture of inter-relationship or community.

The obvious objection is that such writers are too singularly eminent, all highbrow and some dead, in a world that seems more than ever dedicated to youth. This is precisely the point. Industrial, mass civilisation is indeed new; and in psychic terms this newness strangely resembles infantilism. Youth is likely to go on being dionysiac in a man-made mass society freed from the constraints of scarcity, but this cannot continue into later life without being personally as well as socially disintegrating. Mature industrial civilisation may well evolve a culture which explicitly recognises the ages of man, like the Greeks and Hindus, or Shaw, in his own wayward fashion, in the last part of *Back to Methuselah*. If so, the dionysiac side of youth can be recognised, but its transience stressed, which would limit its pretensions. The condition is that there should be some visible progression from the values of youth to those of maturity. Given the values developed by the great romantic intellectuals themselves, this is at present lacking. It is this which gives significance to the various signs of change. One is that the intellectual leaders of the last generation, usually far from fashion and popularity (except for Sartre's short-lived vogue in *Saint-Germain des Prés* in the late Forties) have addressed themselves to this crucial issue in our current culture. Another is that whereas the ideal Romantic artist is a prodigy who dies young, the symbolic time of life of the modern one seems to be middle, or for Yeats even old, age. If ideas meet real needs, they are likely to percolate through to popular culture however unpopular they are in the prophets who beget them. When a Jesuit like Teilhard de Chardin resorts to Noöspheres and Anglican bishops cause regular ripples of scandal with their honest-to-godless prose; while a stubborn nonconformist like Gide preaches 'faith without faith' and an atheist like the dying Orwell concludes that 'the real problem is how to restore the religious attitude while accepting death as final'; one is plainly dealing with reactions foreign to the traditions of secular Liberals and orthodox Christians alike. Auden has written in *The Enchafèd Flood* that 'a man's interest always centres, consciously or unconsciously, round what seems to him the most important and still unsolved problem'.[28] It can hardly be accidental that the spiritual concern which has been a secondary priority among advancing liberals for a quarter of a millennium should now be developing into one of the most distinctive features of liberal humanism itself.

* * *

The cultural relevance of any writer's work is bound to remain speculative until the culture has settled the matter for itself over a period of time. What is tangible and impressive at this point is that Auden has turned the awareness and tensions implied in the dialogue between him and his Romantic heritage into a distinctive poetic style. For near on two centuries the most sentient representatives of European civilisation have considered it their duty to cultivate self-fulfilment. Auden now states the necessity of partial non-fulfilment as the human frontier which, far from being cause for frustration, makes us what we are: 'How should we like it were stars to burn with a passion for us we could not return?'[29] For two centuries, they placed their trust in a spiritual revolution which, if they would only *dare* enough, would suddenly, by a kind of Divine insufflation, transform life and society. Now Auden sees progress as evolution, neither a sudden conversion nor any change that can be predicted from past assumptions; it needs to be invented at every step, as in Spender's remark about Eliot that for him 'work preceded magic and inspiration'.[30] For two centuries the Romantics, faced with the fact of non-fulfilment, made it their vocation to be unhappy, in the name of new continents to be won for the human spirit. Now Auden preaches that 'happiness is not a right; it is a duty. To the degree that we are unhappy, we are in sin.'[31] Reduced to familiar models, the view of happiness as a duty is the traditional view of the tougher Anglican intellectuals. Archbishop Whateley, over a hundred years ago, said that 'happiness is no laughing matter'.[32] Yet ordinary lives have so long been lived by other standards that the pursuit of relative happiness instead of pregnant pain means standing our most cherished habits of thought on their heads. Hardest of all, it means abjuring self-assertion. Self-assertion is so deeply ingrained in our emotional preconceptions that any real departure from it gives a shock. The attitude behind Auden's verse — especially his later verse — is itself a kind of activist manifesto, a militant attack on the reader's prejudices in the guise of self-deprecation and withdrawal. Its assertion of modesty as an aesthetic principle implies a revolution in feeling which, as far as the majority are concerned, has simply not taken place. Even in Eliot, the shock is less. In Eliot, the language speaks of imperative duty, but the music insists on *lacrymae rerum*: it only pretends to be stoic. Auden, on the other hand, has quietly shed the religion of the heroic, attached, even in the denial of poses, to the heightening of life. By the same token, he has shed the current non-Pop conception of poetry. That conception, of art as distillation, as a concentrate of experience, is still heroic even in the denial of heroism. It stands essentially for the case against death and eternity taken over by the artists at the Renaissance: *exegi monumentum*. It is the artist's personal substitute religion.

Indeed, Auden's rejection of all afflatus stands in contrast not to the Romantic and French revolutions, but to the Renaissance, not to two but to five centuries of art. In the *New Year Letter* he says

> That all the special tasks begun
> By the Renaissance have been done[33]

and in 'Kairos and Logos', written shortly after, traces the malady of the modern mind, in Niebuhr's style, back to the Great Discoveries. That was when Man, standing on the edge of new horizons

> Beheld the weights and contours of the earth
> . . . The fatherhood of knowledge stood out there[34]

and thought himself 'the father of his fate'. Auden's dissent is not just from Shelley or Keats, abhorred of the Thirties, but from the baroque poet sighing for country pleasures from an antechamber at court or asserting the townee values to an age of self-made bumpkins, and all the others, since the *Quattrocento*, who have never dreamed of art in any but a high humanistic style. His chosen medium is the low style which has been out of favour ever since Man took to the more or less conscious worship of himself. To find an analogy for Auden's type of poetry one has, therefore, to go back beyond this high style to the end of the Middle Ages. Though exact parallels are out of the question, the loose abundance of Auden's verse, its lack of concern with subjective intensity, its care to place every event and emotion in its total spiritual context, evoke medieval more than post-Renaissance models. Like the poetry of the Middle Ages, Auden's is much preoccupied with the allegory of the religious plight of Man and of his journey through temptation to a certain peace. From the songs to the secular sermons for Marble Arch, from the socially conscious, didactic, verses of the Thirties to the paradigm of the Passion in the 'Horae Canonicae', from the potted essays of *Another Time* to *The Age of Anxiety*, his poems are nearly all fragments for a Progress of the Soul. Even in method, there are hints of medievalism. The tendency to illustrate and personify abstractions, to dramatise ethical situations, not least by playing the buffoon, to couch wisdom in a style compounded of earthy slapstick, scholastic logic and practical precept, all breathe the climate of the medieval moralists and sermon-writers. The grotesque streak in him as in late medieval art is the result of the sense of the individual's situation being stronger than the sense of his individuality. If your sense of his individuality is very strong, you cannot play about with his behaviour: it is too firmly rooted to be arbitrary and mobile. If, however, you have a vivid sense of his situation and of the pitfalls into which he can fall you may build any number of hypothetical *scenae* in which the issue is dramatised. Auden is a schoolman of human behaviour. One would say of him, as he does of medieval man, that he defines 'the individual not as a "character" but as a soul'. Modern as its trappings are, his world, like that of the Middle Ages, is full of allegories. He has sagely said that the intellectual weakness of the men of the Middle Ages 'was an oversimple faith in the direct evidence of their senses and the immediate data of consciousness, an over-simplification of the relation between the objective and the subjective world'. Is that so very different from Auden's auto-matic ascription of any disease to a failure of the psyche? Even as a craftsman, as a conscious professional Maker, he unex-pectedly echoes that long lost age. 'It must be admitted', he has written in the introduction to his anthology of *Poets of the English Language*, 'that, to our taste, the medieval poets are frequently prolix and formless.'[35] He too has been accused of writing too much, of looseness, and of incapacity to fuse his subjects and his forms. His love of pattern in itself, his view of poetry as a game, his wasteful abundance (typical of the professional aware of his social function as an entertainer, neither more nor less than the function of any other professional), his determination, especially today, to put into verse almost anything that occurs to him, are more alien from the Renaissance tradition of our last civilisation than from the Middle Ages of our last-but-one. If one thinks of all life as exemplary of good or bad, and of art as no substitute for the deity, one is not likely to concentrate on each poem one writes one's hopes of a line of credit on eternity. It is no wonder, then, to find Auden writing that 'there has been no time since its own when the literature of the Middle Ages could appeal to readers as greatly as it can today'.[36] This may be premature for the mass of his readers. For Auden himself, it implies little more than fellow feeling for some of the facets of his own work.

Auden, of course, is no medievalist; analogies are not identities. His sense of the evolutionary separation of Man from Nature, though formally traditional if one equates Nature with God, is in practice without precedent. It involves a rejection of millenia of correspondences going back through the Romantics and the chain of being to Pythagoras and the world of sympathetic magic 'before philosophy'. The analogy is useful primarily because it helps to fix the quality and limits of the poet's achievement. Auden certainly lacks what the nineteenth century called 'passion' and the 1940s 'commitment'. Auden's poetry is rarely tight in the passionate, committed way of Hopkins, Yeats or Eliot. He writes obsessively of Love, but could not possibly cry out like Hopkins

> Thou mastering me
> God! giver of breath and bread.[37]

He believes in the existentialist I-and-Thou, but finds it easier to preach than to practice. There is something typical of the high-minded English liberal about his attitude, free as the wind about discussing love in public but obsessively reserved and inhibited about saying 'I love you'. Even Auden's lyricism is, with some exceptions, reflective rather than enthusiastic, melancholy rather than impassioned. His poetry does not, in its own essence, plumb the depths of alienation, sickness or despair though it is much preoccupied with all three. It is the reasonable, balanced man's poetry, always aware in every detail of the world as a whole. Sometimes, this reserve becomes something less desirable, notably when Auden succumbs to the technocratic temptations of his intellect. The technocrat excels at solving 'problems', at bringing order out of chaos or at manipulating people and things when all the elements have been reduced to counters in his head. Such an attitude can blind a man in the very act of seeing, blunt his sympathies and tempt him to an abuse of his mental powers. As soon as Auden is not struggling with some issue larger than his current grasp of it, he gives the impression of living inside his mental machinery and of mistaking its powerful hum for the poet's 'mechanism of sensibility'.[38]

That does not, however, mean a mechanism of sensibility is lacking. Auden's incapacity to utter the naked cry disqualifies him only for one kind of poetry and has driven him to turn his talents to account in another kind. His way is to look from the emotions to the context in which they must fulfil themselves; to encounter the agonising ironies of life and try to come to terms with them. Moderation is one of the natural languages of a troubled age. He is moderate and detached and clings to the middle stance precisely because an immense sense of tragedy, perhaps built into his personal unease and certainly built into the first half of the century, has led him to seek the balance in which suffering is assimilated. Auden's is a comic art, if by comedy one means the effort to encompass and outgrow self-absorption. The temptation of comedy may be complacency, but the process of acquiring this cannot be anything but painful and difficult. Though Auden's work is mainly cast in the form of conclusions, they are shaped by the turmoil of the process. One must not look at the tone in which he writes—its disclaimers are almost mathematically proportionate to the tensions they overcome—but to its implications. Auden's verse may dress casually, even frivolously, but one finds in it most of the experience of alienation which has gone into the theatre of non-communication since the war. His unwilling preoccupation with self may make Auden's achievement narrower than his universal themes, covering virtually the whole range of common human activity, led his first readers to suppose. In particular, it probably explains why his successful passages are either lyrical or elaborately didactic and his one really successful long poem, 'The Sea and the Mirror', is a custom-made juxtaposition of the two. At the same time, this isolation also makes his art much deeper and more compulsive than many have concluded in the postwar reaction to the manifest fact that his intellectual interests are wider than his imaginative illuminations. Auden is a poet of the suffering created by isolation and of the spiritual growth to encompass, or at least neutralise, that suffering.

As an aspect of that, one finds in Auden's work a sense, relatively rare today, of the duty to communicate which must be part of living with others. This makes him more than a poignant artist of the private dilemma and gives him a public dimension which is not a dilution but a necessary part of his vision. It is necessary because it corresponds to the diffuse suffering of a generation at grips with its own peculiar logic of the emotions. Auden is the poet of the greed and fear of 'freedom', and of the disciplines without which a personality cannot be even imperfectly integrated. This makes his comic vision one of the inherent visions of the twentieth century—not the only one, but one without which the range of the others would be sadly incomplete. Moreover, his art has the strengths as well as limitations of its origins. The concern for the social and psychological diversities of the human condition which is one of its hallmarks is not something to be wished away. This has, at the minimum, given it unflagging interest and contacts with the world which make Auden seem universal by contrast with the limited concerns of the Victorian twilight. His verse may lack something in selectivity, but by the same token it is generously inclusive. If behaviour is viewed in terms of its consequences, and the individual in terms of the wide world, the appeal from the particular to the general gives endless opportunities for observation and invention. Auden, at least in his youth, has had a creative fertility unequalled in English twentieth-century verse. He has a range of interests, an informed concern for the world, a wit and a sheer histrionic enjoyment of his own performance, which make him nearly always vital and entertaining even when he is below his best. When he is at his best, Auden is the one poet in England this century who has treated some of the major troubles of his time in ways which measure up to the breadth of their impact on people's daily lives. That he has approached them often as a comic allegorist and that we are so little used to comedy or to allegory that we associate them with lack of involvement or even with laxity, should not conceal either the powerful relevance of the comic vision or the scope of Auden's achievement in re-rooting it in a new environment. He is one of the outstanding figures who have made the thirty turbulent years from 1914 to 1945 a great period of English poetry; and, as a comic artist, he is virtually unique in an age of deliberate self-consciousness worn as tragedy.

Notes and References

A. BIBLIOGRAPHICAL

I. Auden Volumes

Wherever possible, references are made to all the relevant volumes of collected verse; original volumes are quoted only where no collected source exists for a quotation in the form used here. Often, the versions of poems in collected editions differ from the original, or are omitted from one collection to the next.

All volumes refer to Faber & Faber editions and titles, except where otherwise stated.

CP	Collected Shorter Poems, 1930–44 (1950)
CSP	Collected Shorter Poems, 1927–57 (1966)
CLP	Collected Longer Poems (1968)
AH	About the House (1966)
AT	Another Time (1940)
DBS	The Dog Beneath the Skin (1935)
DH	The Dyer's Hand (1963)
EF	The Enchafèd Flood (1951)
FTTB	For The Time Being (1945)
HC	Homage to Clio (1960)
LI	Letters from Iceland (1937)
LS	Look, Stranger! (1936)
NYL	New Year Letter (1941)
O	The Orators (1932)
P	Poems (2nd edn. 1933)
PEL	Poets of the English Language (Eyre & Spottiswoode, 1952)

II. Volumes by Other Authors

Bayley   John Bayley, *The Romantic Survival*, Constable (1957).
        The chapter on Auden offers the most challenging interpretation of Auden's creative psychology.

Callan   Edward Callan, 'Auden's New Year Letter', *Renascence* XVI (1963), 13–19; reprinted in 'Auden', in Monroe K. Spears (ed.) *Twentieth Century Views*, Prentice Hall (1964)

Day Lewis
  BD   Cecil Day Lewis, *The Buried Day*, Chatto and Windus (1960)
  HP   Cecil Day Lewis, *A Hope for Poetry*, Blackwell (1934)

Everett   Barbara Everett, *Auden*, Oliver and Boyd (1964)

214

NOTES AND REFERENCES

Isherwood Christopher Isherwood, *Lions and Shadows*, Hogarth Press (1938)

NV *New Verse*, 1933–9, ed. Geoffrey Grigson

Reed Henry Reed, 'W. H. Auden in America', in *New Writing and Daylight 1945*, ed. John Lehmann, Hogarth Press (1945), 131–5

Skelton Robin Skelton (ed.) *Poetry of the Thirties*, Penguin (1964)

Spears Monroe K. Spears, *The Poetry of W. H. Auden*, subtitled *The Disenchanted Island*, O.U.P. (1963).
This book is a gold-mine of information on Auden's work and working life, and Spears has often consulted Auden himself. I am indebted to it for innumerable facts.

Spender
TCVA Stephen Spender, 'W. H. Auden and His Poetry', *Atlantic Monthly* CXCII (1953), 74–9, reprinted in 'Auden', in Monroe K. Spears, (ed.) *Twentieth Century Views*, Prentice Hall (1964)

WWW Stephen Spender, *World Within World*, Hamish Hamilton (1951)

Symons Julian Symons, *The Thirties*, Cresset Press (1960)

B. TEXTUAL

Prologue

1. DH 337–8
2. CSP 282
3. CLP 73
4. Spender, TCVA 26
5. Eliot, *The Waste Land*
6. DH 55, quoting Charles Williams, 'Witchcraft'
7. CP 43; CSP 49
8. CLP 344
9. O 57
10. CP 244
11. Spears, 146–7
12. CP 232; CSP 90
13. CP 28
14. DH 51
15. Introduction to *An Elizabethan Song-Book* (1955), xv
16. Eliot, *Ash Wednesday*
17. Everett, 25
18. Everett, 3
19. Spender, TCVA 28–9
20. Spender, TCVA 38
21. John Holloway, *Encounter*, August 1968, 79
22. DH 34
23. Geoffrey Grigson, NV Nov. 1937, 16
24. DH 57–8
25. DH 196
26. E.g., CP 69, 127, 251; CSP 75, 72
27. AH 33
28. *Encounter*, Nov. 1963, 49
29. AT 114

30. CSP 231-2
31. CP 125
32. CP 70
33. CP 64; CSP 72
34. CP 60; CSP 19
35. CP 50; CSP 51
36. Bayley 139
37. DH 55
38. DH 59
39. CLP 295
40. Spears 66, quoting 'A Literary Transference' (1940)
41. AT 7
42. CP 50; CSP 51
43. CP 120
44. CP 191
45. NYL 160

46. E.g. CP 113; CSP 148
47. CLP 87
48. CSP 265
49. Richard Hoggart, *W. H. Auden*, Longmans (1957), 8; also *Introduction to W. H. Auden, a Selection*, Hutchinson Educational Ltd (1961), 17-41, speaks of 'little touch, taste or smell'.
50. CLP 58
51. Spender, WWW 54-5
52. DBS 118
53. CP 94-5; CSP 28.
54. R. H. Tawney, *Religion and the Rise of Capitalism*, Ch. V
55. CP 159; CSP 151

Chapter 1

1. CP 58-9; CSP 20-1
2. CP 94; CSP 28
3. PEL III, xvi
4. CP 49-50; CSP 51
5. CP 55-6; CSP 62
6. CP 119; CSP 33
7. CP 21; CSP 25
8. Robert Bridges, *Testament of Beauty* I, 6-7 and 120-1
9. CP 137; CSP 43-4
10. CLP 68
11. CP 84; CSP 39
12. 'T. S. Eliot: A Question of Speech', in B. Rajan (ed.), *T. S. Eliot: A Study of his Writings by Several Hands*, Dennis Dobson (1947), 109
13. CP 44-5; CSP 22
14. Walter Allen, *The Listener*, 17 April 1952, 640 et seq.

15. CLP 74
16. Isherwood, Ch. V
17. CP 59; CSP 21
18. CP 207-8, 215; CLP 19, 27
19. CP 83; CSP 38
20. CP 218-19; CLP 30
21. CP 143; CSP 30
22. CP 119; CSP 33
23. CP 222-3; CLP 34
24. CP 215; CLP 27
25. P XXII 76
26. CP 84
27. CP 60; CSP 19
28. CP159; CSP 29
29. Sartre, *La Nausée*; Roquentin's ex-mistress is a devotee of 'perfect moments'.
30. CP 161
31. Isherwood, NV, Nov. 1937

32. Spears, 15. Six of the pieces in 'Paid on Both Sides', were included in *Poems 1928*, printed on Stephen Spender's private press in the summer vacation of 1928.
33. P 7
34. CLP 74
35. CP 60; CSP 19
36. CP 183; CSP 22–3
37. Isherwood, Ch. V.
38. Spender, TCVA 27
39. CLP 74
40. CP 208; CLP 20

41. CP 83; CSP 38
42. CP 184–5; CSP 23–4
43. CP 83; CSP 37
44. CP 201; CLP 13–14
45. CP 202; CLP 14
46. Isherwood, Ch. V
47. CLP 47
48. CP 117; CSP 153
49. CP 218; CLP 29
50. Everett, 3
51. Gabriel Hanotaux, quoted in P. Geyl, *Napoleon: For & Against*, Peregrine (1965), 364
52. CP 74

Chapter 2

1. Skelton, 18
2. Symons, 15, 94
3. Day Lewis, BD 176
4. Skelton, 13
5. David Gascoyne NV, Nov. 1937, 24
6. Louis MacNeice, NV, Nov. 1937, 12
7. Skelton 249. This stanza omitted DBS, CP, CSP
8. Symons, 14, 17
9. Day Lewis, HP 44
10. Geoffrey Grigson, NV, Nov 1937, 1
11. Symons, 173
12. Skelton, 18, 36–7
13. *W. H. Auden: A Bibliography. The Early Years through 1955*, B. C. Bloomfield, Virginia Univ. Press
14. Dylan Thomas, NV, Nov. 1937, 25

15. Reed, 131
16. Spears, 49
17. O 95
18. George Orwell, *Inside the Whale*.
19. O 30
20. Everett, 102
21. O 29
22. O 14
23. O, 3rd edn. (1966), 7
24. Day Lewis, HP 56
25. O, 3rd edn. (1966), 7
26. CP 89; CSP 77
27. Day Lewis, HP 46
28. CP 147; CSP 59
29. Day Lewis, HP 46
30. Isherwood, Ch. V
31. This incensed Joseph Warren Beech in *Making of the Auden Canon*, Minnesota Univ. Press (1957), Ch. 14, 177–80

32. LS 11. This poem, itself still cast in the shadow of revolution, was first published in the *New Statesman*, 16 July 1932
33. Symons, 78; Spears, 92; O 66
34. DBS 155
35. Symons, 83–4
36. Oxford Book of Light Verse (1938), Introduction
37. *Dance of Death* (1933) 11
38. CLP 60
39. DH 388
40. Spender, WWW 53
41. CP 32–3
42. CP 69
43. CP 34
44. CP 109; CSP 74; Spears 161, n. 56
45. HC 85
46. LS Prologue, 12

47. CP 238; CSP 108
48. Skelton, 14–15, 18
49. CLP 81
50. Day Lewis, BD 205–6
51. LS XVII, 46
52. DH xi
53. DH 19
54. CP 82; CSP 37
55. Isherwood, NV, Nov. 1937, 4
56. CLP 69
57. CLP 85
58. CLP 102
59. Symons, 150
60. CP 173; CSP 168
61. Skelton, 31
62. Spender, WWW 53
63. CP 125
64. CP 112; CSP 71
65. CP 243; CSP 88
66. CP 247

Chapter 3

1. *Modern Canterbury Pilgrims*, James A. Pike, ed., Morehouse-Gorham, New York, 1956. Quoted Spears, 173–177. Spears says the 'Anglican layman' was Charles Williams.
2. CP 177–8
3. O 98
4. CP 70
5. CLP 52
6. CLP 111
7. CSP 225
8. CP 117; CSP 153
9. CP 137; CSP 144
10. CP 244; CSP 82
11. CP 239; CSP 108

12. CP 192
13. LS XIV, 37
14. Spender, WWW 248
15. AT 114; CP, CSP omit
16. CP 153; CSP 147
17. Isherwood, NV, Nov. 1937
18. CP 25–30
19. Spears, 183–4
20. CLP 118
21. Stephen Vizinczey, *In Praise of Older Women*, postscript to 2nd edn.
22. CP 19; CSP 123–4
23. LS XXII, poem 1, 53
24. CP 231; CSP 89
25. CP 127; CSP 75

NOTES AND REFERENCES

26. Isherwood, Ch. V.
27. CLP 40
28. CP 118; CSP 154
29. CP 228; CSP 86
30. CP 98
31. CP 244–5
32. LS XXXI, 67
33. CP 62
34. CP 271–2
35. CP 102
36. Review of 'Either/Or', *New Republic*, 1941, quoted Spears, 178
37. CP 39; CSP 203
38. CP 118; CSP 154
39. CP 113; CSP 148
40. CP 104
41. CLP 125
42. Everett, 1
43. A. Alvarez, *The Shaping Spirit*, Chatto (1958), 88
44. CP 171–2
45. John Lehmann, *I Am My Brother*, Longmans (1960), 64
46. CP 63–4
47. CP 96–8
48. Reed, 135
49. NYL 174; CSP 184
50. NYL 93
51. CLP 85
52. Symons, 74
53. CLP 92
54. CP 99; CSP 149
55. NYL 119
56. CP 21; CSP 25

Chapter 4

1. Callan, 153
2. Reed, 131
3. Callan, 152–9
4. CSP 318
5. CLP 120
6. CLP 130
7. CLP 87
8. CLP 83; Spender, WWW 51
9. NYL 108–9
10. NYL 83
11. CLP 104
12. CLP 121–2
13. CLP 93
14. NYL 109
15. CLP 109
16. CLP 106
17. CP 182
18. CLP 90
19. CLP 163
20. CLP 133
21. CLP 166
22. CLP 134
23. CLP 137
24. CLP 204
25. O 91
26. CP 97; CSP 98
27. CLP 203
28. CLP 259–60
29. CLP 207
30. CLP 206
31. CLP 215
32. CLP 218
33. CLP 216
34. CLP 237, 239
35. CLP 248
36. CLP 249–50

37. CLP 183
38. CLP 218
39. CLP 246
40. CLP 239
41. Sartre, *L'Age de Raison*, Ch. III
42. CLP 203
43. *The Ascent of F6*, Act II, Scene I
44. Sartre, *La Nausée*
45. CLP 154
46. CLP 208
47. NYL 91

48. CLP 109
49. CP 184–5; CSP 24
50. CLP 196
51. CLP 219
52. CLP 210
53. CLP 287
54. CLP 264
55. CLP 346
56. Spender, TCVA 38
57. CP 181
58. FTTB, blurb (written by Spender)

Chapter 5

1. DH 5
2. There is a good discussion of this in John G. Blair's *The Poetic Art of W. H. Auden*, Princeton (1965) 38–45. Two of the principal statements of Auden's attitude to poetry are 'Art and Psychology', in *The Arts Today* (1935), ed. Grigson and 'Squares and Oblongs' in *Poets at Work* (1948), partly taken into DH.
3. CSP 255
4. Walter Allen, *The Listener*, 17 Apr. 1952, 640
5. CSP 258
6. CSP 265, 262
7. CSP 164
8. CLP 109
9. CSP 260
10. Robert Browning, 'Two in the Campagna'
11. CSP 325
12. CSP 225
13. E.g., 'The Old Man's Road', CSP 304–5

14. AH 5
15. CP 147; CSP 59
16. CSP 333–5
17. DH 7
18. CLP 352
19. CSP 333
20. Polybius, Bk. IV, Ch 20, translated Arnold Toynbee in *Greek Civilisation and Character*, Mentor Books (1953)
21. CSP 335
22. CSP 295
23. CP 112–13; CSP 147
24. CSP 334
25. CLP 243; AH 7
26. Spender, WWW 299–300
27. LI 202
28. CP 205; CLP 17
29. CSP 227
30. O 86
31. Bayley, 52
32. AH 10
33. AH 11
34. CSP 270
35. CSP 281

36. CSP 258
37. CSP 249
38. CSP 273

39. CSP epigraph
40. CSP 310
41. CLP 284

Epilogue

1. CP 9
2. Gerhard Masur, *Prophets of Yesterday*, Weidenfeld (1963) 150
3. CLP 203
4. CLP 248
5. CLP 213 and 245
6. HC 78
7. PEL I, xxviii–xxx
8. NYL 112
9. DH 273
10. CP 28
11. DH 274
12. Stravinsky, *Memories and Commentaries*, 147, quoted Spears, 63
13. Spender, TCVA 30
14. CLP 246
15. EF 125
16. Auden, Introduction to Sydney Smith, *Selected Writings*, (1956), xix
17. CSP 239
18. DH 88
19. Sartre, *La Nausée*, last section, 'Une heure Plus Tard'
20. Ibid.
21. E. F. Schumacher, 'Economics in a Buddhist Country', in *Roots of Economic Growth*, Gandhian Institute of Studies (1962)

22. Balzac, *Etudes sur M. Beyle: Analyse de la Chartreuse de Parme*, Skira 14
23. Baudelaire, *Fleurs du Mal*, 'Le Voyage'
24. Edward Shils, 'Of Plenitude and Scarcity', *Encounter*, May 1969, 42
25. Leopold von Ranke, *Die Grossen Mächte*, concluding paragraph
26. Robert J. Lifton, *The Endless Crisis* (ed. Duchêne), Simon and Schuster (1970) 160–1
27. Pierre Emmanuel, ibid. 184
28. EF 83
29. CSP 282
30. Spender, 'Remembering Eliot', *Encounter*, April 1965, 7
31. DH 432
32. Richard Whately, Archbishop of Dublin (1787–1863), Apophthegms 218
33. CLP 116
34. CP 28
35. PEL I, xxiv
36. PEL I, xxx
37. Gerard Manley Hopkins, 'Wreck of the Deutschland'
38. Bayley, 55, quoting Eliot

Index

INDEX

225

INDEX